NEIGHBORS AND STRANGERS

Studies in Legal History

Published by The University of North Carolina Press

in association with the

American Society for Legal History

BRUCE H. MANN

NEIGHBORS

AND STRANGERS

LAW AND COMMUNITY IN

EARLY CONNECTICUT

THE UNIVERSITY OF NORTH CAROLINA PRESS

CHAPEL HILL AND LONDON

© 1987 The University of North Carolina Press

All rights reserved

Manufactured in the United States of America

Library of Congress Cataloging-in-Publication Data

Mann, Bruce H.

Neighbors and strangers.

(Studies in legal history)

Bibliography: p.

Includes index.

1. Dispute resolution (Law)—Connecticut—History.

I. Title. II. Series.

KFC4160.3.M36 1987   347.746'09   87-6001

ISBN 0-8078-1756-2   347.46079

FOR MY PARENTS,

Donald and Geraldine M. Mann

CONTENTS

ACKNOWLEDGMENTS

Every scholar accumulates debts. Some—student loans, for example—we can repay given adequate employment. Others, the stuff of acknowledgments, we cannot. For those, public confessions of indebtedness such as the ones that follow have to suffice, accompanied by the hope that the proper parties read them.

I did most of my research at the Connecticut State Library in Hartford. Robert Claus, former state archivist, and his successor, Mark Jones, made the library a welcome place to work. The present and former members of the staff—Ann Barry, Eunice DiBella, Peg Giguere-Davis, Kristin Johnson, Sandi Perlman, and Ted Wohlsen—never seemed to tire of my many requests. At the Connecticut Historical Society, the director, Christopher Bickford, extended the same courtesies, as did Elizabeth Abbe and Ruth Blair. I am also grateful to the Connecticut Conference of the United Church of Christ and to the librarians of the New Haven Colony Historical Society, the William L. Clements Library, Sterling Memorial Library, and the Beinecke Rare Book and Manuscript Library for the use of their collections.

Mark Baronas, Ilona Crosswhite, Linda Francois, and Paul Nowosadko, former students at the University of Connecticut School of Law, assisted in gathering the quantitative data that underlies much of the first three chapters. When I finally accepted the necessity of using a computer, I would have foundered but for the patient, expert guidance of Alida Metcalf and, in the later stages, Richard Zuraski. Their labors as well as mine were supported by grants from the National Endowment for the Humanities, the American Bar Foundation, the American Association for State and Local History, and the University of Connecticut Research Foundation. Colleagues at Brown University, the American Bar Foundation, and the law schools of Northwestern University, Boston University, and the University of Illinois invited me to try out my ideas at various workshops and were gracious hosts as well as good critics. The editors of the *Law & Society Review*, the *New York University Law Review*, and the *Michigan Law Review* permitted me to include revised versions of material that first appeared in their pages. Dorris Johnson, Barbara Aumer, and Bruce Ching typed the manuscript with more good cheer than my handwriting deserves.

Fellow travelers in the field are few but exceedingly congenial. I am grateful for their company on what proved to be a longer journey than I had anticipated. Christine Heyrman, David Konig, and Avi Soifer did not have to prove their friendship by reading the manuscript, but they did, and the book is better for their efforts. Barbara Black, Robert Gordon, Stanley Katz, and Hugh Macgill helped me in more ways than I can begin to recount, let alone repay. At a particularly difficult time, Lawrence Friedman, whom I had not yet met, offered encouragement that proved more important than he could have known. My greatest collective debt is to my friends and former colleagues in the law school at Washington University, St. Louis, but for whom I would not have had the opportunity to finish the book.

From all these friends and others, I have learned what it means to be part of an academic community. For teaching me what it means to be part of an academic tradition, I am indebted to David Underdown, Gordon Wood, Jack Hexter, and, above all, Edmund Morgan, under whose watch and care I first asked some of the questions I have attempted to answer here.

My children, Amelia and Alexander Warren, have grown up with this book, a fate they have borne well. My wife, Elizabeth Warren, believed in the book when I did not. She also prodded, encouraged, and threatened—always lovingly, of course—until I finished it, all the while teaching her own classes and doing her own research and writing. She knows what matters.

ABBREVIATIONS

Acts and Laws 1715	*Acts and Laws of His Majesties Colony of Connecticut in New-England* (New London, 1715)
Acts and Laws 1750	*Acts and Laws of His Majesty's English Colony of Connecticut in New-England in America* (New London, 1750)
Conn. Arch.	Connecticut Archives, Connecticut State Library, Hartford
Conn. Rec.	J. Hammond Trumbull and Charles J. Hoadly, eds., *The Public Records of the Colony of Connecticut, 1636–1776*
CtAR	Court of Assistants Records, Connecticut State Library, Hartford
HCCR, HCCF	Hartford County Court, Records and Files, Connecticut State Library, Hartford
HCPCR	Hartford County Probate Court Records, Connecticut State Library, Hartford
NHCCR, NHCCF	New Haven County Court, Records and Files, Connecticut State Library, Hartford
NLCCR, NLCCF	New London County Court, Records and Files, Connecticut State Library, Hartford
SCR, SCF	Superior Court, Records and Files, Connecticut State Library, Hartford
WMQ	*William and Mary Quarterly*

NEIGHBORS AND STRANGERS

INTRODUCTION

EZRA STILES, while minister at Newport, Rhode Island, heard a story of two churchmembers who "had unhappily got into a Lawsuit" that proved acrimonious. The two brethren became "guilty of such Indiscretions and broken peace, as that it came into the Church—and seemed impossible to reconcile." Two other churchmembers observed the contention and "marvelled that such irreconcileable Enmity should arise among Christs Disciples for a Lawsuit." Surely such heat was avoidable. To prove that people could go to law and not quarrel, the two observers sued one another "for sake of Trial." Their experiment, however, went awry. They "soon embroiled their Spirits, and the Thing proceded and ended in a total Breach of Friendship and most irreconcileable Enmity." For Stiles, the moral was clear: "Dangerous to tempt Satan, and try our own Strength!"[1]

The story, which Stiles heard at best thirdhand, was probably apocryphal. But even if it were not true, it would warrant inventing. As a cautionary tale, it captured deeply rooted anxieties and ambivalences about law and community. The puritanism to which Stiles was heir had once inspired church and town covenants that enjoined members and inhabitants from suing one another before the community could attempt reconciliation. Yet people turned to law anyway—sometimes as a last resort, often at first instance, but always in large numbers.

What did they seek? Did they share Stiles's preoccupation with whether or not their differences were "reconcileable," or did they simply want redress? Was law inimical to community, as Stiles seemed to think, or was the relationship between the two more complex? Did that relationship, whatever it was, remain constant, or did it change as the seventeenth century turned to the eighteenth and the eighteenth moved toward the Revolution? These are large and difficult questions. Large, because how people attempt to resolve the disputes that inevi-

1. *The Literary Diary of Ezra Stiles*, 1:144, entry for 19 Aug. 1771.

tably roil human relations is an elemental issue in any society. Difficult, because the raw legal data required to answer them can most
charitably be described as Augean and do not readily yield their social
or economic significance. Nonetheless, they must be answered if we
hope to explore the fundamental relationship between law and society
and deepen our understanding of community in early America.

The book I have written attempts to answer those questions. It is a
study of legal change and community from the middle of the seventeenth century to the eve of the Revolution. In it, I have tried to
accomplish two tasks—first, to identify how law and the ways people
used it changed, and, second, to explain those changes in the context
of other, often related, changes in economy and society. To these ends,
the book melds legal history and social history and offers a rethinking
of the relationship between law and society in, if not western civiliza-
tion, at least early Connecticut.

The connections between law and community are difficult to identify, let alone explain. "Community" is an elusive concept, all the
more so for being an evocative one. In loose, modern parlance, it
conjures images of a simpler time when relations were close and famil-
ial, when people mattered more than things, when neighbors truly did
love one another as they loved themselves. We may not know quite
what community means, but we are certain that our ancestors had it
and that we do not. This veil of romanticism lends special peril to the
historical study of community.[2]

To historians of early America, community has meant the town,
preferably the New England town. To inhabitants of Connecticut in
the seventeenth century, community probably meant the same thing.
There, the world for most people was the town in which they lived.
Except for a few traders and officials, social and economic relations
were largely local. Such broader ties as there were were irregular, their
very irregularity underscoring the essential smallness of society. For
much of the population, that smallness was reinforced by the intense
tribalism of early puritanism. For everyone, it was heightened by the
exigencies of life in a hostile environment. Individual families could
not supply all their needs, material or otherwise, but towns more
nearly could. They made possible the things that lifted daily existence
above the rude level of individual subsistence—a setting for coopera-

2. The best theoretical critique of the concept of community in American
history, to which I am particularly indebted here, is Thomas Bender, *Community and Social Change in America.*

tive exchanges of goods and services, a pastor who ministered to the entire town, a schoolmaster so "that Learning may not bee buried in the Grave of our Forefathers," a militia to ease the threat of Indian attack, a gristmill to which everyone brought their grain. These qualities and others made the town synonymous with community in the seventeenth century.[3]

Inevitably, towns grew, neighbors moved away, economies matured, churches divided. What these changes meant for notions of community is unclear. Perry Miller suggested declension as a theme of puritan studies, so it perhaps seemed natural that historians of community would also find, and sometimes lament, the decline of community. Trying to identify when community began its decline has been a growth industry, despite the occasional dissent from studies of towns where the traditional indicia of community never existed or, more heretical still, intensified.[4]

"The decline of community" has an appealingly rueful ring, but is it accurate? The best community studies at least acknowledge, if they do

3. The quotation is from the Connecticut Code of 1650, which required towns of fifty households or more to support a schoolmaster. *Conn. Rec.*, 1:554–55. For an excellent discussion of the ideal of community in seventeenth-century New England, see Stephen Foster, *Their Solitary Way: The Puritan Social Ethic in the First Century of Settlement in New England*. Connecticut has been a historiographic as well as a historical backwater. There is only one published town study of any merit, Charles S. Grant, *Democracy in the Connecticut Frontier Town of Kent*, and one social history of distinction, Richard L. Bushman, *From Puritan to Yankee: Character and the Social Order in Connecticut, 1690–1765*. There is also valuable material for the seventeenth century in Richard S. Dunn, *Puritans and Yankees: The Winthrop Dynasty of New England, 1630–1717*; Robert C. Black III, *The Younger John Winthrop*; Robert G. Pope, *The Half-Way Covenant: Church Membership in Puritan New England*; and Paul R. Lucas, *Valley of Discord: Church and Society along the Connecticut River, 1636–1725*; and for the eighteenth century in Jackson Turner Main, *Society and Economy in Colonial Connecticut*. Much of the best work remains that of the nineteenth-century antiquarians listed in the Bibliography.

4. The roster of community studies is well known and does not require full recapitulation here. Good historiographic assessments of the literature include an early one by John M. Murrin, "Review Essay," and a recent one by Darrett B. Rutman, "Assessing the Little Communities of Early America." Of the town studies that describe decline, the best ones are also among the earliest: Darrett B. Rutman, *Winthrop's Boston: Portrait of a Puritan Town, 1630–1649*; Philip J. Greven, Jr., *Four Generations: Population, Land, and*

not avoid entirely, the hazards of typological theories of social change borrowed from modernization theory and are circumspect in their use of polar dichotomies of status and contract, traditional and modern, puritan and Yankee. Yet most fall prey to the related, if less obvious, fallacy of regarding community as a unitary concept that can admit only one meaning and one manifestation, the town. Community, however, was more than merely a place. It was also a network of social relations, often but not necessarily among people who lived near one another. More particularly, it was the mutual obligations and shared experiences that bound people together.

In Connecticut, community did not decline so much as it was redefined. It would take another book to explain what happened, but, as my principal concern is with legal change, an outline will have to suffice. Population growth, migration, economic development, war, and religious revival transformed the nature and context of social relations in the first half of the eighteenth century. People were drawn outside their towns for the first time. No longer "little commonwealths," towns lost the insularity and homogeneity that had made them the embodiment of community. In addition to changes in economic and social relations, religious dissent and the dispersal of settlement contributed to the new diversity of towns. Town inhabitants in the seventeenth century had gathered in the same meetinghouse to hear the same minister and had sent their children to the same school,

---

Family in Colonial Andover, Massachusetts; Kenneth A. Lockridge, *A New England Town, The First Hundred Years: Dedham, Massachusetts, 1636–1736*; and Paul Boyer and Stephen Nissenbaum, *Salem Possessed: The Social Origins of Witchcraft*. John Demos emphasizes communal stability in the seventeenth century in *A Little Commonwealth: Family Life in Plymouth Colony*. The studies that have been most persuasive in finding continuities in community in the eighteenth century are Michael Zuckerman, *Peaceable Kingdoms: New England Towns in the Eighteenth Century*; Robert A. Gross, *The Minutemen and Their World*; and Christopher M. Jedrey, *The World of John Cleaveland: Family and Community in Eighteenth-Century New England*. Community in the traditional sense may never have existed in the proto-capitalistic Springfield depicted by Stephen Innes, *Labor in a New Land: Economy and Society in Seventeenth-Century Springfield*. The best recent entry in the field, Christine Leigh Heyrman, *Commerce and Culture: The Maritime Communities of Colonial Massachusetts, 1690–1750*, argues that communalism persisted and even strengthened in the face of commercial development.

all supported by the town. In the eighteenth century, these community obligations devolved upon smaller territorial units organized for that purpose, the ecclesiastical society or parish. By the eve of the Revolution, only nine towns—out of sixty-eight in the colony—contained just one parish. Four encompassed as many as nine.[5]

The emergence of multiple parishes within towns symbolized the redefinition of community. Each parish interposed a layer of authority between individual inhabitants and the town. It provided a smaller body through which neighbors could administer concerns that were more local than the town and no longer the business of the town as a whole. Many parishes eventually became towns, but as parishes they were not the all-encompassing communities that towns had been. They were, to be sure, communities. But they were smaller, less complete, and, in that respect, less wholly communal than the town communities of the seventeenth century. Community grew more specialized, more particular, as towns grew larger.

Although the literature of community studies has suggested what happened to community, it has said almost nothing of law. Many social historians have, to be sure, used legal sources, occasionally to brilliant effect, but only rarely have they studied law.[6] The distinction is important. It is akin to mining church records for information without at least occasionally coming to terms with religion. The analogy is a fitting one. Law and religion had much in common in early New England. Both were intellectual systems as well as social processes. Both were mediums through which people defined and attempted to assure what they valued as a society—what behavior was permissible, how people should act toward one another, how people could resolve their differences without resort to violence, and, in the case of law,

---

5. Bruce C. Daniels, *The Connecticut Town: Growth and Development, 1635–1790*, p. 98.

6. Easily the most striking use of legal records as a source for social history is John Demos, *Entertaining Satan: Witchcraft and the Culture of Early New England*. The only recent historian of the colonial period to address law and its relation to society squarely is David Thomas Konig, *Law and Society in Puritan Massachusetts: Essex County, Massachusetts, 1629–1692*. There is also a sensitive study of the legal profession in Virginia by A. G. Roeber, *Faithful Magistrates and Republican Lawyers: Creators of Virginia Legal Culture, 1680–1810*, as well as a fine treatment of the formal law of women's property rights by Marylynn Salmon, *Women and the Law of Property in Early America*.

what property was and what rights attached to it. Both were fundamental to society. It does not demean religion to suggest that historians should attend to law for many of the same reasons.

This is not to suggest that historians of early America have neglected law altogether. Criminal law, in particular where it concerned the regulation of morality, has always excited interest.[7] But the law that touched most people, especially in the eighteenth century, was civil, not criminal. It was the questions of debt, contract, and property that underlay everyday social interactions. These were the issues that constituted the vast majority of court business and defined the major area of interaction between law and society. Like death and taxes, two events that generated the records so essential to social historians, civil law visited everyone. Yet most historians ignore it.[8]

In fairness, records of civil law matters tend to be less tractable than most sources of the historian's trade. Civil litigation is often dull and drily technical, with none of the endearing prurience of criminal law. One might, therefore, forgive historians for leaving the field to lawyers, who bring to the fray a tolerance for tedium lovingly nurtured in law school. But lawyers have not served the legal history of the colonial period well, either. They have, it is true, contributed to an older tradition of historical still lifes, which capture and freeze slices of a social and legal past but which do not attempt to deal with change. Alongside that tradition, however, exist casual dismissals of colonial law as rude or irrelevant, as well as more recent studies that in their eagerness to demonstrate the special role of law after the Revolution—often with stimulating insight—unintentionally trivialize or misrepresent what went before. Law in the colonial period was not, as most legal historians would have it, static or derivative. On the contrary, it was changing, complex, and, by the eve of the Revolution,

7. For example, see Douglas Greenberg, *Crime and Law Enforcement in the Colony of New York, 1691–1776*; Gail Sussman Marcus, " 'Due Execution of the Generall Rules of Righteousnesse': Criminal Procedure in New Haven Town and Colony, 1638–1658"; and John M. Murrin, "Magistrates, Sinners, and a Precarious Liberty: Trial by Jury in Seventeenth-Century New England."

8. The most prominent exception is still Richard B. Morris, *Studies in the History of American Law, with Special Reference to the Seventeenth and Eighteenth Centuries*. If one stretches the category of things civil to include public law, there is also Hendrik Hartog, *Public Property and Private Power: The Corporation of the City of New York in American Law, 1730–1870*.

quite ready to sustain the stresses and growth of the decades that followed.[9]

To redress the imbalance, and because of its very ordinariness, I have concentrated on civil law. The core of my data for the first three chapters is a coded sample of 5,317 civil cases drawn from the records of the Hartford County Court at five-year intervals from 1690 through 1760 and from the New London County Court at ten-year intervals from 1720 through 1750, not to mention several hundred other cases from elsewhere in the colony that I left mercifully uncoded.

The county courts were the workhorses of the Connecticut judicial system. They had original jurisdiction over all civil matters, real or personal, as well as local administrative authority and criminal jurisdiction over misdemeanors. Each county court was a panel of three to seven magistrates appointed by the General Assembly. They met twice a year in regular sessions and usually twice more in adjourned sessions. With only minor exceptions, all civil disputes came initially before the justices and juries of the county courts.[10]

Above the county courts was the superior court of judicature, which succeeded the court of assistants in 1711. A chief judge and four

9. The best of the older work is represented by George L. Haskins, *Law and Authority in Early Massachusetts: A Study in Tradition and Design*, and the essays in David H. Flaherty, ed., *Essays in the Early History of American Law*. The most famous dismissals, which still rankle, are Roscoe Pound, *The Formative Era of American Law*, and Grant Gilmore, *The Ages of American Law*. Two influential legal historians who implicitly reject the significance of colonial law are William E. Nelson, *Americanization of the Common Law: The Impact of Legal Change on Massachusetts Society, 1760–1830*, and Morton J. Horwitz, *The Transformation of American Law, 1780–1860*. For a historiographic overview, see the lament of Stanley N. Katz, "The Problem of Colonial Legal History."

10. The county court was not the lowest trial court. Individual justices of the peace had concurrent jurisdiction with the county court over all actions in which title to land was not in issue and where the amount sued for as debt or damage did not exceed forty shillings. Justices usually tried these "small causes," as they were called, in their own homes. On the criminal side, their authority to try cases extended only to the minor misdemeanors that fell under the rubric of "delinquency"—drunkenness, profane swearing, sabbath-breaking, breach of peace. In more serious offenses, they questioned the accused and weighed the evidence to determine whether there was sufficient reason to bind the suspect over to the county or superior court for prosecu-

puisne judges rode circuit, sitting in each county twice annually to hear pleas of felony, divorce, and all other actions brought by appeal, review, or writ of error. In the eighteenth century, judgment of the superior court was final.[11] Further redress could only come by a writ of error or a petition to the assembly for equitable relief.

Most of the cases in the sample are debt actions of various kinds. That, however, is simply a function of the overwhelming predominance of debt cases in civil litigation generally. It does not make this a book about debt litigation, any more than the use of estate inventories would render it a disquisition on inheritance. The records are merely one source, albeit the major one, for learning how people attempted to resolve their differences with one another. One must, of course, be wary of extrapolating from court records to the population at large. Except only indirectly, litigation did not reflect disputes that did not reach court, whether because the parties settled their differences themselves or resorted to the time-honored technique of "lumping it."[12] Still, with proper caution, court records are a valuable and largely untapped source for a society in which most people, or at least most adult males, wound up in court at one time or another—whether as litigants, witnesses, jurors, or observers.

My approach to the material has been that of a social historian. I have been interested in patterns more than in individual cases, although I have tried to remember that people speak more colorfully, if less authoritatively, than numbers. Some of the patterns I found are ones only a lawyer could love. By themselves, matters of legal techni-

---

tion. *Acts and Laws 1715*, p. 15. Good primers on the legal system of Connecticut in the eighteenth century are Zephaniah Swift, *A System of the Laws of the State of Connecticut*, and John T. Farrell's introduction to *The Superior Court Diary of William Samuel Johnson, 1772–1773*.

11. It had not always been so. In the eighteenth century, dissatisfied litigants could carry their appeals from the county court through the court of assistants to the General Assembly—if, of course, they paid the requisite fees and gave the required bonds at each level. In 1697, the assembly ordered that civil cases appealed to the court of assistants from the county courts should have one review there with no further appeal. *Conn. Rec.*, 4:200. Appeal to the Privy Council in England was a theoretical possibility, but only nine litigants in Connecticut—seven in civil cases and two in probate cases—did so in the years between 1693 and 1783. Joseph H. Smith, *Appeals to the Privy Council from the American Plantations*, pp. 667, 670.

12. On "lumping it," see William L. F. Felstiner, "Influences of Social Organization on Dispute Processing."

cality rank exceedingly low in intellectual sex appeal. Mindful of this, I have tried not to study technical legal change for its own sake. For example, if I were to report that the defendant's plea of choice in civil actions changed from the general issue to pleas in abatement and then to demurrers, the finding would be of justifiably limited interest. But if I were to explain it, as I do in chapter 3, as part of a transformation from a communal model of disputing in which the procedures acknowledged the individuality of disputes, to a system hedged with technical rules that homogenized disputes by subordinating facts to abstract, generalizable principles of law—the finding then assumes significance for determining the changing role of law in society in general and in communities in particular.

How to divine the interactions between law and society is not a simple task. After all, law is not a perfect mirror of society. One cannot ponder legal phenomena and intuit their social or economic significance through crude functionalist analyses. Instead, we must look for patterns in how people used law—what legal forms and procedures they chose, how they pleaded their cases and had them decided. We must examine these patterns in the context of what people sought from law and what it gave them, recognizing always that the two might not coincide. Only then can we see the continuities and discontinuities between changes in law and in society.

Following my own advice, what I discovered was that law in Connecticut did change from the seventeenth century to the eighteenth.[13] Among other changes, debt litigation became formalistic and unforgiving, pleading grew more technical and less expressive of the facts of individual disputes, and the civil jury faded from predominance to comparative insignificance. Some of the changes were closely tied to the growing commercialization of the economy and to the changing social context of economic relations. Others were related to the stirrings of legal tradition as a fledgling legal profession approached law as an autonomous system rather than as a contingent social process. Taken together, as they must be, the changes marked a transformation from a legal system that allowed litigants to address their grievances in ways that were essentially communal to one that elevated predictability and uniformity of legal relations over responsiveness to indi-

---

13. This may not be surprising. As Gary Nash recently observed, "No historian labors in the eye-straining, frustratingly incomplete, and sometimes nearly intractable sources of local records in order to prove the changelessness of the society he or she is studying." See Gary B. Nash, "Social Development."

vidual communities. The transformation is one that other legal historians, notably Morton Horwitz and William Nelson, have placed in the nineteenth century. In Connecticut, at least, it occurred much earlier.

Perhaps the strongest testament to the changing relationship between law and community came from outside the legal system. As legal anthropologists know, formal legal rules and institutions are not the only ways people handle disputes. Arbitration and church disciplinary proceedings, the principal alternatives to legal process, were deeply rooted in the communities they served. Yet, as I argue in chapters 4 and 5, they, too, changed in the eighteenth century. They grew more formal, more legalistic, and ultimately less communal. As they became less distinguishable from law, they lost the qualities that had made them distinctive in the first place.

Law increasingly became the standard by which all forms of disputing were measured. By the middle of the eighteenth century, the formal legal system established its hegemony over the ways people resolved their differences. Once-neighborly modes of disputing yielded to a legal system that treated neighbors and strangers alike, with few concessions to the communal spirit of the seventeenth century. That did not, of course, mean that neighbors in fact treated one another as they did strangers. But the opportunity to do so now existed where before it had not. Ways of disputing that once were the norm had become the exception. They persisted, but they no longer suited the generality of legal relations. The implications of these changes for society on the eve of the Revolution were far-reaching. Ultimately, they are the implications that all historians of community have been trying to discern.

I

DEBTORS AND CREDITORS

TOWARD the end of the summer of 1695, Hannah Cowell, a widow who ran a shop in Farmington, set aside cloth goods worth thirty pounds for James Lewis, a neighbor and fellow trader. Cowell's daughter learned who the goods were for and warned her mother not to trust Lewis, "for he owes Mr. Banister Fifty pounds." Later, when Lewis returned to pick up the materials, Cowell refused to give them to him. She confronted him with his indebtedness to Bannister and said that "she could not Trust, being a woman was not able to ride up and down to get in debts."[1]

Cowell was right not to trust Lewis. Lewis had purchased cloth, material, buttons, and ribbons worth nearly fifty pounds on credit from Thomas Bannister, a prosperous Boston merchant. Bannister's evidence of the debt was his account book, which contained a continuous record of his transactions with his customers. Lewis appears to have overextended himself, and Bannister was not his only creditor. When Bannister finally sued to recover his due in September 1696, Lewis produced his own account book, in which he had recorded payments to Bannister of all but a fraction of his debt. Bannister had remained in Boston, and the attorney who acted for him in court had only his book to counter Lewis's. Lewis swore to the accuracy of his book, whereupon the jury awarded Bannister only the reduced amount that Lewis claimed remained unpaid. Lewis's book, however, was a forgery. Bannister learned of the deception and appealed to the court of assistants. His petition suggests that he regarded Lewis's behavior as more a professional affront than a personal one—"it is a thing contrary to all methods of marchants dealing when they trust men with considarable quantitis of goods to take their pay in that

1. Deposition of Hannah Cowell, 25 Sept. 1696, Conn. Arch., Private Controversies (1st ser.), 4:308. The following discussion is based on the documents at ibid., 4:307–31.

specie[,] a man after [he] becoms a debtor to turn him self round and to enter payments in a book and make o[a]th to said acount. [T]his seems to be an esy way of payment though a dangerous way."[2] For Bannister, as for Hannah Cowell, trust was the irreducible core of the relationship.

Bannister won his appeal, but only because witnesses testified that Lewis had admitted owing Bannister a substantial sum after the pretended payments he had marked in his book. Without that testimony, the case pit Lewis's word against Bannister's. Lewis's reputation may not have been spotless, but his oath had been good enough for a local jury, at least against an outsider.

The nature of book debt not only permitted this result, it fairly compelled it. Book accounts were informal. They did not contain explicit promises by the debtor to pay the amounts listed. Nor did they stipulate any time for payment. Instead, accounts charged on book created obligations for which the law implied a promise to pay. This seems a rather vague and risky basis for credit relations. Yet as late as the second decade of the eighteenth century book accounts were the preferred means of evidencing indebtedness in Connecticut, whether the indebtedness was that of a husbandman to his hay mower or a merchant to his factor. Within a generation, however, book debt had fallen from favor and been replaced by formal credit instruments—bonds and promissory notes that detailed the debtor's obligations with cold specificity. The shift did not occur because of changes in the substantive or procedural law of debt. Rather, it occurred because the social and economic determinants of debt relations changed in ways that exposed the weaknesses of book accounts and made the strengths of formal instruments more serviceable.

I

The predominance of debt cases in civil litigation throughout the period—usually 90 percent of all civil actions—suggests the importance of credit in a society that had little hard currency and where income was tied to the vagaries of harvests and the sea. Until well into the eighteenth century, the majority of the population were farmers who produced primarily for their own households, with only small sur-

2. Bannister's Appeal to court of assistants, Hartford, 1 Oct. 1696, ibid., 4:317.

pluses available for trade. Their failure to produce for the market stemmed not from lack of interest or aversion to commercial activity, but rather from conditions of land, labor, and transportation. Poor transportation, rocky soil, and the high cost of labor relative to the price of land hindered production of a commercial surplus and kept trade within well-worn local channels. The economy was "pre-commercial" of necessity, not by choice.[3]

Subsistance, however, is not the same as self-sufficiency. For what farmers could not grow or make themselves, whether cooking utensils or fineries, they relied on local shopkeepers, merchants, and chapmen. Payment was rarely in cash, which was chronically scarce. Instead, people used agricultural produce as money. For public transactions such as payment of taxes, the General Assembly assigned values at which the treasurer would receive and disburse specified commodities. In this form, commodity money was known as *country pay* or *current money* and was, strictly speaking, a means of payment rather than the medium of exchange. Private transactions, on the other hand, were different. Individuals there used the goods designated as country pay, although not necessarily at the rate set by the assembly for public business. They also exchanged a wide variety of other goods that the assembly had not sanctioned and bargained over the values they would attach to them. For merchants, accepting produce in payment for purchases was essential. Only by collecting the small surpluses of many farmers through commodity money exchanges could a merchant accumulate enough produce to trade in distant markets. One should not, however, equate payment in kind with trading for beads and trinkets. People figured their book accounts in pounds, shillings, and pence rather than bushels and pecks. Produce was the medium of exchange, not the object of the transaction.[4]

Book accounts were well suited to such transactions, as well as to transactions with blacksmiths, coopers, carpenters, tanners, taverners,

3. Richard L. Bushman, *From Puritan to Yankee: Character and the Social Order in Connecticut, 1690–1765*, pp. 25–32; Bruce C. Daniels, "Economic Development in Colonial and Revolutionary Connecticut: An Overview"; Isabel S. Mitchell, *Roads and Road-Making in Colonial Connecticut.*

4. Curtis P. Nettels, *The Money Supply of the American Colonies Before 1720*, pp. 208–11; Henry Bronson, *A Historical Account of Connecticut Currency, Continental Money, and the Finances of the Revolution*, 1:5–10, 22–24; Jackson Turner Main, *Society and Economy in Colonial Connecticut*, p. 42. On the distinction between means of payment and medium of ex-

mowers, drivers, laborers, and anyone else with whom one traded goods for services. Anyone could keep a book, and it may be that most men did at one time or another. The book accounts themselves had an almost organic quality, which nicely mirrored the economic relations they recorded. Each book was a running account of the dealings between the parties. The debtor's account grew, one transaction at a time, perhaps reduced by occasional payments on account or seasonal settlements, until the creditor saw fit to request full payment. Some books were short, others long. Some spanned months, others years. There were no limits to the number or duration of transactions except those determined by the parties as they continued to deal with one another. Book debts did not bear interest, regardless of their size or duration. They were a product as well as a record of face-to-face transactions between traders and farmers, between farmers and laborers, as well as of more distant transactions between traders and the merchants who supplied them, all enmeshed in a web of relations that ran on credit and trust. Creditors knew their debtors and knew them well.

Like book accounts themselves, the procedure for suing to collect a book debt was simple and flexible. A creditor merely declared that the debtor owed him a certain sum on a book account that he had never paid, "though often requested."[5] Both parties could testify. Each was

---

change, see Max Weber, *Economy and Society: An Outline of Interpretive Sociology,* 1:5–76, 78. From mid-eighteenth-century merchants' books, Margaret Martin surmised that there was little bargaining over prices. Merchants doubtless held the upper hand, but competition among them for country produce probably kept bargaining within a limited range. Margaret E. Martin, *Merchants and Trade of the Connecticut River Valley, 1750–1820,* p. 154.

5. In this respect, actions on book differed from actions of assumpsit, which in England had gradually supplanted actions of debt *sur contract* in the sixteenth century. Actions of assumpsit, as well as the more specialized *indebitatus assumpsit,* required the plaintiff to plead that the defendant had promised to pay. See A. W. B. Simpson, *A History of the Common Law of Contract: The Rise of the Action of Assumpsit,* pp. 281–315. Although I have never encountered the word "assumpsit" in the court records of early Connecticut, book debt was in many respects analogous to it. This does not, of course, mean that book debtors never promised to pay their creditors—only that the book itself did not record the promise. In such transactions the promise to pay was implicit, and, perhaps more often than not, explicit as well, as when Nathaniel Foot of Wethersfield sued his fellow townsman Laza-

free to offer whatever evidence he or she thought relevant to the dispute. The book itself was not dispositive of the debt. If the bench or jury found that the amount due differed from the amount demanded, the discrepancy was not fatal to the suit, as it was in actions of debt at English common law. The only statutory constraint was that, unless a debtor signed his book account and thereby acknowledged his obligation, the creditor had to sue within a fixed period after the debt had been incurred. If he did not, he lost his right of action against the debtor. The limitation was hardly onerous. Successive statutes lengthened the recovery period from three years in 1673 to "any time, provided the original debtor be living," in 1705.[6] Moreover, creditors could easily circumvent the restriction by requiring their debtors to sign their accounts as a condition for continued credit or by offering proof of their accounts in court and reducing the accounts to judgments that they could levy executions upon if necessary.

Essential to the ease with which book debts could be contracted and litigated was that they relied on a creditor's willingness to extend credit to people who did not expressly bind themselves to pay the debt. Such reliance implied a measure of trust between creditor and debtor. The trust might be that of friends or neighbors, or that of traders who formed assumptions and expectations of one another's behavior through a series of exchanges, or a combination of the two. Trust could rest as easily on self-interest as on altruism. In an exchange economy, commerce was a system of promises—promises to pay, to deliver, to lend, to forbear, to work. Commercial transactions inevitably rested on trust. For courses of dealing to continue, trust had to imply a commitment to the faithful performance of obligations.[7] Creditors on book accounts trusted their debtors to pay, just as debt-

---

rus Hollister for a book debt of forty shillings, "partly in cash lent and partly for what you promised to pay on Account of the widow Butlar." See Foot v. Hollister, 6 HCPCR 122 (1700). On the action of book debt generally, see Zephaniah Swift, *A System of the Laws of the State of Connecticut*, 2:167–72.

6. *The Book of the General Laws of the People Within the Jurisdiction of Connecticut*, pp. 19–20; *Conn. Rec.*, 4:502. Francis Fane, standing counsel to the Board of Trade and Plantations, thought the life recovery period too liberal and recommended in 1738 that the Board reject a successor statute. English law limited recovery on book debts to six years. See Francis Fane, *Reports on the Laws of Connecticut*, p. 173.

7. See Joyce Oldham Appleby, *Economic Thought and Ideology in Seventeenth-Century England*, pp. 188–90.

ors trusted their creditors to deal with them fairly. The nature and limits of the trust were forged over time. Past exchanges formed the basis for future ones. When James Lewis told Hannah Cowell, "For all what I owe Mr. Bannister, he would trust me £30 more, if I would take it," he was, as it turned out, lying.[8] But he was also stating a truism of commercial practice. Hannah Cowell and Thomas Bannister each traded with Lewis until they decided they could no longer trust him.

Significantly, Cowell's decision not to extend credit to Lewis rested in large part on Lewis's past exchanges with Bannister. Merchants formed communities of interest that linked traders and shopkeepers to merchants with whom they did not deal directly as well as to those with whom they did. Recognition of these ties and of the interdependence implicit in continuing courses of dealing often made even distant merchants reluctant to invoke legal process to settle their book accounts with one another. For example, when Edward Bromfield and Francis Burroughs, two merchants from Boston, finally sent a dunning letter in 1691 to Daniel Shelton, a Stratford trader who had run up a large account with them in the previous six years, they emphasized not the debt but rather the debtor's behavior—"for our Security we did expect better treatment from you when we first gave you credit then now we find we are like to have." Even then, they did not consider relations far enough gone to sue until another four years had passed.[9]

The trust necessary to support dealings on book accounts did not require the parties to share the idealized indicia of community. For example, Humphrey Clay and his wife were, by some lights, quite popular in New London. Theirs was the only place in town where thirsty men could find strong refreshment on the sabbath. For that, as well as for their "entertaining seaverall persons unseasonably by night," for Clay's "notorious Lasivious carriages," and for his wife's "impudent baudye horish practices," a special court of commissioners fined them forty pounds in 1664. The commissioners would, however, abate half the fine if the Clays left the colony within six months. After the court closed his establishment, Clay had to settle his business affairs. His regular customers, it appears, had run up tabs with him.

8. Deposition of Hannah Cowell, 25 Sept. 1696, Conn. Arch., Priv. Controversies (1st ser.), 4:309.

9. Francis Burroughs and Edward Bromfield to Daniel Shelton, 23 Mar. 1691, Conn. Arch., Priv. Controversies (1st ser.), 4:252.

Some paid on demand, others Clay sued on the tabs, which were book accounts. Whatever else linked Humphrey Clay and his customers, the ties that supported dealing on book accounts grew from a regular series of transactions. Those transactions, however illicit, forged a community of interest every much as appropriate for book accounts as was the community of interest among merchants.[10]

The linkage of credit to trust endowed book accounts with a kind of presumptive accuracy—not conclusive, but presumptive. Bannister's attorney did not question the forged book that Lewis presented at the first trial, and the jury accepted the book on Lewis's oath to its accuracy. Similarly, when Gershom Brown, a mariner from New Haven, presented his book against Ebenezer Hobart of Guilford to Caleb Leet, the administrator of Hobart's estate, Leet immediately and apparently without question paid Brown what Brown claimed Hobart had owed him. Leet treated the book as presumptively accurate and trusted Brown, even though the sum involved was sizeable. Only later did he discover that Brown's book was "pretended."[11]

Community is not necessarily a function of place, nor does spatial proximity alone guarantee community. Nevertheless, the trust that underlay book accounts occurred most often among neighbors. Book debts were, to a large extent, community matters. Almost 90 percent of all book debt actions filed in the Hartford County Court in 1700 were between residents of the county. In 60 percent of the cases, both debtor and creditor lived in the same town.[12]

The local nexus of book debt is significant. Connecticut in the seventeenth century was a small society. The population nearly tripled in the last four decades of the century, but the 31,500 inhabitants of the colony in 1700 would be poor attendance at many a modern football

10. In re Clay, 1 NLCCR 26 (1664); Clay v. J. Waterhouse, 1 NLCCR 33 (1664); Clay v. I. Waterhouse, 1 NLCCR 33 (1664); Clay v. Chapel, 1 NLCCR 33 (1664); Clay v. Hendy, 1 NLCCR 33 (1664); Clay v. Lothrop, 1 NLCCR 34 (1664); Clay v. Stafford, 1 NLCCR 36 (1664). Since Clay was seeking to recover debts incurred in activity later punished as illegal, it took a special resolution of the court of commissioners to grant him "Liberty to prosecut according to Law any that shall refuse to pay him there just debts for Liquors sould by retale or otherwise."

11. Leet v. Brown, 3 NHCCR 52 (1715).

12. Of the fifty-one actions for debts filed in all sessions of the Hartford County Court, thirty-two were for book debts. Twenty-eight of the book debt actions matched litigants from within the county. In nineteen of those the parties came from the same town.

game.[13] The world for most people was the town in which they lived. It is difficult now to imagine what this meant. The average town contained perhaps a hundred families, five or six hundred people, most of whom lived within a few hundred yards of the center of town. Where houses stopped, field and forest began.[14] People not only knew one another, they knew one another in a variety of contexts. Of course, there are times when knowing one's fellow townspeople may be small comfort. Yet trust can rest on naked self-interest as well as on friendship. The interdependence of the early settlers, born partly of choice and partly of necessity, gave the first towns a powerful cohesiveness.

Debtors and creditors did not, indeed could not, limit their relations to single transactions. They might also be neighbors, relatives, fellow church members, companions in the local militia company, suppliers of goods and services that each needed, rivals for the affection of the same widow, parents whose children had quarreled or whose livestock had eaten each other's grain. In short, they were people whose courses of dealing with one another stretched across time as well as across several roles.[15]

13. Bruce C. Daniels, *The Connecticut Town: Growth and Development, 1635–1790*, pp. 45–50.

14. John Demos, *Entertaining Satan: Witchcraft and the Culture of Early New England*, p. 311. This picture of the physical scale of community life in seventeenth-century New England is a familiar one to historians. For other descriptions, see David Grayson Allen, *In English Ways: The Movement of Societies and the Transferal of English Local Law and Custom to Massachusetts Bay in the Seventeenth Century*; Paul Boyer and Stephen Nissenbaum, *Salem Possessed: The Social Origins of Witchcraft*; John Demos, *A Little Commonwealth: Family Life in Plymouth Colony*; Philip J. Greven, Jr., *Four Generations: Population, Land, and Family in Colonial Andover, Massachusetts*; Richard P. Gildrie, *Salem, 1626–1683: A Covenant Community*; Kenneth A. Lockridge, *A New England Town, The First Hundred Years: Dedham, Massachusetts, 1636–1736*; Sumner C. Powell, *Puritan Village: The Formation of a New England Town*; and Darrett B. Rutman, *The Husbandmen of Plymouth: Farms and Villages in the Old Colony, 1620–1692*. The picture should be adjusted at least somewhat to take into account the existence of dispersed villages as well as central ones. See James T. Lemon, "Spatial Order: Households in Local Communities and Regions."

15. Demos, *Entertaining Satan*, pp. 311–12. Anthropologists have long recognized the significance of multilayered social relations. For example, see Max Gluckman, *The Judicial Process Among the Barotse of Northern Rhode-

It would be easy to infer from this intricate, multilayered web of social relations that communities were peaceful, harmonious, and uncontentious.[16] And they doubtless were, at least part of the time. On the other hand, the high incidence of intratown litigation suggests that communal tranquility was an occasional state rather than a continuous one.[17] Communalism, however, does not require the absence of conflict any more than the presence of conflict negates it.[18] People may have found it easier to trust neighbors with whom they had a variety of relations and knew well, albeit perhaps not favorably, than it was to trust strangers. The exigencies of life in a hostile environment also made people dependent on one another in ways that had nothing to do with trust in the benign sense of the word. Both elements—trust and necessity—were at work in communities in seventeenth-century Connecticut.

The multiplicity of social relations in traditional communities can be a source of quarrels as well as of cohesion. When people deal with one another in several capacities—when their relationships embrace a variety of interests—it is difficult to contain disputes to the particular transactions that produce them. Disputes that arise in one context may send tremors throughout the spectrum of the parties' relations.

For example, six lawsuits between George Denison and John Carr at the June session of the New London County Court in 1665 began with Carr's agreement to perform some work for Denison. Or perhaps they grew from Carr's dalliance with Denison's daughter, Ann. At this remove, it is impossible to determine how the dispute began. It is abundantly clear, however, that the dispute rapidly spread well beyond its flash point. At that one session of the county court it encompassed Denison's complaint against Carr "upon suspicion of felloni-

---

sia, pp. 18–20; Laura Nader, "Choices in Legal Procedure: Shia Moslem and Mexican Zapotec," p. 397.

16. For example, see Michael Zuckerman, *Peaceable Kingdoms: New England Towns in the Eighteenth Century*, pp. 48–50; William E. Nelson, *Americanization of the Common Law: The Impact of Legal Change on Massachusetts Society, 1760–1830*, pp. 1–10.

17. John M. Murrin, "Review Essay"; L. Kinvin Wroth, "Possible Kingdoms: The New England Town from the Perspective of Legal History," pp. 326–30.

18. On the integrative functions of conflict in seventeenth-century Massachusetts, see Demos, *A Little Commonwealth*, and David Thomas Konig, *Law and Society in Puritan Massachusetts: Essex County, 1629–1692*.

ous takeing away" from his house various small items, Denison's suit
on behalf of his daughter "for defamation of her by scandelous
words," Denison's further suit "for attempting to draw away the af-
fections of his daughter . . . two or three times under a pretence of
mariag without her parents consent or allowance," Carr's action "for
a debt due by bill or agreement," Carr's claim that Denison had
broken his written promise to abide by the appraisal made by two
men of the work Carr had done for him, and Carr's fine for cursing
(this last may have come after the court fined Carr five pounds for
attempting to marry Ann Denison without her parents' consent).[19]

Whatever the origin of the dispute—and the causes may very well
have been cumulative—it ramified throughout the range of personal
and professional relations between Denison and Carr. The very fact
that we cannot pinpoint the origin is a significant reflection of the
number of ties that linked the two men. Disputes in such circumstances can be particularly nasty precisely because the personal relations are close and frequent.[20] The informal multiplicity of social ties
may, in fact, leave law as the only vehicle available to the parties to
resolve their differences.

Even with this unromanticized view, the principal influence of
multilayered social relations on the way people handle their disputes
lies in the fact that such ties bind communities together. The preserva-
tion of such ties may be more than individually desirable—it may be a
community necessity. Anthropologists have noted that courts proceed
differently in disputes when the parties are tied in a web of relationships than they do when the parties are comparative strangers to one
another. In the former instance, reconciliation is important to enable
the parties to continue to live together, as they must in small communities where their paths necessarily cross. In the latter, reconciliation is
less important because there is nothing valuable to preserve.[21]

This is not to suggest that litigants from small communities seek
compromise rather than victory when they sue or that courts always
prefer to reconcile the parties rather than award the spoils to one or

19. Denison v. Carr, 1 NLCCR 46–47, 49–51 (1665); Carr v. Denison, 1
NLCCR 47 (1665). At the same sessions, Denison also traded lawsuits with
Thomas Shaw. Denison sued Shaw for defamation, and Shaw sued Denison
for a book debt of "victualls drincke and lodging." Denison v. Shaw, 1
NLCCR 47 (1665); Shaw v. Denison, 1 NLCCR 48 (1665).

20. See Weber, *Economy and Society*, 1:360–63.

21. See Gluckman, *Judicial Process Among the Barotse*, pp. 20–21, 55.

the other. Some disputes are not susceptible to compromise, and some disputants do not seek compromise. Nathaniel Johnson, for example, filed over two dozen lawsuits from 1710 to 1715 while administering the estate of William Hoadly of Branford. One was against a widow named Mary Foot, also of Branford, for a book debt of some eight pounds. Johnson sued despite a plea from Foot "to Reckon with her, and . . . that if shee owed him any thing shee would pay him every penney and rather then go to Court shee wold pay him 20s more." Johnson, however, who from the lawsuits emerges as a rather hard-hearted sort, replied that "he had no need of her Gifts, but wold go to Court and Recon before honest judetious men." Yet for every creditor like Nathaniel Johnson, there were others for whom litigation was a last resort. A Mr. Condie's recovery against Edward Stallon in New London in 1664 included what was in effect additional interest for "two yeeres forbeareance." Samuel Raymond of New London waited fourteen years for his fellow townsman, Lester Strickland, to pay a bill, which Strickland did in 1693. Estate inventories are full of old, long-unsolicited debts.[22]

If courts proceed differently in cases where the litigants have had a range of dealings with one another, it is because the parties themselves structure their legal relations in ways that permit the different procedure. Where social relations serve several interests at once, the range of facts relevant to a dispute may be broad. If reconciliation is important, the factual inquiry necessary to resolve the dispute must be equally broad. Narrow conceptions of relevance are appropriate only where the social relations at stake are themselves narrowly defined.[23]

In book debt actions, the range of potentially relevant evidence was such that witnesses other than the parties themselves commonly testified. For example, when Daniel Collins of East Haven sued his neighbor, John Robinson, in 1716 for a book debt of thirty shillings, the judges of the county court listened to four witnesses before deciding how much Robinson owed. The court costs alone, which the court

22. Johnson v. Foot, 3 NHCCR 22 (1714); Deposition of Daniel Collins and William Roberts, n.d., NHCCF 2; Condie v. Stallon, 1 NLCCR 36 (1664); Raymond v. Strickland, bill dated 20 May 1679, NLCCF 174. David Konig has an excellent discussion of the phenomenon of "neighborly loans." See Konig, *Law and Society in Puritan Massachusetts*, pp. 82–88.

23. See Gluckman, *Judicial Process Among the Barotse*, pp. 20–21, 78; Richard L. Abel, "A Comparative Theory of Dispute Institutions in Society," pp. 289, 294.

assessed against Robinson, were over two pounds—more than six times the unpaid debt. Similarly, when John Guy, a merchant from Branford, sued his former servant, Mary Kirkham, in 1713 for a book debt of £5 11s. 4d., the evidence included not only Guy's book, but also the sworn testimony of three witnesses.[24]

The dispute between Guy and Kirkham nicely illustrates the evidentiary and procedural flexibility of book debt, as well as the circumstances that can give rise to dealings on book in the first place. Guy had hired Kirkham in June or July 1712 to help care for his ailing wife and child. Shortly after entering Guy's service, Kirkham purchased a number of items from him on credit. Guy's book lists twenty-four entries, mostly for fineries such as lace, handkerchiefs, gloves, snuff, buckles, ribbons, and silver buttons. Kirkham's service proved unsatisfactory, and Guy "turned her a way" in October. Guy sued Kirkham for the debt six months later, in April 1713. The case came to the New Haven County Court in June after preliminary proceedings before a justice of the peace. The principal evidence of the debt, Guy's book, was not decisive. In fact, despite the book, Kirkham won a jury verdict at the first trial in June on her plea that she had paid Guy five pounds and that no balance was due.

Books were not conclusive evidence of the debts they recorded. They were, instead, merely a starting point for discussing the range of dealings between debtor and creditor in open court. For Mary Kirkham, that discussion eventually led to the testimony of Hannah Butler, who said that Kirkham had "Served nather as nursh nar maid but in podering her head and walking abroad was mose of her work."[25] Butler's testimony came at the retrial on review of the case in November 1713. The jury weighed conflicting testimony about when Kirkham had entered Guy's service, what the wage agreement had been, whether she had performed the duties expected of her, and how much of her wages had been credited against her debt. Of these, the only evidence supplied by the book was the credit for wages. Everything else that the parties, the judges, and the jury regarded as relevant to the issue of what, if anything, Kirkham owed Guy came from sources other than the evidence of the debt itself. No one felt constrained by narrow conceptions of relevance.

24. Collins v. Robinson, 3 NHCCR 73, NHCCF 1 (1716); Guy v. Kirkham, 3 NHCCR 9, 17–18, NHCCF 1 (1713).

25. Deposition of Hannah Butler, 9 Nov. 1713, Guy v. Kirkham, NHCCF 1 (1713).

The procedural and evidentiary flexibility of book debt invited the parties to explain their dispute in ways that would place the legal issue of indebtedness in the larger context of their social relations. Liability on book debts turned—at least potentially—far more on the facts of the dispute than on any fixed conception of the law, as one debtor discovered when he complained that the jury that decided a book debt action against him considered evidence that the court had excluded.[26] The procedural framework of book debt litigation rested on the assumption that each dispute was unique. Because they were unique, cases were decided only after the parties had aired all the evidence they thought relevant. This doubtless explains why so many book debt litigants submitted their cases to the jury for decision rather than to the judges of the bench. It also explains why the vast majority of contested book actions, whether decided by bench or jury, turned on factual issues rather than legal ones.[27] Debtors and creditors who used book accounts committed themselves to a course of dealing that, as a trade-off for not requiring an express promise to pay, permitted a broad inquiry into the nature of their obligations. Such inquiries were appropriate when the relations between debtor and creditor were not limited to the individual transactions that created the debt.

The qualities that made book debt so suitable for credit relations between people who dealt with one another regularly also enabled litigants to use book accounts to air grievances that might be only tangentially related to the issue in litigation. Disputes played out in the social context of multilayered, interdependent relations often stirred up an array of grievances that had accumulated over many years.[28] For example, when Daniel Barker of Branford sued two of his fellow townsmen, Nathaniel and Daniel Page, for a book debt of £23 11s. in November 1710, the Pages did not deny the debt, only that they were jointly liable. After they lost, both in the county court and

26. Petition of James Poisson, 10 May 1711, Conn. Arch., Priv. Controversies (1st ser.), 6:222; *Conn. Rec.*, 5:210. The assembly rejected the petition.

27. Juries decided 52 percent of the contested book debt actions in the Hartford County Court in the period 1710 to 1715, but only 25 percent of the contested actions on written instruments in the same period. Of the contested book debt actions in the same period, 81 percent turned on factual issues. For the significance of whether judges or juries decided cases and whether on factual or legal issues, see Chapter 3.

28. Max Gluckman observed this among the Lozi of present-day Zambia. See Gluckman, *Judicial Process Among the Barotse*, pp. 21–22.

on appeal to the court of assistants, Nathaniel and Daniel Page struck back. Each sued Barker on book, one of them for expenses he claimed to have incurred five years earlier for wintering a horse and cattle for Barker. Neither man recovered what he had lost to Barker in the first lawsuit, but it is unlikely that either would have acted had Barker not sued first.[29]

This is not to suggest that judges or juries used book actions to resolve grievances other than those at issue in the particular case at bar, merely that the evidentiary catholicity of book debt allowed the parties to air them. Airing such grievances could serve a valuable social function. For people linked by multilayered relationships, the mere act of dragging an adversary into court and holding him up for judgment on something—anything—represented a victory over someone against whom the plaintiff had other complaints, whether or not those other complaints were on trial.[30] That done, the parties could resume their normal quarrelsome—but mutually dependent—neighborly relations.

Consider, for example, the dispute in East Haven between a brother and sister, Thomas and Hannah Hitchcock, on the one hand, and their brother-in-law, Jacob Robinson, on the other.[31] Robinson was administrator of the estate of his mother-in-law, Sarah Hitchcock,

29. Barker v. N. Page and D. Page, 2 NHCCR 446 (1710), 3 CtAR 196 (1711); N. Page v. Barker, 2 NHCCR 467 (1711); D. Page v. Barker, 2 NHCCR 490, NHCCF 2 (1712), 3 CtAR 272, 293 (1713).

30. In a similar vein, John Demos has offered an intriguing explanation of intracommunity litigation in seventeenth-century Plymouth colony. Houses in early Plymouth were too small and families too large to permit anything approaching privacy as we know it. The potential for family discord was great but was, as far as anyone can tell, largely unrealized. On the other hand, court records reveal a surprising volume of acrimonious litigation between neighbors. Demos advances the hypothesis—and he stresses that it is only a hypothesis—that such litigation stemmed from displacement of the anger and aggression generated by cramped living conditions. The family was the fundamental unit of puritan society—its equilibrium had to be maintained. Although not verifiable, Demos's suggestion that "a man cursed his neighbor in order to keep smiling at his parent, spouse, or child" is persuasive. Demos, *A Little Commonwealth*, pp. 48–51.

31. The following account is based on the records and files of Robinson v. H. Hitchcock, 3 NHCCR 33–34, 45, NHCCF 3 (1714); T. Hitchcock v. Robinson, 3 NHCCR 32, 38, NHCCF 1 (1714); Robinson v. T. Hitchcock, 3 NHCCR 37, NHCCF 3, 3 CtAR 369, 1 SCR 14 (1714); Robinson v. T.

mother of Thomas and Hannah. Thomas and Sarah had been coad-
ministrators of the estate of the patriarch of the family, Sarah's husband Eliakim. In mid-March 1714, Thomas Hitchcock sued Robinson
for book debts that totaled £4 14s. 7d. pay.[32] The first suggestion that
the debt represented a deeper grudge came at the county court in April
when Robinson pleaded payment of all but £1 11s. 8d., for which he
had made a "reckoning" in 1704 with Sarah and Thomas Hitchcock
in their capacity as administrators of Eliakim's estate and which was
now due to Sarah's estate. Robinson used his account of Hitchcock's
indebtedness as a counterclaim against Hitchcock's suit. The accounts
the two men exhibited against one another in court were primarily for
various labor services that each claimed to have performed or procured for the other—mowing, harrowing, planting, spinning. Some of
Robinson's items against Hitchcock went back almost seven years,
while part of the debt Hitchcock sought to recover was ten years old.

Thomas Hitchcock's suit against Robinson for the book debt arose
within a relationship of long standing that had many elements to it.
The immediate trigger of the suit appears to have been Robinson's
conduct as administrator of Sarah Hitchcock's estate. After Sarah died
sometime in late 1713, Robinson quarreled with Thomas and Hannah
Hitchcock over Sarah's household goods and personal effects. Robinson tried to play Thomas and Hannah against each other by offering
to release one from liability and proceed against the other. Thomas
Hitchcock responded by resurrecting the old book debts against
Robinson.

A jury award of 13s. 10d. and costs settled Thomas Hitchcock's
book debt action against his brother-in-law. It did not, however, settle
the underlying grievances. That, of course, had not been the point of
the litigation. The book debt action was only one episode in a family
squabble that began before and continued after the book debt itself
had been adjudicated. The lawsuit aired grievances rather than settled
them. The procedural and evidentiary informality of book debt allowed the parties to use the litigation to let off steam. In doing so, they
acted in a manner that supports what modern anthropologists have
noted about the importance of time as a variable in handling disputes.

Hitchcock, 3 NHCCR 45 (1714); T. Hitchcock and H. Hitchcock v. Robinson, 3 NHCCR 50, NHCCF 1 (1715); Robinson v. T. Hitchcock, NHCCF 2
(1715); Robinson v. T. Hitchcock, 3 NHCCR 60, 1 SCR 197 (1716).

32. Both men were cited personally, not as administrators.

When enduring relationships are important, either to the individuals or the community, courts or mediators deal with the grievances in diffuse, informal fashions over extended periods of time, attending to the person rather than the act.[33] In appropriate circumstances, book debt litigation permitted litigants to air grievances without having them adjudicated—a community function of no small importance if the parties must continue to deal with one another. This is not to suggest, of course, that all book debt actions served this hidden social function. In all likelihood, most were exactly what they purported to be—actions to recover debts due on book accounts. What matters is that book debts could and frequently did serve a distinct social function as opposed to a purely economic one. Their ability to do so was what made them so suitable for debtors and creditors who were locked—or, if one prefers, voluntarily engaged—in continuing courses of dealing that extended beyond individual business transactions.

Until after the turn of the eighteenth century, book debts were the primary method of contracting debt obligations. They embodied the credit that ran the local economy. As informal as book debt was, neighbors often resorted to even less formal means of tracing their financial obligations to one another. In all likelihood, a casual promise to pay sufficed much of the time—promises so casual and so widely honored that they rarely rose, or sank, to the level of legal visibility, where they might leave written remains. For example, when Peter Trebye of New London sought payment from Peter Blatchford in 1666 "for not paying him for his labour wherein hee imployed him," he did not file a debt action or submit an account, but "complaineth of" Blatchford, using the term usually reserved for public accusation of improper or criminal behavior. Similarly, John Richards, also of New London, labeled his action against William Thompson in 1664 as simply "for a debt due for work." The obligation that underlay Thomas Lord's claim of debt "for a blacke and a whit steer and a buff coate" against his kinsman and fellow townsman of Lyme, Richard Lord, in 1711 was oral, which is why the parties summoned witnesses. The oral agreement by which Henry Cook of Branford rented

---

33. See Barbara Yngvesson, "Responses to Grievance Behavior: Extended Cases in a Fishing Community," and "The Atlantic Fishermen." By way of contrast, disputes in circumstances in which the "past and future aspects of the relationship are not important"—but not necessarily nonexistent—tend to be processed quickly in a manner that focuses on the act rather than on the relationship. See Yngvesson, "The Atlantic Fishermen," p. 83.

twelve sheep from Tabitha Foot, also of Branford, was sufficiently informal that when Foot sued Cook in 1714 for the money due the closest she could place the agreement was "in the Latter end of [1712] or there abouts."[34]

None of these cases rested on or even involved written evidence of the obligation. The understandings between the parties and all relevant evidence were oral. Yet the informality of the transactions does not imply lack of sophistication any more than one would deride as backward a shopkeeper who accepted an out-of-state check without taking one's firstborn child as security. For example, the promise that John Thomas of New Haven made in 1712 to pay Stephen Perkins, also of New Haven, eighteen shillings "money or Labour Equivalent" was oral and thus, by the standards of contractual obligations, informal. But when Perkins sued Thomas on the promise four years later the pleadings turned on whether the promise was supported by consideration or was instead unenforceable as "a Nude Contract"— hardly the pleading of unsophisticated litigants.[35] Oral transactions, like book accounts, were products of a social setting that assumed the integrity of obligations—an assumption made possible by the interdependence inherent in multilayered relationships. Such assumptions could sometimes be misplaced. That, however, is a risk common to all dealings, formal and informal.

II

Book debt itself did not change during the eighteenth century. Litigation on book accounts, however, changed radically. From 83 percent of all debt litigation in Hartford County in the first decade of the century, book debts fell to 30 percent in the third decade and in the 1730s reached 20 percent, at which level they remained until just before the Revolution. Conversely, actions on written instruments— bonds, bills obligatory, and promissory notes—increased from 17 percent in the first decade to 70 percent in the third and 80 percent thereafter. Scattered records of justices of the peace reveal the same

34. Trebye v. Blatchford, 1 NLCCR 76 (1666); Richards v. Thompson, 1 NLCCR 40 (1664); T. Lord v. R. Lord, 8 NLCCR 35 (1711), summons dated 9 Nov. 1711, NLCCF 178; Foot v. Cook, summons dated 28 Dec. 1714, NHCCF 1.

35. Perkins v. Thomas, 3 NHCCR 75, NHCCF 2 (1716).

pattern at the lowest legal level.[36] Actions on book hardly disappeared—in raw numbers they increased sixfold in Hartford County
from the first decade of the century to the fifth—but they no longer
dominated debt litigation.

There were no substantive or procedural changes that would explain the declining popularity of book debt as a mode of contracting
and contesting debt obligations. In theory, book debt retained its potential social value for people in multilayered relationships. In practice, however, it is clear that debtors and creditors called upon book
debt to perform that function less frequently.

Written instruments were a very different kind of debt obligation
than book accounts. They were formal instruments by which the
debtor, over his own signature, expressly promised to pay a specific
sum to the creditor, either on demand or on a certain date. They were
not local inventions. Conditioned bonds, for example, had long been
a mainstay of bilateral contracts at English law. Promissory notes had
their immediate origin in English goldsmiths' notes of the mid-seven-
teenth century, while a related form, bills obligatory or writings
obligatory, had been used by merchants since the end of the fourteenth
century.[37]

There were, to be sure, differences among the three. Conditioned
bonds, which were more common than single or simple bonds, were
contracts under seal by which the obligor bound himself to pay the
stipulated sum to the obligee on a certain date unless by that date he
had performed a specified condition. That condition, known as a
condition of defeasance, could be either the performance of some act
or the payment of a sum of money. Conditioned bonds could be used
to secure the conveyance of land, the delivery of commercial goods, or
the repayment of loans, to name but a few of their applications. Fail-

36. For example, in a six-month period in 1754, a Windham justice of the
peace heard forty-seven actions on notes and only four on book debts. During
the same period his only other cases were five sabbath offenses, two present-
ments for swearing, one for breach of peace, and a replevin bond. "First
Record Book of Samuel Gray, Esq., of Windham, from June 6, 1754 to April
2, 1761." For the distribution of debt actions in the county court, see Table 1,
Appendix.

37. See Simpson, *History of the Common Law of Contract*, 88–125; J.
Milnes Holden, *The History of Negotiable Instruments in English Law*, pp.
10–12, 66–73; P. S. Atiyah, *The Rise and Fall of Freedom of Contract*, pp.
154–56; Gerard de Malynes, *Consuetudo, vel, Lex Mercatoria: Or, The Ancient Law-Merchant*.

ure to perform the condition made the obligor liable for the full amount of the bond. Since it was customary to execute bonds for twice the amount lent or twice the value of the items to be delivered, the face amounts of the bonds were decidedly penal in nature.

Bills obligatory and promissory notes were not under seal. They were "informal bonds," which originally had no standing at common law. Bills and notes were promises signed by the debtor to pay the creditor a specified sum within a stipulated time or on demand. Bills generally acknowledged the indebtedness and recited what we would now regard as the consideration for the debtor's promise—that, for example, the obligation was for commodities received—whereas notes were simply unadorned promises to pay the named amount. In Connecticut, bills obligatory were also signed by witnesses, while promissory notes were not. For the most part, however, the distinctions between bills obligatory and promissory notes in Connecticut were inconsequential. Relatively few identifiable bills appear in the records. More importantly, it would be misleading to impute the English or modern clarity of the categories of bonds, bills, and notes to colonial practice. For our purposes, the similarities among them are far more important than the differences. As a group, they stand in sharp contrast to book debts.

Written instruments were certainly not unknown in Connecticut before the eighteenth century. Merchants, for example, used bills obligatory as payment or to secure the performance of commercial undertakings. Matthew Beckworth of New London gave "a bill of securitye" for twenty pounds sterling to Samuel Chester in 1665 or 1666 to guarantee the delivery of bills of lading. Deliverance Blackman, also of New London, gave his bill to John Gallop, Sr. in 1674 to secure his promise to deliver two thousand shingles. Thomas Lord of Lyme executed a bill in favor of William Rowlson of Haddam in 1698 "in consederation of the hire of the sloupe Provedence twenty and five dayse at nine shillings per day" and for various goods.[38] Perhaps the only unusual aspect of these transactions is that they wound up in litigation. Neither the bills themselves nor the manner of suing on them indicate anything novel about the use of written instruments. Nonetheless, people did not use bills, notes, or bonds very often. They relied instead on book accounts and oral promises as the bases of their financial obligations to one another.

38. Chester v. Beckworth, 1 NLCCR 71 (1666); Gallop v. Blackman, 3 NLCCR 71 (1674); Rowlson v. Lord, 7 NLCCR 234, NLCCF 174 (1699).

The shift to written instruments in the second and third decades of the eighteenth century constituted a fundamental transformation in the nature of debt obligations. It also marked a change in the uses of written instruments themselves. Bills obligatory largely passed from vogue by 1720, their place taken by promissory notes.[39] Merchants and traders continued to use written instruments—now conditioned bonds and promissory notes—to secure the performance of commercial undertakings, such as the delivery of iron from the mines in Salisbury and Kent, the delivery of horses, lumber, or rum, or construction work. Notes and bonds were also widely used to secure submissions of disputes to arbitration, and bonds were common in land transfers.[40] But as promissory notes grew to overshadow conditioned bonds, which they first did in the 1730s, the primary use of written instruments ceased to be to secure the obligor's performance of an underlying contract and became instead a means of recording his promise to repay a debt.[41]

As we have seen, the internal economy of Connecticut at the turn of the century operated largely on barter transactions. The economy embraced ways of dealing to which book debt was ideally suited. Much of that changed with the advent and spread of paper money, which was both a cause and a symptom of economic transformation. The very appearance of paper currency—first issued by the General As-

39. Bills obligatory comprised 83 percent of the written debt instruments litigated in the Hartford County Court in the first decade of the eighteenth century, 33 percent in the second, and only 4 percent in the third.

40. Cook v. Lamb, 3 NHCCR 517, NHCCF 8 (1738) (bond to deliver iron); Beecher v. Cooke, 4 NHCCR 332, 344, NHCCF 13, 10 SCR 11, SCF 327 (1748–49) (note to deliver iron); McLeroy v. Barnard, 12 HCCR 143, HCCF 134 (1746) (note to deliver a horse); Atwater v. Turner, 4 NHCCR 338, NHCCF 13 (1748) (note for delivery of barrel staves and headings); Atwater v. Hotchkiss, Atwater, and Munson, 4 NHCCR 344, 347, NHCCF 13, 10 SCR 16 (1749) (note for delivery of lumber); Alling and Howell v. Factor, 4 NHCCR 701, 709, NHCCF 20, 11 SCR 231, 280 (1755–57) (note for delivery of rum); Stacy and Tharp v. Peck and Bradley, 4 NHCCR 27, NHCCF 11 (1740) (bond for masonry, plastering, and delivery of materials); Gorham v. Simms, 4 NHCCR 359, NHCCF 15 (1749) (note for lathing, plastering, building chimney); Brown v. Tuttle, 3 NHCCR 81, NHCCF 1 (1717); Harris v. Malbone, 21 NLCCR (Nov. 1750) no. 23, NLCCF 231 (1750); Lord v. Ely, 21 NLCCR (Nov. 1750) no. 86, NLCCF 231 (1750). On the use of written instruments in arbitration, see Chapter 4.

41. See Table 1, Appendix.

sembly in 1709—signaled growing involvement in a commercial economy.[42] Spurred by rapid population growth and by periodic military expeditions to Canada and against the Indians, trade expanded dramatically in the first half of the eighteenth century. Population, which had doubled in the generation between 1670 and 1700, doubled again in the next thirty years. Population density, which had remained fairly stable for the twenty years from 1690 to 1710, increased rapidly after 1710 as the rate of population growth outstripped the availability of new land for settlement.[43] The resulting pressure on land encouraged more specialized cultivation to adapt to the different types of land. Specialization in turn led to commercial farming, both because of the inherent need to market crops and the development of large markets in the West Indies. The nature of the newly settled land and the demand for animal products caused meat and dairy production to surpass grain farming as the principal form of agriculture. Market farming and agricultural specialization did not develop as fully in Connecticut as they did in Pennsylvania or the Chesapeake tobacco country. Nonetheless, the agrarian economy of Connecticut grew enough to change the contours of commercial activity.[44]

Connecticut merchants did not have the transatlantic contacts of their more substantial counterparts in Boston and New York. Instead, they directed their ventures to the West Indies and to the coasting trade—profitable, to be sure, but not the stuff of commercial empire. Local merchants chafed at the lock that neighboring colonies had on direct trade with Europe, but, despite efforts to form trading compa-

---

42. *Conn. Rec.*, 5:11–12; James A. Henretta, *The Evolution of American Society, 1700–1815: An Interdisciplinary Analysis*, p. 7. See also Jacob M. Price, *Capital and Credit in British Overseas Trade: The View from the Chesapeake, 1700–1776.*

43. Daniels, *Connecticut Town*, pp. 47, 50.

44. Jackson Turner Main goes so far as to describe the years between 1710 and 1730 as an "economic boom." Main, *Society and Economy in Colonial Connecticut*, pp. 115–51. On the growth of overseas trade, see Glenn Weaver, *Jonathan Trumbull: Connecticut's Merchant Magistrate (1710–1785)*, pp. 32–34. On the development of commercial farming, see Daniels, "Economic Development in Colonial and Revolutionary Connecticut," pp. 432–34. See also James T. Lemon, *The Best Poor Man's Country: A Geographical Study of Early Southeastern Pennsylvania*, and Gloria L. Main, *Tobacco Colony: Life in Early Maryland, 1650–1720.*

nies, they never succeeded in breaking into the mainstream of European trade.[45]

Agricultural expansion did not alter this pattern, but it did add an entirely new local dimension. With more products available for export, secondary ports along the Connecticut River and Long Island Sound and market towns on the road to Boston grew to accommodate the demand for markets and transportation. The concentrated population and market orientation of these towns encouraged the appearance of artisans and merchants and the specialization of business enterprise. The lure of greater local trade opportunities encouraged people to enter the lists as small traders and challenge established merchants. Farmers and craftsmen often took to trading on the side. With the kind of optimism possible in an atmosphere of prosperity and expansion, many new traders began business with little capital support and ran marginal operations. They favored the easy credit that paper money represented. Partly in response to the growing political influence of the new traders, the assembly authorized new issues of paper money after the first one in 1709. As the scarcity of currency eased—and before the shadow of inflation lengthened—new merchants were able to enter towns and compete with established traders by offering farmers cash for their goods. Farmers could then use the cash to repay debts they owed to the merchants with whom they usually ran up long book accounts.[46]

45. The most ambitious effort was the New London Society for Trade and Commerce, which the General Assembly chartered in 1732. The society, however, attempted to raise additional capital by issuing bills of credit in the form of promissory notes backed by mortgages given by subscribers to the company, thus in effect presuming to issue their own paper money. The bills actually announced on their face that they were "in Value Equal . . . to Bills of Publick Credit of this or the Neighbouring Governments." The assembly quickly suspended the charter, and the society collapsed. See Bushman, *From Puritan to Yankee*, pp. 124–27. A copy of a society bill of credit appears in Wyman W. Parker, *Connecticut's Colonial and Continental Money*, p. 20. The best general accounts of the society are Andrew McFarland Davis, "A Connecticut Land Bank," and Bruce P. Stark, "The New London Society and Connecticut Politics, 1732–1740."

46. Bushman, *From Puritan to Yankee*, pp. 107–23; Henretta, *Evolution of American Society*, pp. 36–37, 78–81; Martin, *Merchants and Trade*, p. 14. Charles Grant noted the speculative nature of the widespread indebtedness in Kent. See Charles S. Grant, *Democracy in the Connecticut Frontier Town of Kent*, pp. 66–74.

Cash was attractive to farmers. Credit with local traders could resemble economic bondage. Individuals whose purchases on book accounts outstripped their capacity to pay had to mortgage their futures to receive credit to pay for past advances. As Solomon Stoddard lamented, "Multitudes of people in the Country are not beforehand, they spend their Money before they have it; the extravagancy of their expenses forces them to lie in debt."[47] Cash did not miraculously free farmers from debt—one historian has calculated that the number of debt cases in the courts increased nineteen-fold in the first three decades of the century, nine times the rate of population growth.[48] Nor did people cease doing business on book—in an economy and a society that were still primarily agrarian, that would hardly have been possible.[49] Nonetheless, debt obligations took a new form.

Paper currency answered the demands for capital of farmers who wanted to buy land or livestock and of traders who needed goods to trade. As paper money supplanted commodity money, direct extensions of credit in return for written promises to repay became the dominant mode of contracting debt obligations. These promises were the bonds and promissory notes that pushed book debt aside in the 1720s.

47. Solomon Stoddard, *An Answer to Some Cases of Conscience Respecting the Country*, p. 2. The same pattern of borrowing against anticipated ("prayed for" might be more accurate) future profits characterized the relations of Virginia tobacco planters with their factors. See Price, *Capital and Credit*.

48. Bushman, *From Puritan to Yankee*, p. 136. In the Hartford County Court, the number of debt cases increased fifteenfold in the same period.

49. For evidence of local book debt transactions later in the eighteenth century, see Fred Anderson, *A People's Army: Massachusetts Soldiers and Society in the Seven Years' War*, pp. 29–32; and Christopher M. Jedrey, *The World of John Cleaveland: Family and Community in Eighteenth-Century New England*, pp. 91–93. Christopher Clark notes the persistence of noncash exchange networks in western Massachusetts in the early nineteenth century. See Clark, "Household Economy, Market Exchange and the Rise of Capitalism in the Connecticut Valley, 1800–1860," pp. 173–75. Account book mavens can always produce evidence that traditional forms of exchange continued into a so-called "modern" period. My favorite is my father-in-law's description of a grocery-store owner in Wetumka, Oklahoma, named Bill Shaber, who in the 1930s kept his customers' accounts in a cheese box hidden in a barrel of beans. Such stories merely illustrate what should be a truism—that "traditional" social relations frequently coexist with "modern" ones. See Abel, "A Comparative Theory of Dispute Institutions," p. 294.

Even people who continued to trade on book felt the influence of signed credit instruments when creditors demanded that their debtors make their book accounts over into notes or bonds as a condition of further credit or of forbearance on the existing debt. For example, when Simon Scripture, "a Shop keeper and Retailer of English Goods" in Coventry, insisted that James Jackson of Windsor acknowledge a book account that was larger than Jackson had anticipated and give him a note for it at a usurious rate of interest, Jackson felt he had no choice but to agree, "being then unable to pay said Debt and fearing the displeasure of" Scripture.[50] Merchants naturally became the heaviest investors in notes and bonds, both because they were more likely to receive them in commercial transactions and because of the private banking functions that many of them performed.[51]

What made written instruments so popular was their certainty. The debtor's liability on written obligations rested primarily on whether the instrument itself met the legal requirements of form. Actions on written instruments did not admit the range of evidence that was customary in actions on book accounts. The debtor's options were few. He could plead *non est factum*—that the instrument was not his deed, but that it had been altered or that his signature had been forged. He could plead performance of the condition, if the bond was conditional or the note had been given to secure performance of a promise. Or he could plead payment. He could not plead that there had been a mistake or that he was entitled to a set-off from other dealings with the creditor or that he had intended something other than what he had signed or that the creditor had promised not to sue. In short, except for pleas that were limited in scope and often technical in nature, written instruments bound debtors to what they had signed. This quality made notes and bonds more definite and less controvertible than book accounts. With their precise forms and express promises, written obligations embodied the debtor's liability more completely and to a greater certainty than book accounts.

50. Defendant's plea in bar, Jan. 1756, Scripture v. Jackson, 14 HCCR 211, 237, HCCF 150 (1755–56).

51. See generally Bushman, *From Puritan to Yankee*, pp. 127–30; Martin, *Merchants and Trade*, pp. 27, 156–63, 176. Herbert Johnson noted a similar transformation in New York from a barter economy to one based on credit, and the consequent importance of credit instruments. Herbert A. Johnson, *The Law Merchant and Negotiable Instruments in Colonial New York, 1664–1730*, pp. 4–14.

Creditors understood the greater certainty of written instruments. Occasionally, they acknowledged it expressly, as when William Southworth of Stratford remarked in a petition against his former partner, Richard Alsop of Middletown, that a note was "a Stronger lien and Security in the judgment of Law then the plaintiff had by the original Contract [on book]."[52] Usually, however, the knowledge was implicit in their actions, by their very use of the instruments.

It is important to emphasize that this recognition of the more precise qualities of written instruments was not a sudden revelation of the 1720s, when creditors first flocked to notes and bonds. As early as the 1690s it was apparent that creditors who sued on bills obligatory only had to prove their bills to win judgment if the debtor did not appear to defend the action, whereas when the debt was on book the court would continue the case to its next session to give the debtor another chance to appear.[53] In 1695, when Edward Bromfield and Francis Burroughs of Boston lost patience with Daniel Shelton of Stratford for his inability to pay book debts of seven-to-ten years' standing, they instructed their attorney to give Shelton a choice between going to court or executing a bond to pay the balance due in six months. The parties had done business on book, but in the end the security of a written credit instrument was the only way for the debtor to forestall litigation.[54]

The certainty with which written credit instruments embodied the debtor's liability made the outcome of litigation on them more predictable than was the case with book accounts. Procedural restrictions on actions based on written instruments narrowed the range of relevant evidence to the instruments themselves. Nothing mattered other than the piece of paper with the debtor's promise and signature. Thus, when Nathaniel Collins of Enfield engaged an attorney in New London in 1711 to sue a debtor on a bill obligatory, he could write the attorney that "its needless to insist uppon any thing farther, because the bill is the turning point."[55] When the assembly in 1725 barred any

52. Petition of William Southworth, May 1758, Conn. Arch., Priv. Controversies (2d ser.), 26:58a.

53. Nest v. Tanner, 7 NLCCR 69 (1691); Chandler v. Wickware, 6 NLCCR 216 (1699).

54. Edward Bromfield and Francis Burroughs to Nathaniel Foote, 1695, Conn. Arch., Priv. Controversies (1st ser.), 4:260.

55. Nathaniel Collins to George Denison, 23 May 1711, in Collins v. Fearman, NLCCF 178.

review or appeal from the first trial in the county court in actions on bonds, bills, or notes for the payment of money only, it was only recognizing that instruments that could be adjudicated on their formal attributes did not require substantive review.[56] Actions on book accounts, on the other hand, were entitled to a full complement of reviews and appeals, each of which represented a new trial at which the parties could wrangle over whatever evidence they thought relevant.

The importance of a rational, predictable legal system to economic activity is a staple of the modernization literature.[57] One need not address the simplistic and misleading question of whether Connecticut was undergoing modernization in the eighteenth century to accept that mercantile transactions can proceed more smoothly and on a grander scale when the impediment of individuality is removed. If the terms, conditions, and obligations of each agreement are unique to the underlying transaction and thus subject to interpretation in the context of the particular case—as was true of book debt—the scale of economic activity is perforce limited.

An expanding economy requires that individual transactions be governed by generally applicable rules. Because of the sheer number of such transactions and the distances they may involve, they have to be conducted in a routine fashion. Their form and the legal rules that direct them must be uniform and calculable. Rational economic exchange requires the assurance that like cases will be treated alike. To provide that assurance, general rules override the individuality of particular cases and force them into a common mold. Formal requirements that limit litigation to the instruments themselves and restrict appeals homogenize the underlying transactions and give them a uniform, predictable legal character.[58]

---

56. *Conn. Rec.*, 6:559, 7:15. Eleven years later, in 1736, the assembly retreated and barred appeal only where the amount demanded did not exceed forty shillings. *Conn. Rec.*, 8:55.

57. For example, see David M. Trubek, "Toward a Social Theory of Law: An Essay on the Study of Law and Development," pp. 6–7 and nn. 17–19.

58. It is in this context that the transitional qualities of bills obligatory and conditioned bonds are most interesting. Each instrument contained on its face language that admitted limited defenses—the recital of consideration in the bill and the condition of defeasance in the bond. Debtors could escape liability on the instrument if they could plead and prove a failure of consideration or performance of the condition. These defenses were narrower than

The formal rationality of written instruments made them better suited than book accounts to credit transactions in the expanding economy of eighteenth-century Connecticut. An important symbol of their suitability was that, unlike book accounts, written instruments were assignable—that is, the creditor could transfer the instrument, usually by endorsing it, to a third party who would then have the right to collect the amount due on it from the debtor.

Assignability is not simply a legal matter. It has significant economic and social import. A proper credit system requires that debts be transferable. The ability to transfer a debt facilitates collection by a third party on the creditor's behalf. More importantly, it permits assignors to pay their own debts. For debts to be transferable, promises to pay must be detached from the transactions that gave rise to them and treated as essentially fungible.[59] When the law recognized such promises as assignable, local traders, for example, could satisfy their debts to their suppliers by transferring the promises to pay that their local customers had made to them in the form of bills or notes given in payment for goods received. The plaintiff in a suit to collect the debt would then be the more distant supplier, not the local trader with whom the debtor had originally dealt. Assignment depersonalized the relationship between debtor and creditor, which may be one reason why the common law limited assignments in the fifteenth century by stigmatizing lawsuits on purchased deeds as maintenance.[60] The impersonal quality of assignment is almost certainly what prevented assignability, when recognized, from developing into full negotiability in Connecticut until late in the eighteenth century.

Merchants, of course, had always made their own arrangements for transferring debts. Book accounts, for example, enjoyed a measure of assignability among merchants by force of mercantile custom, though not law, through factoring of open accounts. Factoring became more

---

what was available to book debtors, but broader than promissory notes allowed. The shift from bills to bonds to notes in the opening decades of the eighteenth century—a shift that progressively limited debtors' procedural options—confirms the larger trend from the implicit communalism of book accounts to the formal rationality of written instruments generally. I am grateful to David Konig for this observation.

59. See Atiyah, *Rise and Fall of Freedom of Contract*, pp. 135–38; Holden, *History of Negotiable Instruments*, pp. 10–12.

60. Holden, *History of Negotiable Instruments*, pp. 13–14. "Maintenance" was interference, usually financial, in a lawsuit in which one had no interest.

common as book accounts developed into accounts receivable and payable.[61] Bills were assignable in Connecticut at least as early as 1650, when the assembly ordered that "any Debt or Debts due upon Bill or other specialty, Assigned to another, shall be as good a debt and estate to the Assignee as it was to the Assigner, at the time of its Assignation, and that it shall be lawful for the said Assignee to sue for and recover the said Debt due uppon Bill and so assigned, as fully as the originall Creditor might have done."[62] Despite the liberality of the language, assignment here did not connote full negotiability—that is, transfer of the debt free from any counterclaims or defenses the debtor might have against the original creditor. Negotiability at common law in England developed with respect to bills of exchange in the late seventeenth century. Parliament extended negotiability to notes in 1704 by the Promissory Notes Act.[63] However, true negotiability appears not to have existed in Connecticut, as Elisha Hyde of Norwich discovered when he lost a suit on a bond he had received by assignment on the debtor's plea that the assignor had discharged him from his debt.[64]

Hyde may have known the debtor whose bond he had received. Both men were from the same town. There was, however, nothing to prevent a creditor from assigning his debtor's instrument to a stranger —someone with whom the debtor shared no tie other than that represented by a now-disembodied debt. For example, when Isaac Jones, a New Haven clothier, assigned Samuel Sanford's bill "to my friend" Abraham Bradley, as Jones described Bradley in the endorsement, Sanford's debt ceased to be one with a fellow townsman with whom he had traded in the past and probably expected to trade in the future. It became instead a debt owed to someone who lived two towns distant. Even if Sanford knew Bradley, and he may have, the social con-

61. Gary M. Walton and James F. Shepherd, *The Economic Rise of Early America*, pp. 89–90; Johnson, *The Law Merchant and Negotiable Instruments in Colonial New York*, p. 70 n. 37.

62. *Conn. Rec.*, 1:512. The statute was modeled closely on one enacted in Massachusetts three years earlier. Frederick K. Beutel, "Colonial Sources of the Negotiable Instruments Law of the United States," p. 139.

63. Atiyah, *Rise and Fall of Freedom of Contract*, pp. 137–38; Holden, *History of Negotiable Instruments*, pp. 73–84.

64. Hyde v. Leffingwell, 19 NLCCR (June 1740) no. 322, NLCCF 9 (writ dated 5 Apr. 1740). See also Cook v. Hatch, 12 HCCR 135, 144, HCCF 134 (1746).

text of the original debt was irrelevant. The relations between Sanford and Jones had no bearing on the new relation between Sanford and Bradley. More to the point, if Sanford did not know Bradley, or if any debtor did not know the person to whom his obligation had been assigned, then the ties between debtor and creditor truly had become impersonal.[65]

The potential for impersonality implicit in the assignability of written instruments reflected an important distinction between the exchange recorded by book accounts and the exchange embodied in notes and bonds. The former exchange was often, but not always, commercial in nature. It might represent trading on account with a local shopkeeper, but it could just as easily arise from labor services by a neighbor. The exchange covered by notes and bonds, however, was always commercial. It arose from trade transactions, from direct extensions of credit, or from contractual undertakings. Written credit obligations were instruments of an increasingly commercialized economy. They aided the intrusion of market relations into areas of social life that previously had been governed by customary arrangements, communal norms, and traditional authority. Together with paper currency, which was a public variant of private credit instruments, written instruments forced people not only to calculate in monetary terms, as they had always done, but to deal in monetary terms as well.[66]

Perhaps the clearest indication of the change in social and economic relations that accompanied the shift to written instruments is that most actions on notes and bonds were not disputes at all. Beginning in the 1730s, when promissory notes first eclipsed bonds, debtors never contested more than 10 percent of the actions on written instruments entered against them. In fact, they rarely contested more than 6 percent.[67] Instead, they appeared in court and confessed judgment

---

65. Bradley v. Sanford, 3 NHCCR 57, NHCCF 1 (1715). See also Bradley v. Morris, 2 NHCCR 484–85, NHCCF 1 (1712); Bradley v. Pond, 3 NHCCR 36, NHCCF 1 (1714). One can see another dimension of the impersonality in the rejection by the New Haven County Court of a debtor's plea that the plaintiff could not sue him out of his county by virtue of the assignment of his bond to the plaintiff by the original creditor. Lyron v. Edwards, 3 NHCCR 3 (1713).

66. Joyce Appleby noted a similar consequence of the power of money in seventeenth-century England. Appleby, *Economic Thought and Ideology in Seventeenth-Century England*, pp. 199–201.

67. See Table 2, Appendix.

against themselves, or they did not appear at all and allowed judgment to go against them by default. Either way, the debtor conceded liability to the creditor. All of the confessions of judgment and an indeterminate number of the defaults represent creditors reducing the debts to judgments before they had any intention of trying to collect from the debtor. When such notes later became due, either by their terms or by the creditor's demand, there was no question of the debtor's liability—the judgments had already determined that. If a debtor did not pay, the creditor could procure a writ of execution on the judgment to seize the debtor's property.[68]

Notes and bonds reflected a world of rather different relations between debtors and creditors than those recorded on book.[69] It was a world in which credit was no longer something that grew from transaction to transaction as people dealt with one another without formal promises to pay. Instead, credit had become something extended in single transactions in return for formal admissions of liability. Relations that once were courses of dealing now focused on individual transactions. Although written instruments reflected this underlying change, they did not produce it. Credit instruments, primarily bonds, surpassed book accounts in the 1720s as the most commonly litigated debt obligations. But debtors did not immediately defer to their certainty. As late as 1725 debtors on written instruments contested their liability in nearly a third of the cases brought against them. Similarly, despite the declining popularity of book accounts, debtors on book continued to dispute as many as half of the actions against them until the 1730s, when the rate of contest plummeted under 30 percent,

68. In 1753, for example, Nathaniel Chapman of Saybrook wrote to his debtor, Charles Squire, that "I have agreed with Maj. Elihu Chauncey [a justice of the peace in Durham] that if you will Confess judgment before him upon the above account and also upon the note I have against you and for the sum of sixteen pounds costs that I have paid upon both Writs I will not take out execution before two months are expired." Squire agreed and confessed judgment before Chauncey, who noted the stay of execution, which he granted two months later. Nathaniel Chapman to Charles Squire, 24 Nov. 1753, Chauncey Family Papers, Box 11, Folder 1. The note, dated 18 May 1753, is in Box 1.

69. A forceful symbol of the new order occurred in 1737, when the General Assembly, in its first departure from a century-old policy of making free grants of land, ordered that seven unsettled townships in the northwest corner of the colony be sold at public auction, with the purchasers to secure payment by conditioned bonds. *Conn. Rec.*, 8:134–37. See Grant, *Democracy in the Connecticut Frontier Town of Kent*, pp. 9–15.

where it more or less remained.[70] The intrinsic qualities of written instruments facilitated the new relations between debtors and creditors. They did not make those new relations inevitable.

I I I

The structure of a society shapes the way people handle their disputes. The expansion of the economy in the eighteenth century did not mean that all commercial dealings had become faceless and impersonal. That was never the case. However, population growth, migration, and economic development drew people beyond town and county boundaries and changed the way they did business with one another. Multilayered relations and the dealings appropriate to them did not disappear—the continued use of book accounts suggests that they persisted. But they now shared the stage with single-interest, instrumental relations shaped by new patterns of economic behavior.[71]

When written instruments first appeared in significant numbers in the second decade of the eighteenth century, nearly two-thirds linked debtors and creditors from different towns.[72] Transactions conducted

70. See Tables 1 and 2, Appendix.

71. It is important to emphasize the juxtaposition of multilayered and instrumental relations, rather than a dichotomous succession from one to the other. The persistence of traditional social and economic relations is clear, even into the nineteenth century. For example, see James A. Henretta, "Families and Farms: *Mentalité* in Pre-Industrial America"; Michael Merrill, "Cash Is Good to Eat: Self-Sufficiency and Exchange in the Rural Economy of the United States"; Robert E. Mutch, "Yeomen and Merchants in Pre-Industrial America: Eighteenth-Century Massachusetts as a Case Study"; Robert A. Gross, "Culture and Cultivation: Agriculture and Society in Thoreau's Concord"; and Clark, "Household Economy." Yet it is equally clear that rural farmers had been drawn into external markets well before the Revolution. See Winifred B. Rothenberg, "The Market and Massachusetts Farmers, 1750–1855"; Carole Shammas, "How Self-Sufficient Was Early America?" The recent work of Bettye Hobbs Pruitt suggests the importance of recognizing the juxtaposition and interconnectedness of reciprocal local exchanges and provincial market relations. See Pruitt, "Self-Sufficiency and the Agricultural Economy of Eighteenth-Century Massachusetts." The same dual focus would clarify our view of what was happening to social and economic relations in the eighteenth century.

72. Of the actions on written instruments filed in the Hartford County Court in 1710 to 1715, 64 percent involved debtors and creditors from differ-

at such a physical remove narrowed the range of possible dealings between the parties and increased the likelihood that the relationship between them did not extend much beyond the exchange in question. Distance made the development of multilayered relations unlikely. If book accounts implied a measure of trust between debtor and creditor, it was a trust made possible by the smallness of an economic universe in which people knew and dealt with one another in several capacities. But when people traded with strangers rather than neighbors, or at least with people whom they knew less well, the basis for trust was more limited.

Notes and bonds gave credit transactions an intrinsic predictability that rested on legal form rather than on trust. This is not to say that trust was irrelevant to dealings on written instruments. Promises to pay by note or bond were only as good as the debtor's ability to satisfy them. Creditors had to assess the creditworthiness of their debtors and trust in their debtors' continued ability to repay. Sometimes creditors misjudged, as Benjamin Phelps of Goshen discovered when his agent took a note from Josiah Stanley of Wallingford in payment for a horse. Phelps's agent had received contradictory reports on Stanley's creditworthiness, but hazarded the deal nonetheless. Stanley proved "to be a man of little credit and less money" and defaulted on his note. Phelps predictably won his suit on the note. Stanley, however, had absconded, leaving Phelps with a worthless judgment and no horse.[73] Trust, then, was still present in credit transactions on notes

---

ent towns. As a methodological matter, one must, of course, exercise caution in extrapolating from litigation patterns to the behavior of debtors and creditors generally. With respect to actions on written instruments, there are some useful connections between the worlds of litigation and nonlitigated compliance. As noted earlier, by the 1730s most actions on written instruments did not represent disputes at all. Instead, they were uncontested actions in which the creditor filed suit and the debtor acknowledged the indebtedness to facilitate later collection by the creditor if the debtor defaulted. As notes and bonds spread in intratown credit relations, one would expect to find an increase in the proportion of intratown actions on written credit instruments and a corresponding decrease in the proportion of intertown actions on written instruments, not because notes and bonds were becoming less suitable for long-distance transactions but because local debtors could more easily appear at the county court to confess judgment against themselves. That is precisely what happened.

73. In desperation, Phelps sued the man who had recommended Stanley as creditworthy, but lost on a well-argued demurrer. Phelps v. Porter, 12 HCCR

and bonds, but it was neither the kind nor degree of trust common in book dealings.

The increasing intrusion of written instruments in intratown credit transactions, together with the sharp drop in the frequency of disputed debts, suggests the acceptance of new forms of credit relations. Debtors and creditors who used written instruments may have shared communal ties beyond their individual business transactions, but because they used formal credit instruments, such ties were not necessary. Nor did they matter. Written credit instruments permitted impersonal market exchanges, where, as Weber noted, "there are no obligations of brotherliness or reverence, and none of those spontaneous human relations that are sustained by personal unions."[74] Connecticut at mid-century was still a small society. Its inhabitants retained a communitarian model of social life even while their commercial behavior became more impersonal.[75] But the nature of their relations and the legal forms that embodied them were fundamentally different from those that prevailed a generation or two earlier.

If the formal rationality of notes and bonds fit the new structure of social and economic relations, it was not a fit that suited everyone. Merchants, for example, whose dealings among themselves were traditionally characterized by distinctive customs and even informality, continued to conduct much of their trade with each other on book. Within the community of merchants, rigorously observed formality could be a hindrance.[76]

Outside that community, however, different considerations controlled. Credit instruments insinuated themselves into book relations

---

137, 9 SCR 49, SCF 87 (1746). Alan Everitt has a good discussion of what he describes as "the essentially *personal* conception of credit." See Everitt, "The Marketing of Agricultural Produce," pp. 567–68.

74. Weber, *Economy and Society*, 1:636.

75. See J. E. Crowley, *This Sheba, Self: The Conceptualization of Economic Life in Eighteenth-Century America*, p. 6; Patricia J. Tracy, *Jonathan Edwards, Pastor: Religion and Society in Eighteenth-Century Northampton*, p. 92.

76. One example of merchants continuing to use book accounts among themselves is Richards and Bache v. Robbins, 15 HCCR 72, 84, 108, 131, 161, HCCF 159 (1760–61), in which the executors of the estate of a New York merchant sued a merchant from Wethersfield to collect a commercial book debt. For good discussions of merchants' dealings with one another, see William T. Baxter, *The House of Hancock: Business in Boston, 1724–1775*; and Weaver, *Jonathan Trumbull*.

when creditors required their debtors to make their book accounts over into notes or bonds as a condition of further credit. The General Assembly noted abuses of this practice in 1734 when it enacted penalties against "ill minded persons" who compelled their debtors "to give mortgages, bills, bonds or notes under hand, for the payment of great and unlawful sums for forbearance, or to trade further with them, upon unreasonable advance, to the great oppression and undoing of many families."[77] The legislation permitted debtors who were sued on their written obligations to turn the creditor's action into an equitable proceeding on the bond or note. If the debtor claimed that the instrument was usurious and had not been given for adequate or just consideration, the court would go behind the formal sufficiency of the instrument and examine the factual circumstances of the obligation. If the court decided that the note was usurious, it would ignore the creditor's claim on the note and award him only the value of the goods sold or the principal sum of the debt.

The statute attempted to soften the harshness that could result from rigid adherence to the formal attributes of notes and bonds. The potential for such strict formalism was inherent in the procedural restrictions that circumscribed litigation on written instruments. When the range of relevant evidence was limited, the formal sufficiency of the instruments mattered more than the substance of the underlying transactions.

On the one hand, formally rational credit instruments facilitated the establishment of routine commercial transactions in an expanding economy. However, they also gave creditors power over their debtors that some creditors used unscrupulously. Samuel Smith of Suffield, for example, counted on the formal sufficiency of a bond that Charles Hazelton had executed in his favor when he snatched it from the table and refused to deliver the papers that were to have been his part of the bargain. As Smith left the room, he said to Hazelton, who by the bond became his debtor, "Father Hazelton look to yourself for I intend to cheat you." Samuel Darling of New Haven also used the formal nature of bonds to his advantage when he induced James Barnes to sign a bond for an amount larger than Barnes thought they had agreed upon. Barnes, "being an illiterate man and unskilfull in reading, Writing," had relied on Darling's "Fidelity in that behalf to draw and record the Bond" according to their agreement. Smith's fraud was egregious enough to cost him a judgment. Darling's was not.[78]

77. *Conn. Rec.*, 7:514.
78. Deposition of Curtis Fairchild, 21 Mar. 1740, Smith v. Hazelton, 19

Unless debtors such as Hazelton and Barnes could plead and prove fraud, which was not a simple matter to do, their signatures to formally sufficient bonds were enough to obligate them to their creditors. The formal rationality that made credit instruments so useful in a commercial economy did not, and could not, admit individual, differential treatment of cases. To have done so would have stripped the instruments of the uniformity and calculability that made them useful. There was, of course, a price for such slavish attention to form. Mechanically applied formal rules may compel inequitable results. The law could sometimes offer relief, but only by abrogating law and invoking equity to redress the imbalance. Such was the effect of the statute in 1734. Debtors who, like Joseph Pratt of Saybrook, found their "necessity being then so Great" and "fearing the Displeasure" of their creditors had signed notes or bonds for usurious sums, could at least hope that equity would intervene and reform their otherwise-binding instruments to just amounts.[79] Debtors who could not plead usury or any of the traditional equitable defenses such as fraud or duress—which is to say, most debtors—had to suffer the rigor of formal credit instruments. It was, of course, a rigor that appealed more to creditors than to debtors, but that doubtless was the point.

Unlike notes and bonds, book debts did not require statutory amelioration. The accuracy of the accounts and the legitimacy of any counterclaims were facts to be determined rather than presumed or excluded. These qualities, however, were not enough to allow book accounts to continue as the debt obligation of choice—a choice which, in any event, belonged to creditors. Changes in the economy and in the basis of social relations undercut the conditions that enabled book accounts to serve the majority of creditors well. As the use of written instruments spread from transactions across town lines to dealings within towns, as debtors conceded liability before payment for their creditors' convenience, as the legal forms people used to memorialize their economic relations changed, it is clear that notions

---

NLCCR (Nov. 1739) no. 13, 7 SCR 472, SCF 9 (1739–41); Darling v. Barnes, 4 NHCCR 247, NHCCF 13 (1745) (defendant's plea).

79. Defendant's bill of complaint, Schellenex v. Pratt, 12 HCCR 143, HCCF 134 (1746). For other pleas of usury, see Cook v. Orvis, 3 NHCCR 459, NHCCF 8 (1736); Collins v. Leming, 4 NHCCR 47, 49, NHCCF 8 (1740); Comstock v. Ford, 21 NLCCR (June 1750) no. 74, NLCCF 230 (1750); Kilborn v. Mygatt, 8 HCCR 118 (1736); Bulkeley v. Hinnan, 10 HCCR 21 (1740); Gibbs v. Boardman, 10 HCCR 21 (1740); McLeroy v. Barnard, 12 HCCR 143 (1746); Solomon v. White, 14 HCCR 208 (1755).

of community—of what was appropriate in dealing with one's neighbors—were also changing. One sign of the change was that notes and
bonds, which originated in the urban centers, became more common
in country towns than they were in the more developed market towns
and ports.[80] The social and economic implications of that phenomenon are far-reaching, but there are other pieces to the puzzle, and we
must assemble them before we can study the picture.

80. Actions on written instruments constituted 86 percent of the intratown
debt litigation in country towns as early as the 1720s, rose to 93 percent in the
1730s, and remained at that level for another decade before settling back to
87 percent in the 1750s. In urban towns, however, they never approached that
level of predominance and only in the 1750s came as close as 80 percent, after
rising from 61 percent in the 1720s to 77 percent in the 1730s and 69 percent
in the 1740s. See Tables 3–5, Appendix.

2

THE GEOGRAPHY OF

LEGAL CHANGE

T H E commercialization of the economy in Connecticut in the decades between 1710 and 1740 did not affect each town equally. Factors such as land quality, population, length of settlement, and, above all, location, influenced how each community participated in the economic changes. One important consequence of the development of intertown transportation systems, the specialization of agriculture, the growing diversity of artisans, and the spread of trading networks—in sum, the transformation from a comparatively homogeneous economy of largely subsistence farmers to a more complex commercial economy— was the widening economic differentiation among towns.

By 1740, towns in Connecticut had separated into three distinct economic types—urban centers, secondary market towns, and country towns.[1] The distinctions were not a function of population or population density or of taxable property, although such differences did exist. Rather, they were determined by the nature, quantity, and importance of the economic activities conducted in each town. Every town, regardless of type, included some merchants, all were rural in greater or lesser degree, and the number of artisans tended to be proportional to population.[2] The towns differed, however, in the relative propor-

1. The scheme is that used by Bruce C. Daniels, *The Connecticut Town: Growth and Development, 1635–1790*, pp. 140–70. I have used Daniels's three-tier hierarchy of town types rather than Edward Cook's more finely honed five-tier ranking for the sake of simplicity. See Edward M. Cook, Jr., *The Fathers of the Towns: Leadership and Community Structure in Eighteenth-Century New England*. For a brief critique of both, see James T. Lemon, "Spatial Order: Households in Local Communities and Regions," pp. 107–9.

2. Daniels, *Connecticut Town*, pp. 159, 194–95.

tions of merchants and farmers, the concentration and variety of artisanal activity, and the importance of merchants and their trade to the
town and the surrounding region. To be sure, the ranks of the different town types were not fixed, and the variations within them were
considerable. But the typology is useful and reflects distinctions that
were discernible to contemporaries.

The four urban centers—Hartford, New Haven, New London, and
Norwich—were major entrepôts for the towns around them. All were
heavily engaged in direct export trade.[3] Their prominence rested primarily on their locations. Each was a strategically located port. Hartford sat on the Connecticut River at the highest navigable point for
oceangoing vessels, ideally situated for transshipment of goods along
secondary river systems. New London had the finest harbor in the
colony, which enabled it to withstand the competition of Norwich,
located twelve miles upstream at the natural access point to the eastern Connecticut hinterland. Only ships of thirty tons or less could sail
up the Thames to the headwaters at Norwich, but at New London "a
ship of 500 tunn may go up to the Towne, and com so near the shore
that they may toss a biskit ashoare."[4] The harbor at New Haven was
less commodious, but it was well situated for the coasting trade to
New York.

Favorable geography, properly exploited, conferred commercial
success on the urban centers. Each town had a large merchant community and a compact town center that was devoted largely to retail
activities. The towns were recognizably urban, even to English visi-
tors, and were sufficiently cosmopolitan that three of them boasted
newspapers by 1764.[5] Nonetheless, they remained towns rather than
cities, even by colonial standards. None of them ever broke out of the
economic orbits of Boston or New York. In Connecticut, however,
they were preeminent. They controlled the flow of trade into and out
of the colony. All four were county seats or coseats, and Hartford and

3. Daniels includes Middletown as a fifth urban center. Since it only attained that status at the very end of the period discussed here, I have treated it
as the secondary market town that it was for most of the period.

4. Answer of the colony, 15 July 1680, to inquiries of the Committee for
Trade and Foreign Plantations, *Conn. Rec.*, 3:297.

5. Daniels, *Connecticut Town*, pp. 148–50. The *Connecticut Gazette* began
publication in New Haven in 1755, the *New London Summary* in 1758, and
the *Connecticut Courant* in Hartford in 1764. The *Norwich Packet* followed
in 1773.

New Haven were cocapitals of the colony. Everything of economic, political, legal, and social importance in their respective counties turned on the urban centers.[6]

The secondary market towns, of which there were approximately twenty-five on the eve of the Revolution, performed only one of the two principal economic functions of urban towns. Towns along the Connecticut River and Long Island Sound engaged in direct trade outside the colony and were centers of commercial activity, but none of them figured prominently in the commerce of the towns around them. By way of contrast, four inland market towns—Windham, Litchfield, Danbury, and Lebanon—did serve as market centers for the surrounding towns. They were not ports, however, and so did not participate in the coasting trade.

The secondary towns varied widely in numbers of merchants and amount of commercial activity, but all shared the status of economic subordination to the urban centers. The commercial development of the secondary ports, both river and coastal, was limited by geographic constraints—inferior harbors, distance from producing areas, or an urban center that was too close to permit competition. Geography also hindered the inland market towns, because merchants required access to the ocean to ship goods by sea. These conditions restricted commercial activity in the secondary centers, but they hardly prevented it. The lesser ports and inland market towns performed valuable economic functions and participated fully in the newly commercialized economy. Three of them were county seats. The secondary market towns may have contained fewer merchants and proportionately more farms than the urban towns, but the differences were largely matters of scale rather than of kind.

The forty-three country towns were, in a sense, a residual category of towns that were not urban centers or secondary market towns.

6. Daniels identifies another index of urbanization—the declining number of rattlesnakes killed and presented to the selectmen of Norwich for the ten-shilling bounty. From a high of seventy-eight in 1738, the number of rattle-snakes brought in for the bounty declined until, by the Revolution, rumor had it that only one rattlesnake remained. Daniels, *Connecticut Town*, pp. 150–51. See also Francis Manwaring Caulkins, *History of Norwich, Connecticut: From Its Possession by the Indians, to the Year 1866*, pp. 297–99. However, rattlesnakes still exist in Connecticut to challenge accepted definitions of suburbia. See "Fight in a Hartford Suburb: Residents versus Rattlesnakes," *New York Times*, 17 July 1985, sec. b, p. 1.

They were the towns that were not central places for the towns around them and did not lie on waterways that were navigable by anything larger than a canoe or a flatboat. Stony, hilly land predominated in virtually every town settled after the turn of the century—only one of the towns incorporated after 1737 had land comparable in productivity to the median land quality of the towns settled before 1675.[7]

This depiction implies a false measure of economic isolation. People who were not merchants were not thereby excluded from or ignorant of the market. The parsimony of the land discouraged subsistence farming, but it did not preclude cultivation. Instead, its limited fertility encouraged farmers to specialize in whatever the land would support and to market the surplus. For example, the more recently settled land was best suited for grazing. Meat and dairy production soon surpassed grain farming as the basis of the export trade of the colony.[8] Farmers in country towns produced for a market that merchants in urban and secondary centers mediated for them. They were as much a part of the commercial economy as the merchants with whom they traded.[9] The towns they lived in sometimes did not have town centers, but most did, and all had artisans, mills, retail shops, and taverns. Farmington, for example, was the largest town in physi-

7. The one exception was Goshen. The comparison rests on a correlation of the productivity figures in Daniels, *Connecticut Town*, pp. 186–90, with his lists of towns by period of incorporation, pp. 181–84. The median productivity of land in the towns settled in the first period (1635 to 1675) on a scale of zero through twelve was five, that of towns settled in the second period (1686 to 1734) was three, and that of towns settled in the third period (1737 to 1766) was two. Following Daniels, I have included Woodstock in the second period, when it was settled as part of Massachusetts, rather than the third period, when it was incorporated by Connecticut.

8. Bruce C. Daniels, "Economic Development in Colonial and Revolutionary Connecticut: An Overview," p. 432. Variations in soil types produced other kinds of agricultural specialization, most notably in Wethersfield, where the agricultural economy rested almost entirely on onions, ibid., p. 433. See also Percy Wells Bidwell and John I. Falconer, *History of Agriculture in the Northern United States*, pp. 97–101; Albert Laverne Olson, *Agricultural Economy and the Population in Eighteenth-Century Connecticut.*

9. Winifred Rothenberg has noted similar ties of farmers to a commercial economy in Massachusetts at a slightly later period. See Winifred B. Rothenberg, "A Price Index for Rural Massachusetts, 1750–1855," and "The Market and Massachusetts Farmers, 1750–1855."

cal area and the third most populous town in the colony. Yet in terms of economic development it was a country town. Nonetheless, in 1750 it had sixteen taverns, each one of which was a central place for the surrounding area.[10]

Economic differentiation should not obscure the fundamental similarities that continued to exist among towns. Urban and secondary towns always included sizeable farming populations whose daily routines closely resembled those of farmers in country towns. The economic activities that made such towns urban or secondary were clustered in the village centers of the towns, which occupied only a small portion of the area of a town. The rest of the land, as suitable, was cultivated. Urban and secondary towns thus had within their borders continual reminders of their noncommercial origins. Moreover, agricultural specialization did not produce landscapes that were dominated by one or two crops to the exclusion of others. Land use everywhere was mixed. Market crops, whatever they were, shared the land with crops used for local subsistence. Commercial farming and livestock raising grew with the development of markets, but they did not alter the need for subsistence, which farmers continued to supply themselves and through cooperative neighborly exchanges.[11]

Despite these similarities, the economic differentiation among urban towns, secondary towns, and country towns was significant. It was readily definable in terms of the mixture and scale of economic functions. Moreover, different patterns of wealth distribution characterized each town type. Mercantile activity led to concentrations of wealth, which was, of course, its goal. In urban towns, in particular, the presence of merchants and professional men at one end of the economic spectrum and of poor laborers, sailors, and apprentices at the other created economic inequality that was reflected in the large gap between average wealth and median wealth and in the concentration of personal wealth in the hands of successful merchants. Country towns, on the other hand, were more egalitarian. The extremes of

10. Daniels, *Connecticut Town*, pp. 157, 191. However, Farmington's ratio of one tavern per fourteen square miles was, for the customers at least, considerably less favorable than Hartford's of one per 3.4 square miles in 1776.

11. Richard L. Bushman, "Family Security in the Transition from Farm to City, 1750–1850," pp. 240, 242; Christopher Clark, "Household Economy, Market Exchange and the Rise of Capitalism in the Connecticut Valley, 1800–1860," pp. 173–75; James A. Henretta, "Families and Farms: *Mentalité* in Pre-Industrial America," pp. 15–16.

wealth in terms of personal property that characterized urban centers did not occur in country towns, which lacked the mercantile activity to generate such concentrations of personalty. Land remained the principal source of wealth in country towns. Land-holding was not uniform, but neither was it subject to the disparities of personal property. Unlike profits from trade, land was a finite resource. Inequalities did exist in country towns and may have increased in the decades immediately preceding the Revolution. But there were limits to inequality that did not exist in trading centers and that prevented country towns from attaining the degree of stratification of urban towns.[12]

I

The spatial dimensions of litigation become apparent when one examines the differences between cases in which the litigants were neighbors, in the sense that they lived in the same town, and those in which they were not. The perspective grows more detailed when one considers the type of town in which the parties lived, whether urban center, secondary market town, or country town. Debt actions provide the best basis for comparison, both because they were so numerous and because, of all civil actions, they were most likely to cross town boundaries as well as arise within towns. Other kinds of civil actions, because of the circumstances that occasioned them, tended to be disproportionately intratown matters and did not cross town lines often enough to study quantitatively.[13]

Some of the observations are hardly surprising, such as the fact that juries regularly decided a higher proportion of contested intratown actions than they did of contested intertown actions. Others, however, raise rather curious and difficult questions. Why, for example, did defendants contest intratown actions more often than they did intertown actions? Why did book debt—that quintessential community-based action—persist longest and most vigorously in urban towns,

12. Jackson Turner Main, "The Distribution of Property in Colonial Connecticut," pp. 75–77; Bruce C. Daniels, "Long Range Trends of Wealth Distribution in Eighteenth-Century New England," pp. 129–31.

13. Nondebt civil actions included property disputes, slander, and claims for various kinds of damage to persons or property. Except where absentee landowners were involved, most such actions were almost necessarily intratown matters.

while promissory notes of hand were far more common in intratown actions in country towns than they were in the urban centers? Why did urban creditors face less resistance from their debtors on written instruments than did creditors from secondary centers or country towns? What was the significance of the increasing concentration of creditors in urban towns and of debtors in country towns? To answer these questions, we must consider the data.

Most civil litigation, whether contested or not, spanned comparatively short distances. This is not to say that most litigants in the county courts were from the same town—in point of fact, most were not. But most civil actions were conducted within a radius of one town—that is, most involved residents of the same town or of adjoining towns. In New London County, for example, in the years from 1720 to 1750, inhabitants of the different towns sued town neighbors or people in the abutting towns in 83 to 88 percent of the civil actions, depending upon the town.[14]

Intertown actions were always more frequent than intratown ones, but the proportions between them did not remain constant. Actions on book accounts, for example, increasingly became matters between inhabitants of the same town, a trend that was more pronounced among contested actions than it was among uncontested ones. By way of contrast, debt actions on written credit instruments became less likely to involve fellow townsmen, especially in contested actions, although the changes were less pronounced.[15] As we saw in the last chapter, actions on notes and bonds outnumbered actions on book

14. Although the proportions of what one might call "localized" litigation, in which the parties lived no farther apart than one town, were fairly uniform among towns, the incidence of purely intratown litigation varied widely. In Norwich and New London, the two commercial centers of the county, 86 percent and 83 percent, respectively, of the civil cases that involved residents of the town were geographically localized, and roughly half of the cases (49 percent in Norwich, 53 percent in New London) were intratown disputes. In the less developed towns of Lyme and Groton, similarly high proportions of the cases were localized (88 percent in each), but intratown disputes comprised 44 percent of the actions involving Lyme residents and only 24 percent percent of those involving Groton residents.

15. See Tables 6 and 7, Appendix. Historians should pay closer attention to the geographic dimensions of debt litigation. David Konig, in his study of seventeenth-century Essex County, found that creditors were more likely to sue their debtors the farther away they lived. For the eighteenth century,

accounts by roughly four-to-one after 1730. The increasingly inter-town nature of written credit instruments suggests a general lengthening of the geographic reach of credit relations. At the same time, the fact that book debtors contested their creditors' claims far more often than did debtors on notes and bonds indicates that the increasing rate of contested intratown book actions marked a significant shift in the nature of intratown credit relations.

An important element of that shift was that book debt persisted as a substantial portion of intratown debt litigation far longer in urban towns than it did in either secondary market towns or in country towns. Actions on written instruments, on the other hand, attained a level of predominance between fellow townsmen in country towns that they never did in urban towns.[16] In fact, written instruments, from the time they appeared in large numbers in the 1720s, were proportionately more numerous in actions between country-town neighbors than they were in debt actions generally. The scant surviving evidence of debt litigation before local justices of the peace modifies the picture only slightly.[17] The different structure of intratown debt litigation in urban and country towns seems anomalous—that promissory notes, which were urban in origin, should become more widespread in country towns while book debt, the epitome of traditional, communal relations between debtors and creditors, should persist longer in urban towns. The beginnings of an explanation of the anomaly lie in examining how the mix of debt actions in intratown litigation in Hartford County changed over time.

Christine Heyrman found a consistently low level of intratown litigation in Gloucester and a pattern of litigation in Marblehead that went from almost feverish to more moderate intratown levels. As chapter 1 demonstrates, one can glean useful information not only from the fact of the lawsuit, but also from the kind of debt at issue and whether it was disputed. See David Thomas Konig, *Law and Society in Puritan Massachusetts: Essex County, Massachusetts, 1629–1692*, pp. 79–88; Christine Leigh Heyrman, *Commerce and Culture: The Maritime Communities of Colonial Massachusetts, 1690–1750*, pp. 69–73, 235–41, 244–47, 337–38.

16. See Tables 3 and 5, Appendix.

17. For example, Thomas Hart, a justice of the peace in the country town of Farmington, heard twenty-three debt actions from 1741 to 1750. Only six of them were on book accounts, while sixteen were on promissory notes. Farmington, Justice Court Records, 1741–50.

The distribution of actions on book accounts, bonds, and promissory notes was fairly uniform in the second decade of the eighteenth century, regardless of the town. Promissory notes had made an initial, slight appearance in Hartford, the most developed town in the county, but they were too few to distinguish the composition of debt litigation in Hartford from that of, say, Farmington, a town that remained rural and commercially undeveloped throughout the period. Actions on book accounts outnumbered actions on conditioned bonds in all towns by between three- and four-to-one.[18]

In subsequent decades, the proportion of book debt actions in intratown litigation declined as the use of written credit instruments gained greater currency, but the decline was far less precipitous in Hartford than it was elsewhere. Book accounts dropped to 39 percent of the intratown debt actions in Hartford in the period 1720 to 1725, but to 23 percent in the other towns of the county. During the same period, conditioned bonds dominated intratown debt litigation in the nonurban towns of the county, whereas in Hartford they were outnumbered by book accounts.[19]

By the 1730s, and for the remainder of the period, the focus of intratown debt litigation shifted to promissory notes. Conditioned bonds persisted as a significant minority of intratown debt actions longest in the urban centers of Hartford and, after 1730, Middletown, but even there only until the 1750s. Actions on book declined to where they constituted roughly one-quarter of the intratown debt litigation in the commercially developed urban towns and one-tenth in the country towns. The newly emergent secondary market towns—Windsor, Wethersfield, Glastonbury, and Haddam—lay in between, with actions on book comprising a fairly constant one-fifth of the intratown debt actions. The correlative concentration of promissory notes in intratown debt litigation within the country towns—nearly 90 percent after the virtual disappearance of bonds—is extraordinary.

18. In Hartford, the one urban town in the county, from 1710 to 1715, the distribution of intratown debt actions among books, bonds, and notes was 76 percent, 22 percent, and 2 percent, respectively. In the other towns of the county—and at this early date one can safely treat country towns and what later became secondary market towns together because the commercial development that came to distinguish the two was only just beginning—the distribution was 71 percent, 29 percent, and 0 percent.

19. Conditioned bonds comprised 36 percent of the intratown debt actions in Hartford in the 1720s, but 65 percent in the other towns of the county.

By way of contrast, promissory notes never comprised more than three-quarters of the intratown debt actions in Hartford and Middletown, as they did in the 1750s, and more commonly accounted for 60 percent or less.[20]

The distribution of actions among book accounts, conditioned bonds, and promissory notes in intratown litigation in Hartford County thus changed from a distribution that varied little from one town to another to one that varied according to the commercial development of the town. Written credit instruments came to prevail everywhere. Their spread, however, was slower and less complete in the urban towns than in the secondary riverports, which in turn lagged behind the relatively uncommercialized country towns in the speed and completeness with which their inhabitants turned first to bonds and then to notes. If the trend described intertown actions, one might explain it in terms of urban creditors who, holding the majority of credit in the colony, distinguished between neighboring and distant debtors and who reserved formal credit instruments for the latter. But the trend was in intratown actions, where it presented the anomaly of book debt, which was better suited to communal settings, remaining most vital in the more developed urban towns, while written credit instruments, which first appeared in commercial transactions in those same urban towns, became more dominant in the less developed country towns.

To be sure, not all intratown debt litigation occurred in the county courts. Individual justices of the peace had concurrent jurisdiction over actions in which the debt or damage did not exceed forty shillings. They could also take confessions of judgment on any debt of twenty pounds or less.[21] These jurisdictional facts raise the possibility that the greater concentration of book debt actions in urban towns may have been a function of the ease of access of urban creditors to the county courts, which in Hartford, New Haven, and New London counties met in the urban towns of Hartford, New Haven, New London, and Norwich. That does not appear to be the case, however. If the disparity were a consequence of more convenient access to the county court, then one would expect to find in the county courts large numbers of book actions for small amounts between residents of the

20. See Tables 3–5, Appendix.
21. *Acts and Laws 1715*, p. 15; *Acts and Laws 1750*, pp. 4, 105–6; *Conn. Rec.*, 8:458–59.

county seats, for whom the county court was only slightly less convenient than a justice of the peace. That, however, was not so. Any explanation for the different distributions of intratown debt actions among the different types of towns has to consider factors more subtle than distance from the court.

Intratown book actions do appear to have arisen in proportionately greater numbers before local justices of the peace than they did in the county courts, although the evidence is too spotty to determine how much greater. Justices of the peace kept their own records, some less diligently than others. What records they kept tended to disappear with the rest of their personal effects. The ones that survive are few and often scant. Thomas Hart, for example, a justice of the peace in Farmington, recorded nine years of cases in only seventeen uncrowded pages.[22] Another Farmington justice, this one unnamed, left the only detailed set of justice of the peace records from a country town. There, just before the Revolution, 29 percent of the intratown debt actions were on book accounts and 71 percent on written credit instruments, figures which were at least broadly comparable to the closest year of the sample of intratown litigation in country towns in the Hartford County Court.[23] In Glastonbury, a secondary riverport across the Connecticut River from Wethersfield, 24 percent of the intratown debt actions before a local justice of the peace from 1753 to 1765 were on book accounts, while notes and bonds comprised the remainder, figures which also compare favorably with similar litigation in the county court.[24]

There is some indication that debtors in intratown actions were more likely to contest their creditors' claims when sued before a local justice of the peace than they were when they were summoned to the county court.[25] Because of the low jurisdictional maximum for justice

22. Farmington, Justice Court Records, 1741–50.

23. Farmington Inferior Court Records, 1770–73. The total number of debt actions was 110. In 1760, 21 percent of the intratown debt litigation in country towns in the Hartford County Court was on book and 79 percent on written instruments.

24. Glastonbury Inferior Court Records, 1753–65. The total number of debt actions heard by the justice, whom the records do not identify, was 232. In the decade from 1750 to 1760, 22 percent of the intratown debt litigation in secondary market towns in the Hartford County Court was on book and 78 percent on written instruments.

25. Rates of contest among Windsor residents in the local justice court from 1719 to 1734 were 45 percent of the actions on book and 21 percent of those

courts, this meant that debtors were more likely to resist payment when the stakes were smaller. At first glance, this seems contrary to what one would expect. It may, however, be explainable in terms of the community dynamic of local litigation.

Justices of the peace did not hold regular sessions. They could call court whenever occasion required. Procedure before them tended to be informal. Hearings often resembled discussions, or arguments, between the parties refereed by the justice. County courts, on the other hand, had only two sessions a year at which plaintiffs could file new actions. Moreover, as we will see in the next chapter, pleading in them became increasingly technical and restrictive after 1720. The immediacy of justice court sessions meant that disputes could escalate far more quickly before justices of the peace than they could before the county court, where the parties might have to wait up to six months for the court to meet.

The freshness of the disputes and the discursiveness of the hearings gave justice courts a special place in the social functions of litigation. Debtors may have contested their creditors' claims more frequently before local justices because the comparatively small amounts in issue were only part of the dispute. The individual debts sued upon were only the excuses for invoking legal process, which, when represented by a justice of the peace, could be done quickly and with a minimum of formality. On the other hand, debt actions in the county court were more often for amounts that were large enough to be the primary focus of the dispute rather than simply the last straw in a web of transactions that encompassed other grievances. In addition, the weeks and months that passed before the county court could hear the case allowed the parties more time to reach an agreement out of court, which would then appear in the records as the defendant's default in appearance or confession of judgment or as the plaintiff's withdrawal of the action.

The justice court records with the greatest concentration of intra-town book debt actions at mid-century were from an urban town, New London. Joshua Hempstead left a record of the cases he heard as a justice of the peace from 1739 to 1758.[26] Of the debt actions that he

---

on written instruments, while in the county court from 1720 to 1735 the rates were 37 percent and 13 percent, respectively. See Windsor Inferior Court Records, 1719–34.

26. New London Justice Court Records, 1739–74 (Joshua Hempstead, 1739–58), Record Group 3, Box 565.

recorded between inhabitants of New London, 44 percent were on book accounts and 56 percent on notes and bonds. Virtually all were uncontested. During the same period in the New London County Court, slightly under a third of the intratown debt actions from New London were on book accounts. In Norwich, the other urban center in New London County, the incidence of intratown book debt litigation was higher still, by one-third. The concentration of book debt in urban towns was noticeable everywhere, but it was particularly pronounced in New London County.[27] The exaggerated concentration of book debt actions in New London and Norwich suggests an explanation for the "urbanization" of book debt generally.

New London was by far the most active port in the colony. It boasted the largest number of registered ships and the most vessels entering and clearing the harbor.[28] Only merchants in New Haven approached those of New London in the range of their commercial ventures, and none rivaled them in their ambitions. Such ventures required money, which was in particularly short supply in New London and Norwich. For a brief time a group of New London businessmen issued their own paper money through the New London Society for Trade and Commerce, until the General Assembly halted the practice.[29]

Credit relations in New London and Norwich were characterized by a dual focus. Compared with other towns in the county, inhabitants of the two commercial centers were more likely to engage in litigation that reached beyond the adjoining towns and at the same time were more likely to sue their fellow townsmen.[30] Thus, when inhabitants of New London and Norwich went to law in the county court, there was likely to be both more and less geographic distance

27. By way of comparison, actions on book accounts averaged only 26 percent of the intratown debt litigation in Hartford and Middletown in the same period.

28. Daniels, *Connecticut Town*, p. 153; Gaspare J. Saladino, "The Economic Revolution in Late Eighteenth-Century Connecticut," pp. 395–96.

29. See Chapter 1, n. 45.

30. On average, cases in which residents of Norwich or New London were parties and which reached beyond the radius of the immediately adjoining towns comprised 16 percent of all civil litigation, compared with 12 percent in the other towns of the county. Intratown actions comprised 52 percent of the civil litigation in the two commercial centers, but only 37 percent in the other towns.

between them and their opponents than was the case for inhabitants of the less developed towns in the county. This seeming paradox was a function of the commercialization of the two towns.

As urban centers, New London and Norwich had central business districts with several streets of closely spaced commercial buildings and dwelling houses for merchants, professional men, artisans, and shopkeepers. The population density and the concentration of business activity distinguished these districts from the village centers of less developed towns. In 1774, over one-fifth of the population of the urban towns lived in the town centers, compared with less than one-tenth in the secondary market towns and one-twentieth in the country towns.[31] The greater commercial activity of the urban towns brought their residents into closer and more regular contact with distant traders and suppliers, whereas the concentration of commercial activity in them created webs of business transactions that far exceeded in complexity the legal relations within less developed towns.

The concentrated populations of the town centers and the regularity of the commercial relations within them created a social and economic environment that was as suitable for dealings on book accounts as the insular, subsistence farming communities had been in the seventeenth century. The nascent urban towns of Connecticut were more diverse than the country towns in their ethnic composition and religious conformity, as well as in their commercial activity. They were not characterized by the interdependent relations that distinguished earlier, more homogeneous and insular communities. However, the trust that underlay book debt in the earlier towns could also arise in relations that were frequent and repeated, even if instrumental. People in the town centers of New London and Norwich may not have had the range of personal contacts with one another that people in smaller, more traditional communities often had, but their commercial relations were well developed and likely to be continuing.

"Urban" in this context did not mean impersonal or faceless. The urban towns of Connecticut were still small enough that merchants, shopkeepers, and artisans did business with the same people on a continuing basis through series of transactions rather than single exchanges. These courses of dealing represented continuing relationships that, although limited in social range to the economic tie between the parties, were nonetheless more significant than the individual transactions that comprised them. Moreover, the concen-

31. Daniels, *Connecticut Town*, pp. 160–61.

trated size and population of the urban town centers meant that the people in them lived and worked in closer proximity to one another than did people in other towns, with correspondingly greater opportunity for frequent contact, however casual. Residents of the urban centers may also have shared a sense of uniqueness, of leading lives that set them apart from their country cousins by virtue of being more worldly.

The continued use of book accounts by inhabitants of urban towns in dealings with their fellow townsmen was a mark of community—not community as traditionally defined, but the community of the marketplace. One measure of how different this community was lay in the fact that conditioned bonds, which were not at all like book accounts, also remained more common in urban towns than they did elsewhere. Merchants and artisans used bonds to secure long-term obligations that involved comparatively large sums of money, whether in the form of loans or the value of performance on a contract. Commercial transactions on such a scale were primarily urban phenomena. They represented a dimension of community in the marketplace that was not present elsewhere.

II

The persistence of book accounts in urban towns appears to have been a natural consequence of commercialization, albeit at first a somewhat surprising one. It is rather more difficult to explain why such a disproportionately large share of intratown debt litigation in country towns involved promissory notes. One can understand the procedural advantages of notes and bonds over book accounts. But those advantages did not necessarily carry over to credit relations between fellow townsmen—unless, of course, the nature of those relations had changed. That they did change is suggested by the fact that debt was becoming a rural phenomenon. The proportion of rural debtors steadily increased, fed largely by a surge in the actions against them by creditors from other towns.[32] Moreover, whereas debtors from country towns had once been rather compliant, after 1740 they grew restive and began to contest their creditors more often than urban debtors did.[33]

32. See Tables 8 and 9, Appendix.
33. See Table 10, Appendix.

The increasing concentration of debtors in country towns is not surprising. Commercial expansion brought with it—indeed, rode the crest of—a rising tide of indebtedness.[34] The spread of indebtedness reflected the confidence of prosperity as farmers and traders alike borrowed against anticipated profits to finance the undertakings that they expected would create them. Farmers, in particular, incurred debts to buy land and livestock. The division of the last common lands in the older towns and the settlement of the new towns in the western part of the colony meant that farmers who wanted land, whether to start a farm or to expand their holdings, had to buy it, which most of them could do only with borrowed money.

The sharp increase in uncontested debt actions in the 1730s, in particular the sudden tendency of debtors to confess judgment against themselves to facilitate collection by their creditors should they fail to repay, underscored not only the massive increase in indebtedness but also the acceptance of indebtedness as a necessary cost of doing business.[35] Some observers cautioned against the trend. Jared Eliot, for example, in his election sermon to the General Assembly in 1738, lamented, "We know indeed our present Ability, but we depend greatly on what we think may be hereafter. Thus many run into Debt without measure, and without end, hoping they shall be able to Pay next Year, when they have no visible means for a ground of their hope."[36]

Eliot's fear was well founded. Borrowing against future returns is a strategy that works only if the future returns materialize. Whether they do normally depends on prices continuing at or rising to the anticipated level. However, prices for farm products fell in Connecticut in 1740.[37] Debtors who had counted on continued high prices to repay their loans were caught short and wound up in court by the hundreds. The rate at which debtors contested their creditors' claims,

34. See Richard L. Bushman, *From Puritan to Yankee: Character and the Social Order in Connecticut, 1690–1765*, pp. 128–34.

35. See Table 2, Appendix. Before 1730, debtors who chose not to contest their creditors' claims did not bother to appear in court and instead allowed judgment to go against them by default. After 1730, many debtors continued to default in appearance, but for the first time large numbers of debtors appeared in court and confessed judgment against themselves.

36. Jared Eliot, *Give Cesar his Due. Or, The Obligation That Subjects are under to their Civil Rulers*, p. 43.

37. Bushman, *From Puritan to Yankee*, p. 129.

a rate that had dropped precipitously in the preceding decades, now increased and continued to climb through the next decade as well.[38] Debtors in country towns began to contest their creditors' actions in record numbers. The most common response among debtors, however, was to borrow more money. The volume of uncontested debt actions, which essentially represented creditors recording their claims, swelled in the 1740s to the highest levels reached before the Revolution.[39]

The economics of commercial agriculture and the consequences of a decline in prices explain the growing concentration of debtors in country towns. They also explain the increasing reliance on promissory notes. Trading on book accounts did not, of course, disappear from country towns. In all likelihood, the figures derived from the county court records understate the incidence of book dealings. Estate inventories and scattered account books indicate the persistence of book accounts in both intratown and intertown transactions.[40] Moreover, book accounts were less likely than written credit instruments to leave legal remains. They were not single obligations for specific amounts. They were cumulative accounts that were fixed only as of the most recent transaction. There was no reason for a book debtor to go to court and confess judgment to facilitate later collection by his creditor unless they had concluded their dealings on book—in which case the creditor would be more secure if they made their book accounts over into a promissory note upon which the debtor then confessed judgment.

Because the court records understate the use of book accounts in urban towns for the same reasons, the recorded disparity between urban and country towns in the relative concentrations of book debts and written instruments suggests differences in credit relations. The nature of indebtedness in country towns was different from that of the commercial centers of urban towns. In part, the difference was that between borrowing sums in single, fixed obligations to finance the

38. The reversal was clearest in actions on written instruments. The proportion of contested actions on written instruments rose from 4 percent in the 1730s to 6 percent in the 1740s and 9 percent in the 1750s. The number of contested actions, of course, remained small.

39. See Tables 1 and 2, Appendix.

40. Account books of Jacob Witter, Norwich, 1758–1811; Account Book of George Stillman, Wethersfield, 1725–84 (most entries 1725–28); Account Book of James Harris, Saybrook, Day Book 3, 1733–47.

purchase and development of land and conducting business on a continuing basis with a localized clientele. The economic adversity that
distressed rural debtors in the 1740s also put them in arrears with
local traders with whom they dealt on book. The high concentration
of promissory notes in intratown debt litigation in country towns in
part reflected debtors and creditors who customarily traded on book
accounts but who, for the greater security of the creditors, made their
accounts over into formal credit instruments as the price for further
dealing. The sudden increase in intratown promissory notes in country towns in the 1740s and their persistence in the first half of the
following decade support this explanation. So does their decline in
frequency and the rise of book accounts by 1760, as the French and
Indian War created greater demand, and thus higher prices, for foodstuffs.[41] As prosperity returned to farmers in Connecticut, it would
appear that their creditors once again regarded them as sufficiently
creditworthy to deal with on book without the additional security of
formal credit instruments.

In the midst of these changes, the secondary ports and market
towns were islands of comparative stability insofar as the legal relations of their inhabitants were concerned. All of the most noticeable
shifts in the patterns of legal activity—concentrations of creditors and
debtors and of different types of actions, rates of contest, and the
like—occurred in urban or country towns. Residents of the secondary
towns, on the other hand, experienced considerably less change, both
over time and in relation to inhabitants of urban and country towns.
The rates at which debtors in secondary towns contested debt actions
against them declined only slightly, while rates of contest in urban
towns dropped sharply.[42] Moreover, the proportions of intratown actions on both book and written instruments changed less over time in

41. Promissory notes rose from 78 percent of the intratown debt litigation
in country towns in the 1730s to 87 percent in the period 1740 to 1755 before
dropping back to 78 percent in 1760. Actions on book, on the other hand,
stayed at 7 percent to 8 percent in the 1730s and 1740s, rose to 13 percent in
the 1750s, and climbed sharply to 21 percent in 1760. See Table 3, Appendix.
On the economic upturn of the 1750s, see Saladino, "The Economic Revolution in Late Eighteenth-Century Connecticut," pp. 1–42.

42. From the twenty-year period before 1740 to the twenty-year period
after, rates of contest in book debt actions dropped from 49 percent among
urban debtors and 32 percent among secondary town debtors to 28 percent
and 29 percent, respectively.

secondary towns than in either urban or country towns.[43] This is not to say that legal relations within the secondary market towns remained unaffected by the general legal changes discussed thus far, only that they changed far less than those in urban and country towns did.

The comparative stability of credit relations within secondary towns may have been related to the age and economic structure of the towns. The secondary port and market towns were among the older towns in the colony. Their inhabitants had divided all the arable land well before the beginning of commercial agriculture. The scarcity of unoccupied land left farmers fewer opportunities to expand their holdings within the town and thus less need to incur the kind and amount of debt that farmers in the more recently settled country towns did. Secondary towns resembled urban towns in terms of the commercial activities conducted within them, although the scale was more limited. They did not have the range and concentration of artisanal activity that urban towns did, and their town centers were not as developed. They could not replicate the patterns of business that shaped credit relations in the urban towns, nor did they suffer the conditions of land-holding that shaped credit relations in country towns. In sum, it appears to have been the very middling nature of secondary towns that contributed to the comparative stability of the legal relations within them.

Two other trends merit brief notice. First, with only occasional, insignificant exceptions, debtors contested the claims of creditors who lived in the same town more frequently than they did those of creditors who did not. The margins of contest between intratown and intertown actions were greater in book actions than they were in actions on written instruments, which underscores once again the stronger community nexus of book debt.[44]

Second, not only were debtors more likely to contest the claims of their fellow townsmen, they were also more likely to try their cases to a jury when the creditor was a town neighbor. As the next chapter will make clear, juries decided progressively fewer contested civil actions in the eighteenth century. The rate of decline was far sharper in intertown actions than it was in intratown actions. The proportion of jury verdicts in contested actions sank as low as 10 percent in inter-

43. See Tables 3–5, Appendix.
44. See Table 11, Appendix.

town litigation, but it never dropped below 20 percent in intratown cases. The gap widened in the first half of the century until the 1740s, when juries decided more than twice the proportion of intratown cases than they did of intertown actions. With the puzzling exception of the second decade of the century, the same patterns applied to contested debt actions. The proportion of jury verdicts tended to be lower in contested debt actions than in civil actions generally, and, with one important exception, the margin between intratown actions and intertown actions tended to be smaller. That one exception was the decade of the 1740s, the decade of economic distress, when juries decided three times the proportion of intratown actions that they did of intertown ones.[45]

If these numbers and patterns teach anything, it is that one cannot speak of law as something that meant the same thing to everyone or affected everyone in the same manner. The ways in which people used law—or found themselves caught up in it—varied from time to time and from place to place. Geographic distance and the relative commercial development of the towns in which people lived not only influenced how people did business with one another and evidenced their transactions, but also how likely debtors were to fight their creditors in court and whether cases would be tried by juries. For better or worse, people treated neighbors and strangers differently, and not always to the advantage of the former.

45. See Table 12, Appendix.

3

PLEADING AND THE

DECLINE OF THE JURY

On 18 November 1713, Stephen Pierson, Jr., of Derby found a stray gray horse in a field where it did not belong. He impounded it and, when no one claimed it, had it sold. The horse, it seems, belonged to Stephen Perkins of the neighboring town of New Haven. Perkins did not learn of the sale in time to reclaim the animal. So he did the next best thing—he sued Pierson and demanded four pounds in damages for impounding the horse, "notwithstanding the said feild or inclossure was not fenced according to Law or in any Manner sufficient," and "under Colour of Law" causing it to be sold. As was the practice, Perkins drafted the complaint himself in the form of a summons and paid a justice of the peace to sign it, a ministerial act that constituted formal issuance of the writ.

When the day set aside for pleading at the next session of the New Haven County Court arrived in January 1714, Pierson was represented by an attorney, John Read of New Milford. Perkins spoke for himself. Read began by pleading that the writ should abate because it misspelled Pierson as "Pierce." Perhaps suspecting that the court might not think the error substantial, which it did not, Read offered an alternate plea without waiting for the court to rule on his plea in abatement. The plea he fell back on was a demurrer—a claim that the facts alleged by the plaintiff, even if true, did not state a legal cause of action, and that therefore the defendant did not have to answer the complaint, at least not in a court of law.

Read gave two reasons for the demurrer. First, that "no action can ly for causing a horse to be sold or stolen etc. for frequently the cause is not the blame." And second, that "if it were not [Pierson's] fence that was faulty (which [Perkins] has not alledged) he cannot be in fault if he were ever so much the cause of selling the horse." Perkins replied that these reasons were not sufficient to maintain a demurrer.

He argued that "the causing of an horse to be sold or stollen is not the cause laid but . . . the unjust taking of him whereby a colour of law was obtained for the sale of him." Perkins then characterized Read's second reason as tantamount to saying that "the law is so, that if a man dos impound out of his own inclosure that the impounding is good though the fence be insufficient, so that the poundage must be paid by the Owner of the Creature and then the Owner of the Creature must sue the same man for the money back again." Perkins closed his reply in a large, angry hand with the cry, "The law hates Circuit of Action." The judges of the county court agreed, overruled Read's demurrer, and awarded Perkins damages and costs. The judges of the superior court, however, to whom Read appealed, thought differently. They sustained the demurrer and awarded Pierson the costs he had incurred.[1]

Perkins's frustrated outburst was that of a man playing a familiar game, the rules to which were changing in unfamiliar directions. He argued his own case at a time when lay pleading, although still the norm, was beginning to yield to pleading by lawyers. At the same time, the structure of the pleadings themselves was changing, from pleas that left the parties free to dispute the facts to pleas, such as Read's demurrer, that debated the legal significance of those facts. By the same token, the role of the jury in civil litigation had already begun to decline when Perkins filed suit. By ever increasing margins, fewer cases were decided by juries and more by judges. Taken together, as they must be, these trends point to a transformation from a legal system that assumed the uniqueness of individual disputes to one that subordinated individuality to comprehensiveness and predictability. The transformation was by no means complete when Perkins sued Pierson—by later standards of technicality Perkins's writ should have failed because of the misspelling. Moreover, the contrary assessments of Read's demurrer by the judges of the county and superior courts suggest that standards of legal sufficiency were not yet uniform. Once begun, however, change proceeded quickly. To understand the transformation, one must examine its three major strands—the decline of the jury, the growing legalism of pleadings, and the appearance of lawyers and people who held themselves out as lawyers.

---

1. Perkins v. Pierson, 3 NHCCR 27, 3 CtAR 321, NHCCF 2 (1714).

I

The jury has long occupied a central position in the pantheon of common law mythology. The symbol of twelve respectable jurors applying their collective judgment, understanding, and empathy to the determination of questions of right and wrong is a powerful one, so powerful that it transcends whatever the reality may be. That reality is difficult to recapture. Juries had been used in civil actions in Connecticut from the beginning of settlement. They first appear in the records, without fanfare or special notice, at the third meeting of the magistrates commissioned by the General Court of the Massachusetts Bay Colony to "govern the people at Connecticut."[2] At that meeting, on 1 September 1636, a Sergeant Seely, "plaintiff against the inhabitants of the Towne of Watertown defendants" in a dispute over his right to a proprietary share of the town division lands, agreed "that a Jurer shalbe withdrawen." At the next session two months later, the jury found in Seely's favor.[3] From that point forward, juries appear regularly, as triers of cases and as objects of regulation.

The first regulation, in April 1643, took note of "the diversity of mens judgments amongst Jurors," which meant "divers tymes that no verdict is given in, or else with great difficulty." To correct the problem, the General Assembly ordered that when jurors could not agree, they should tender the reasons for their disagreement to the court for advice, "and then they are to consult togather agayne." If they still could not agree on a verdict, the majority of the jurors "shall give yt in by their voate, and yt shall be deemed to all intents and purposes a sufficient and full verdict." In the event of an equal split, the jurors were to report their vote to the court "with their reasons." The court would then draw up a special verdict, argue it, and enter judgment on a majority vote of the magistrates.[4]

2. Nathaniel B. Shurtleff, ed., *Records of the Governor and Company of the Massachusetts Bay in New England*, 1:170–71. Most historians have focused on the criminal jury. Two of the best studies are John M. Murrin, "Magistrates, Sinners, and a Precarious Liberty: Trial by Jury in Seventeenth-Century New England," and Thomas Andrew Green, *Verdict According to Conscience: Perspectives on the English Criminal Trial Jury, 1200–1800.*

3. *Conn. Rec.*, 1:4–5.

4. *Conn. Rec.*, 1:84–85. Only one such split appears in the records, in an action by a buyer of a horse that he later discovered was lame. The six-man jury divided on whether the seller knew of the lameness. The records report

The second regulation, in February 1645, was occasioned by questions that "hath rysen concerneing unnessary tryalls by Jury." The new rule limited the use of juries as of right to actions entered for forty shillings or more. Actions entered for lesser amounts were to be tried by the magistrates "as they shall judge most agreable to equity and righteousnes." Their discretion appears to have included the power to impanel juries in the smaller cases as they saw fit. The assembly also empowered magistrates to direct jurors to reconsider a verdict "if they doe not conceave the Jury to have proceeded according to their evidence," and to impanel a second jury if the first one persisted in a verdict the magistrates thought erroneous. The assembly further enhanced the power of the magistrates by giving them authority "to vary and alter the dammages given in by the Jury, as they shall judge most equall and righteous."[5] A year later, it modified this last order by directing that any such mitigation or increase "shalbe in open Courte before plaintiff and defendant, or affidavit made that they have bine sommoned to appeare."[6]

These regulations established the formal constraints within which juries operated for the next fifty years. In theory, the limitations were considerable. Judge and jury were not coequal. Judges had the power to override jury verdicts that were not to their liking. In practice, judges invoked their authority infrequently. Except for occasional modifications of a jury award, as when the justices of the New London County Court reduced by a third Richard Ely's recovery against John Robbins for seizing his horses, judges generally left juries to their own devices.[7] Most litigants doubtless preferred it that way, at least until they lost.

---

the disagreement, but not what the court then did. Whatly v. Fellows, *Conn. Rec.*, 1:145.

5. *Conn. Rec.*, 1:117–18. The same orders allowed the magistrates to impanel juries of six or twelve men "as they shall judge the nature of the case to require," verdicts in either case to be by a majority vote of two-thirds. The town of Fairfield objected to a jury of six, but accepted the order that juries of twelve could decide by a two-thirds majority. *Conn. Rec.*, 1:138.

6. *Conn. Rec.*, 1:138. I can find only one instance before the establishment of the county courts in 1665 in which magistrates altered the damages awarded by a jury. Significantly, though, it was not the magistrates of the particular court, in which the case was tried, but the magistrates and deputies of the general court, to whom the aggrieved party had appealed. *Conn. Rec.*, 1:211.

7. Ely v. Robbins, 3 NLCCR 65 (1674).

A great advantage of juries is that they do not articulate the grounds for their verdicts. They are free to apply whatever standard they wish, or even no standard, in answering the questions put to them. In that respect, the mystery of their inner workings resembles the formal irrationality of the oracle or the ordeal.[8] Yet jurors, unlike the omniscient gods who rendered judgment through oracles or the ordeal, are not themselves mysterious. In Connecticut in the seventeenth century they were neighbors or from nearby towns. In background, experiences, and outlook they were much like the litigants whose disputes they determined, and not very different from the judges who oversaw them. They applied the same standards in their deliberations that the litigants themselves would apply in similar cases involving others, which is to say standards shaped by a template of common beliefs and expectations as to how neighbors should treat one another. It was this commonality that gave substance and meaning to the traditional description of jurors as "men of the neighborhood." It doubtless also explains why juries, not judges, decided almost all civil cases from the creation of the county courts in 1665 through the end of the century.

Commonality did not, of course, make for a perfect process or, for that matter, a neutral one. The community ties that linked jurors and litigants, together with the virtual unaccountability of jurors in their deliberations, could make litigants wary of the potential for partiality among jurors, particularly when the dispute was a festering one that affected people beyond the immediate parties. For example, when John Wheeler of New London sued John (Fitz-John) Winthrop, the son and grandson of eminent governors and later himself governor of Connecticut, in September 1691 for pulling down a fence on land they both claimed, the jury returned a verdict of nominal damages in Wheeler's favor. Winthrop, who cared less about the damages than about the underlying assumption that the land was Wheeler's, protested "against the verdictt of the jury by Reason of John Wheeler his saying in Court he knew the verdict of the jury before the jury gave theire verdictt." Wheeler admitted the rashness of his words, assured the court "that he had not discoursed with any of the jury in the Least" about the case, and apologized to the jury, although rather haughtily, for suggesting that he had.

The case then appears to have been tried again at the same session, with the same result. This time the court, "upon some Reasons and a

8. See Max Weber, *Economy and Society: An Outline of Interpretative Sociology*, 2:762.

statute quoted," ordered the jury to reconsider its verdict. Before the jury could announce its second verdict, Wheeler again asserted "openly in Courte he Knewe the jurys verdict Before it was given in." Winthrop then objected "against any verdictt frome that jury," whereupon the court adjourned until the next day, ostensibly because of the lateness of the hour but one suspects also in exasperation. When the court reconvened the next morning the jury made a surprising display of independence. To the demand for a verdict, the jury replied that since Wheeler had "chardged them as if they had not been Faithful to theire oathes" and Winthrop had "protested against any verdictt frome theme," there would be no verdict. In short, a plague on both their houses.[9]

The dispute between Wheeler and Winthrop was part of a much larger dispute between Winthrop and his brother-in-law, Edward Palmes, that had begun fifteen years earlier over the distribution of the elder Winthrop's estate. The larger controversy spread and continued, unresolved, until Winthrop died in 1707. It generated numerous lawsuits between the principals and against surrogates, as well as appeals to the General Assembly in Hartford and New Haven and to the Board of Trade and the Privy Council in London.[10] The parties were prominent, their differences well known, their antipathy implacable. Jurors, who were drawn from the county, could not help but know of the litigants and the context of the lawsuit. Under the circumstances, Winthrop had reason to fear that the jurors might attend to matters other than the instant complaint in their deliberations. He was particularly sensitive to any suggestion that his opponent had gained an illicit advantage with the jury, which would not be required to explain the reasons for its verdict.

The independence shown by the jury in thumbing their noses at Wheeler and Winthrop acquired a measure of statutory legitimacy in 1694 when the assembly repealed the power of judges to replace juries with whom they disagreed. Another measure of jurors' potential for recalcitrance was an order of the assembly a year earlier "to prevent the frustration and unnecessary delay of justice." Thenceforward, immediately upon hearing the pleadings and evidence, juries were to

9. Wheeler v. Winthrop, 7 NLCCR 66, 71–73 (1691). There is no further record of the case.

10. See Richard S. Dunn, *Puritans and Yankees: The Winthrop Dynasty of New England, 1630–1717*, pp. 200–352.

withdraw to a place designated by the court "and their abide untill they are agreed of a verdict."[11] The assembly had acted with criminal trials in mind, but the statute extended to civil trials as well. Occasional complaints of jurors who "broke loose from their confinement" before they had agreed upon a verdict indicate that the concern of the assembly that jurors might discuss their deliberations with others was not an idle one.[12]

All this evidence of the vitality of the jury—its predominance in civil actions, the weakness of formal controls on its deliberations, its ability to apply norms drawn from backgrounds shared with the people whose cases it determined—raises the question of what juries decided. In theory, and by statute, juries in civil actions were to "find the matter of fact, with damages and costs, according to Law, and their evidence."[13] That did not mean, however, that juries were to decide only questions of fact while leaving questions of law to the bench.

The hoary distinction between fact and law is, at bottom, artificial, although often invoked. In 1680, for example, Sir John Hawles, a leading barrister who later became solicitor general to William III, wrote a pamphlet in the form of a dialogue between a barrister and a juror. Hawles put into the mouth of his juror the words, "But I have been told, That a Jury is only Judge of naked *matter of fact*, and are not at all to take upon them to *meddle with*, or regard *matter of Law*, but leave it wholly to the Court." Significantly, Hawles had his barrister recognize the distinction: " 'Tis most true, Jurors are *Judges* of matters of Fact, that is their *proper Province*, their chief business." But he argued forcefully that jurors cannot exclude "the consideration of matter of Law, as it *arises* out of, or is *complicated* with, and influences the Fact." The jury must "also *apply matter of Fact and Law together*."[14]

11. *Conn. Rec.*, 4:98, 129.

12. For example, see Fox et al. v. Haynes, 2 CtAR 259 (1712); Nichols v. Whiting, 3 CtAR 213–14, 4 CtAR 3–4 (1711). Significantly, jurors could not be punished for their dereliction. The court could only refuse to accept any verdict, direct the jurors to return the fees they had received, and continue the case to the next session.

13. *Acts and Laws 1715*, pp. 2–4.

14. [Sir John Hawles,] *The English-mans Right, a Dialogue Between a Barrister at Law and a Jury-Man*, pp. 10–11. The New York *Weekly Journal* reprinted portions of Hawles's tract on the day of the trial of John Peter Zenger in 1735 as a reminder to the jury. See James Alexander, *A Brief Narrative of the Case and Trial of John Peter Zenger*, pp. 15–16.

Hawles understood what philosophers, anthropologists, historians, even some lawyers, have recognized since—that the distinction between law and fact, whatever its heuristic value, is impossible to maintain in practice.[15] Law and fact are not discrete, exclusive entities that have objective reality. They are ways of viewing and rendering the world that are contingent as well as normative.

Juries in Connecticut in the seventeenth century decided cases on the basis of the evidence submitted to them, on their personal knowledge of the dispute, on their understanding of the law in a formal sense, and doubtless also on their sense of what the law ought to be. There is no indication that judges instructed juries on the law to apply, although by the end of the century judges may have made a general charge to identify for the jury the questions they were to consider.[16] Juries could, "in case of some difficulty ariseing among them ... desire farther light or information from the court." In case of terminal doubt, they could render special verdicts.[17] Both of these devices, however, suggest that in all other cases, which is to say most of them, juries decided for themselves how the law should apply—a process that is inextricably linked with, and at times indistinguishable from, deciding what the law is.

The mixture of law and fact was facilitated by the pleadings. Most litigants submitted their actions to the jury under the general issue. Defendants who pleaded the general issue made a blanket denial of all of the plaintiff's allegations without sorting them out or whittling them down to frame a single issue for the jury to determine. Since general denials put in issue the accuracy, veracity, and legal consequence of all facts alleged by the plaintiff, the potential breadth of the allegations implied a corresponding breadth in the evidence that was relevant to evaluating them. Even matters not alleged in the declara-

15. Among the better discussions of the point are Clifford Geertz, "Local Knowledge: Fact and Law in Historical Perspective," and S. F. C. Milsom, "Law and Fact in Legal Development."

16. A statute of 1693 on jury deliberations refers to "the matter given them [the jury] in charge." *Conn. Rec.*, 4:98. William Nelson, who studied Massachusetts in a later period, thinks that jury charges in civil cases were infrequent. William E. Nelson, *Americanization of the Common Law: The Impact of Legal Change on Massachusetts Society, 1760–1830*, p. 26.

17. *Conn. Rec.*, 4:98. For examples of special verdicts, see Whitney v. Hough et al., 1 NLCCR 86, 92 (1667); Young v. Haynes, 7 NLCCR 71–72 (1691) (jury found *non liquet*); Tinker v. Town of Lyme, 2 CtAR 311 (1695).

tion could be relevant if they touched on a good defense to the action. Juries thus heard evidence on a range of issues, often a veritable morass of contradictions from which they had to determine who had done what to whom and why, and what the legal consequences should be. How jurors determined these matters was in part conditioned by their identity as people from similar communities in a communal society.

When given cases under the general issue, juries—because of the comparative weakness of formal controls, because of their discretion, because of the secrecy of their deliberations—filtered the evidence before them through the prisms of their own knowledge, experience, and beliefs, part of a process that Clifford Geertz has described as "the cultural contextualization of incident."[18] In so doing, jurors determined legal issues against a template of community norms and served a mediating function between law and society.[19] In theory and in ideal, such a function is the principal purpose of the jury. It underlies popular notions of the jury as a bulwark against oppression, whether public or private. However, juries can perform their traditional role as purveyors of community norms only if they decide cases. Otherwise, they are ineffectual. It is thus significant that, from early in the eighteenth century, most contested civil actions in Connecticut never reached a jury. Instead, judges disposed of them on points of law.

Through the end of the seventeenth century, juries had decided most civil actions. Shortly after the turn of the century, however, the balance shifted. Judges decided half of all contested civil actions in the half-decade between 1710 and 1715. Ten years later, they decided 70 percent. By 1745, judges decided 80 percent of the contested civil actions in the Hartford County Court, and 95 percent in the New London County Court.[20] The decline of the jury could hardly have been more precipitous. Moreover, the cases decided by judges were not snatched from the jury at the last moment, leaving a wake of frustrated litigants and jurors. Juries had never been impaneled to hear them in the first place. Under rules of practice adopted for the

18. Geertz, "Local Knowledge," p. 181. Nelson has a good discussion of the effect of pleading the general issue. See *Americanization of the Common Law*, pp. 22–23.

19. This quality of juries is an important element of Nelson's argument. See *Americanization of the Common Law*, pp. 20–30.

20. See Table 13, Appendix.

county courts in 1709, jurors in civil actions were summoned to appear on the third day of sessions, after the litigants had made their pleas and joined issue. Only then would the court impanel and swear the jury to hear the evidence.[21]

Although the decreasing resort to juries touched all civil actions, it was not uniform. The variations are instructive. If, for example, one distinguishes between actions on book accounts and actions on written instruments, one finds that debtors and creditors resorted to juries far more often when the debt was on book than when it was on a note or bond. Not until the 1740s did the progressive decline of the jury in book debt actions sink to the level of desuetude that characterized actions on written instruments.[22] For contested civil actions other than debt cases—various actions pertaining to the use or title of land, the recovery of personal property, damages of one sort or another—litigants submitted their cases to juries with decreasing frequency, but always more often than parties to debt actions did. In fact, a resurgence of jury verdicts in non-debt actions in the 1750s was large enough to cause a small increase in the figures for contested civil actions generally.[23]

The decline of the jury was striking. Within the space of half a generation, the scales of civil justice tilted from a system based on verdicts rendered by representatives of individual communities to one that rested on judgments delivered from the bench. It was not a shift that was to everyone's liking. John Collins of Guilford, for example, was fined twenty shillings for contempt in 1713 for his outburst in a tavern after the judges of the superior court had denied him a jury. He had pleaded the statute of limitations as a bar to a book debt action at a time when, as it turned out, the length of the limitations period was in some doubt. The court hesitated for several months before it decided that the statute did not discharge Collins from the debt and entered judgment accordingly. Although the question of which limitations period to apply was a legal one that was exclusively within the province of the bench to decide, Collins had, as he said later in his acknowledgment of fault, "thought it Law and Reason to have a jury." Collins, who was "very much Disappointed and my expectation wholly frustrated in not being allowed a tryall by a jury," had vented

21. *Conn. Rec.*, 5:106.
22. See Table 14, Appendix.
23. See Table 13, Appendix.

his ire with such remarks as "if the king did say that the asses wore horns it must be so" and "if I had known so mutch before I would not have given my money to them for a Tryall from whom I Could expect no Other judgment."[24]

Although Collins was not entitled to a jury, his belief that he was is instructive. The debt charged against him was on a book account, which, as we saw earlier, permitted a wide range of evidentiary and procedural flexibility. Book debts by their very nature resisted the kind of standardization that would allow them to be adjudicated on points of legal form. Their lack of uniformity in fact encouraged juries to evaluate the full course of dealing between debtor and creditor in determining the issue. It should not be surprising that juries decided 52 percent of all contested book actions in the period 1710 to 1715 and 41 percent ten years later, while at the same time they decided only 25 percent and 10 percent, respectively, of the contested actions on written instruments. Book debts intrinsically invited determination by juries, just as notes and bonds lent themselves to adjudication by judges. Considered in that light, it was not the persistence of the jury in book debt litigation that was anomalous, but rather its decline after 1730. John Collins's expectations were simply those of most book debtors—that the dispute would be resolved in a manner that was appropriate to the nature of the obligation, that is, by a jury.

To say that use of the jury declined is not to suggest that the jury itself changed in any fundamental way. Two minor formal changes enhanced the position of the jury slightly. By the statutory compilation of 1715, judges could direct a jury to reconsider its verdict twice. However, the jury that remained adamant through three deliberations, as many did, prevailed. The same compilation made it clear that

---

24. R. v. Collins, 3 CtAR 291, 4 CtAR 164, SCF 323 (1713). The action in which Collins had wanted a jury was Gray v. Collins, 2 NHCCR 477–78, NHCCF 1, 3 CtAR 263, 271, 4 CtAR 104, 121, 163 (1712–13).

The earliest limitation on recovering book debts was three years. See *The Book of the General Laws for the People Within the Jurisdiction of Connecticut*, pp. 19–20. The assembly extended the period to seven years for book debts of forty shillings or less in 1681, a period that it applied to all book debts in 1696. See *Conn. Rec.*, 3:79, 4:66. The seven-year limitation originated in the biblical injunction that loans be canceled every seventh (sabbatical) year (Lev. 25:1–25, Deut. 15:1–2). In 1705, the assembly declared that "all book-debts shall be recoverable at any time, provided the original debtor be living" and provided that a creditor could prove his account simply by

either party to an action in the county court for forty shillings or less could request a jury as long as he was willing to pay its costs. Before, the availability of juries in such small causes appears to have been at the discretion of the bench. Neither of these provisions, however, wrought any major change in the jury. Nor did the first formal articulation of a property qualification for jurors, which was doubtless merely declaratory of long-standing practice.[25]

Juries retained their ability to voice their opinions—and, through them, those of their communities—forcefully. The jury that awarded a prominent attorney less than one-twentieth of what he had demanded in his suit for legal fees against a former client for whom he had won a divorce implied its disfavor of lawyers in general, that lawyer in particular, divorce, or perhaps all three.[26] Similarly, the defendant sued by an attorney for his fee expressed well-placed confidence in the jury when he admitted hiring the attorney but pleaded that "he thinks he demands too much, therefore he desireth to Leave it to the jury"—the jury awarded the attorney little more than a quarter of what he demanded.[27] And the woman who watched a jury on review whittle down to six pence the £500 awarded her by the bench against a man who had publicly called her a witch doubtless left court knowing that

swearing to its accuracy. See *Conn. Rec.*, 4:502. Ten years later, in 1715, the assembly modified its stand and repealed the 1705 legislation. In its place, the assembly declared that book debts incurred since 1697 "shall at any time be recoverable during the natural life of the debtor," and codified long-standing practice by making determination of the sufficiency of a creditor's proof of his account an issue for the jury to decide. See *Conn. Rec.*, 5:505. Curiously, the official compilation of laws published in 1715 printed both the 1715 statute and one embodying the seven-year limitations period. *Acts and Laws 1715,* pp. 26, 204.

25. *Acts and Laws 1715*, pp. 2–4. Jurors were to own freehold worth forty shillings a year or have personal estate in the county of fifty pounds. In all probability, the qualification for jurors had always been the same as those for freemen.

26. Read v. Merriman, 3 NHCCR 96 (1718). Read had sued for fifteen pounds, and the jury awarded him twelve shillings. Although it was common practice to demand more than one reasonably expected to recover, the difference here is more than can be accounted for by an inflated demand. Read appealed to the superior court, but there is no record that he prosecuted the appeal.

27. Mason v. Bacon, 8 NLCCR 8, NLCCF 178 (1711). The attorney does appear to have padded his bill considerably.

whatever the jury thought of her supernatural powers, it was quite certain of her character.[28]

Although the formal powers of the jury did not change, the way juries exercised them, even when they had the opportunity, did. For example, special verdicts were never very numerous, but they occurred more often in the eighteenth century than in the seventeenth. A special verdict stated the facts the jury had found but left final determination of their legal significance to the court. Juries rendered special verdicts when they could not agree on what the outcome should be. The possibility of such disagreement had long been recognized in the rules that permitted special verdicts, but only when use of the jury declined did special verdicts become more common.

The phenomenon of juries admitting that they did not know how to apply the law to the facts they had found was, at the very least, an admission of their limitations. The questions that juries could not answer but instead referred to the bench indicate how some juries defined the limits of their competence—whether a bond given to secure submission to arbitration of a dispute over a book debt was sufficient evidence to prove the existence of the book debt, whether tender of the amount awarded by arbitrators constituted compliance with the award, the construction of a phrase in a bond, whether the facts found gave the defendant's lessor an estate in the land in question, whether allowing a servant to trade constituted an assumption by his master of the servant's debts, whether insertion of a word in a promissory note after execution and delivery invalidated the note, whether failure to object to a proposed arbitration procedure constituted agreement, whether the statute of limitations applied to certain items charged on book.[29] These were all questions of law. They were also questions that had been submitted to juries and were within their power to decide. Indeed, previous or subsequent juries in the same case sometimes answered them.[30] Still, the hesitation of the juries to decide them is instructive.

28. Gould v. Chittenden, 8 SCR 97, 193 (1742–43). The accusation appears in the summons in NHCCF 15.

29. Weed v. Humphreys, 2 NHCCR 468 (1711); Russell and Sperry v. Perkins, 3 NHCCR 2 (1713); Lyron v. Edwards, 3 CtAR 316, 4 CtAR 209–10 (1714); Smith et al. v. Brown, 3 NHCCR 41–42 (1715); Atwater v. Stanley, 7 SCR 243 (1739); Finney v. Howell, 4 NHCCR 19 (1739); Comstock v. Avery, 19 NLCCR (Feb. 1740) no. 1; Wolcott v. Wolcott, 14 SCR 87 (1761).

30. In Russell and Sperry v. Perkins, a second jury on review was able to answer the question itself. 3 NHCCR 24 (1714). And in Lyron v. Edwards, a

With one exception, none of the cases that produced those special verdicts went to the jury under the general issue.[31] Instead, the litigants had framed a narrower issue through their pleadings, and the jury only heard evidence relevant to that issue, not to the case as a whole. The effect of increasingly technical pleading on litigation is the subject of the next section of this chapter. For now it is sufficient to observe that the traditional appeal of the jury rested in no small part on its power to weigh cases in their entirety and to render verdicts according to an internal—and perforce communal—standard that was largely beyond the control of external agencies such as judges. Special or technical pleading, however, prevented jurors from hearing the entire case. It deprived jurors of the context that allowed them to judge the legal significance of the facts they found.[32] Without that context, some jurors felt adrift—they could agree that certain facts had been proven, but they could not agree on what those facts meant.

Special verdicts were not numerous, but their significance does not rest on their numbers. They were symptomatic of the changes wrought by pleading and the declining use of juries. Juries in the eighteenth century were increasingly irrelevant to the resolution of private disputes. They decided fewer cases. Those they did decide often turned on limited issues, as we will see in the next section, or on

---

previous jury had construed the phrase without assistance. 3 CtAR 292–93, 4 CtAR 165 (1713).

31. The one exception was an action of debt on a note in which the general issue of *non est factum* narrowed the question to whether the note was the act of the defendant or had been forged or altered. Finney v. Howell, 4 NHCCR 19, NHCCF 8 (1739).

32. Nelson has a good discussion of the effect of special pleading. See *Americanization of the Common Law*, pp. 21–23. He discusses it in the context of his assertion that few cases in Massachusetts before the Revolution were tried without a jury and that juries were thus able to serve as important agents of community norms and fairness. Jurors can only perform those functions, however, if they receive cases to decide. In Connecticut, it is quite clear that they did not and had not since the 1720s. There, the shift that Nelson attributed to the Revolution in Massachusetts was complete long before the Revolution. John Murrin has suggested to me that the difference between the two colonies on this point may in part be the difference between a corporate colony and a royal colony. Juries may have persisted longer in Massachusetts out of suspicion of royally appointed judges, a suspicion that no one in Connecticut had occasion to share.

special verdicts, which did not determine the ultimate question of liability that the parties had sought to entrust to the jurors in the first place. Juries obviously did not disappear. When Ebenezer Punderson, an Anglican minister in New Haven, won a jury verdict in 1758, for example, he instructed his attorney to "please give my Compliments to the Gentlemen of the jury and give them a custimary treat."[33] Juries remained sufficiently entrenched that victorious litigants could think of tipping them as "custimary." Equally obviously, however, the jury did not occupy the central position that it did in the previous century.

II

Defendants in civil actions had five choices when the clerk called their cases from the docket on the second day of the session—they could confess judgment against themselves, plead the general issue, plead in bar of the action, plead in abatement of the writ, or demur. The first choice ended the litigation and requires no further consideration here. The second, the general issue, was a categorical denial of everything the plaintiff had alleged—not guilty, nothing owed; no wrong or disseisin, or some other denial appropriate to the charge. A general denial did nothing to focus the dispute or narrow the range of relevant evidence, which, as we saw in the previous section, left considerable discretion to the jury. The third, pleading in bar of the action, was not a direct response to the plaintiff's declaration. Instead, the defendant made a counterassertion of fact, which, if true and if legally sufficient, would excuse him from liability in whole or in part. For example, the debtor sued on a conditional bond might plead in bar that he had performed the condition. If the plaintiff then denied that the defendant had performed the condition, the parties joined issue on the narrower factual issue of the debtor's performance or nonperformance. Only evidence on that question would be admissible. Evidence on any other aspect of the case, such as whether the bond was properly executed or whether it was fraudulent or usurious, no matter how relevant in a general sense, had no bearing on the issue of performance.

The fourth choice, pleading in abatement of the writ, avoided the merits of the plaintiff's allegations altogether. It argued that the plain-

33. Ebenezer Punderson to Atwater, 8 April 1758, Punderson v. Baldwin, 5 NHCCR 156, 168, NHCCF 20 (1758).

tiff's writ should abate, and his action with it, because of some technical insufficiency in the writ itself or in its service on the defendant. Improper service, variance between the original writ and the copy served, a vague declaration, inadequate or mistaken identification of the parties, omission of essential information, choice of an inappropriate form of action—all could be grounds for abatement of a writ. Whether they were or not depended on a variety of factors, which, because they lay in the discretion of the judges, were not always fathomable. If the court sustained the defendant's plea in abatement, the plaintiff could amend the offending defects in his writ and proceed with the action after paying the defendant the costs he had incurred in having to answer a faulty writ. Or the plaintiff could appeal to the superior court or simply fold his tent and leave.[34] Because of the last alternative, a well-aimed plea in abatement often ended the litigation, even though legally it was only a caesura in the pleading. On the other hand, the defendant who pleaded in abatement risked nothing. If the court overruled his plea, he could make another plea and continue, or he could appeal to the superior court.

Lastly, the defendant could demur, either generally or specially. A general demurrer admitted the facts alleged by the plaintiff in his declaration but contended that they did not entitle the plaintiff to relief or, in legalese, that they did not state a cause of action. A special demurrer identified the particular objections to the sufficiency of the plaintiff's allegations. In either case, if the court sustained a defendant's demurrer, he won; if it did not, he lost. A demurrer was thus rather like staking everything on one roll of the dice.

In choosing a plea, defendants also chose a procedure. Demurrers, for example, precluded juries entirely. They narrowed cases to a single question of law—were the plaintiff's allegations legally sufficient. The accuracy of the facts alleged was immaterial. Pleas in abatement, if successful, also excluded juries. If unsuccessful, they simply forestalled impaneling a jury until the parties joined issue in subsequent pleadings. The question raised by a plea in abatement—the technical sufficiency of the writ or its service—was a question of law for the bench to decide. The general issue, on the other hand, was triable by jury if the jurisdictional amount of the case qualified it for one or if one party or the other paid for a jury trial. Pleas in bar were also triable by jury, although whether they reached a jury depended on whether the

34. *Acts and Laws 1750*, p. 5.

litigants joined issue on a traverse or a demurrer. For example, to return to the example of the debtor who pleaded that he had performed the condition required by a conditioned bond, the plaintiff could then deny that the debtor had performed—a traverse—or demur, which raised the legal issue of whether performance was a good defense. The former question could be tried by a jury, the latter had to be decided by the bench. Choice of a plea thus determined whether a case would turn on questions that were primarily factual or purely legal and whether the issues would be decided by judges or a jury.

The way litigants pleaded their cases changed markedly in the first half of the eighteenth century. The general direction of the change was from pleas that raised factual issues to pleas that raised legal ones. Until shortly before 1710, virtually all contested civil actions in the county courts were tried under the general issue.[35] Around 1710, however, pleadings took on an entirely different aspect. Factual pleas still predominated, although not overwhelmingly. For the first time, however, a substantial number of defendants offered dilatory pleas—40 percent pleaded in abatement. Most of the technical pleas failed, and the people who made them retreated to pleading the merits of their case. However, the fact that their first line of defense had been a legalistic objection that avoided the merits of the plaintiff's allegations entirely suggests a fundamental change in the way people approached litigation. Moreover, the formal appearance of pleas in bar, with their consequent narrowing of the issues to be tried, was a procedural refinement in what hitherto had been largely unrestricted argument.

The proportion of technical pleas rose quickly in the second decade of the century. By 1720, pleadings on the merits had declined to a scant 15 percent of the initial pleas in civil actions, while pleas in abatement had risen to three-quarters. A smattering of demurrers made up the remainder. Only five years later, pleas in bar and the general issue had recovered to one-third of the initial pleas, pleas in abatement had plummeted to 12 percent, and demurrers had climbed to 55 percent. Thereafter the patterns were clear, if somewhat variable. Defendants pleaded to the merits of the plaintiff's declaration roughly 20 to 30 percent of the time, pleading the general issue some-

---

35. In fact, county court records rarely include any pleas at all much before 1700, not even general issues. The nature of the reported verdicts, however, make it clear that the cases were tried under what amounted to the general issue.

what more often than they pleaded specially. The rest of the time, which is to say most of the time, defendants made pleas in which the legal issues were paramount and the facts were immaterial or admitted. By an increasing margin, most of those pleas were demurrers, which, unlike pleas in abatement, allowed no fallback to another plea if they failed, as most did.[36]

The shift in the structure of pleadings in civil litigation could hardly have been more striking. In a legal system that made a formal, albeit often artificial, distinction between fact and law, a change from a mode of procedure that permitted litigants to have their disputes decided on the merits to one that reduced disputes to abstract principles of law represented a fundamental transformation of the role of law in adjudicating economic and social relations. The decline of the jury, which we can now attribute in part to the growing predominance of technical pleas, was one symptom of that transformation. The change in pleadings was another.

Common law form pleading did not take root in New England, partly because of overt hostility to it, but also because of the dearth of attorneys trained to use it.[37] Pleading could hardly be more technical than the knowledge of the pleaders. Thomas Lechford, for example, the one seventeenth-century lawyer known to all colonial historians,

36. See Tables 15 and 16, Appendix. There is some indication that even pleading the general issue was not what it used to be. In 1742, Jonathan Law, then lieutenant governor of the colony and chief judge of the superior court, wrote to the colony's agent in London about a case. Law had presided over the trial on appeal, which under Connecticut procedure was a trial *de novo*. "As for my own part," Law wrote, "I never found out any other way of proceeding than this: If the Defendant took the general Plea in any Case, a jury was impannelld and then on the Parties conceeding to all the matters of fact layd in the Declaration they proceed immediately to debate the Point or Points of law arising upon those facts and this always verbol . . . and never becomes matter of Record neither can it be filed." Jonathan Law to Francis Wilkes, 24 Mar. 1742, Jonathan Law Papers, 1:270. Law appears to have treated the general issue as a cross between a general denial, in which the evidence was usually submitted to a jury, and a demurrer, in which the facts were undisputed. There is no evidence that Law's mode of procedure applied in any court but his own.

37. See George L. Haskins, *Law and Authority in Early Massachusetts: A Study in Tradition and Design*, pp. 103, 186; and Thomas G. Barnes, "Thomas Lechford and the Earliest Lawyering in Massachusetts, 1638–1641."

was a skillful pleader and conveyancer, but his competence did not affect the general level of pleadings.[38] Other early settlers had some training in law, but none of them applied their technical knowledge to legal practice. Connecticut may not have harbored quite the same antipathy to lawyers that Massachusetts did, but for most of the seventeenth century the records reveal only isolated instances of one person pleading for another. Pleading was so informal that the assembly in 1684 had to order what in more sophisticated procedural systems would have been assumed—that there should be no further pleas or testimony after a case had been committed to the jury.[39]

There was method to the informality. If pleading consisted only of asserting a complaint and denying its validity, anyone could plead for themselves. There were no issues to be "framed" for a jury because the entire dispute was within the province of the jury. Legalistic objections had no place because the social or economic relations behind the dispute were too individual to be dealt with on any basis other than the merits.

In the realm of civil disputes, courts existed to facilitate the resolution of private grievances—by accommodation if possible, by adjudication if necessary. Courts encouraged litigants to resolve their differences privately, either by allowing them to postpone their actions or, occasionally, by referring cases to arbitrators chosen from among the jurors at court.[40] Technical pleading, even if there had been people versed in it, had no place in such a system. That may in part explain why there were no such people.

The same procedural openness characterized the way plaintiffs stated their grievances in the writs by which they began their suits. The primary purpose of the plaintiff's count was to state the details of his grievance. The substance of the complaint took clear priority over its form. James Mugford's recital against Edward Stalling in 1673 is a case in point—an "action of the case for imploying him whilst hee was in the servis to fetch two barells of sugar from Mr. Condyes and not provideing a suffitient boate or cannoe to do [it] with, whereby

---

38. Barnes, "Thomas Lechford."

39. *Conn. Rec.*, 3:158.

40. There appear to have been four such references before 1665. *Conn. Rec.*, 1:83, 107–9; *Records of the Particular Court of Connecticut, 1639–1663*, p. 109. In what is probably a fifth example, the particular court approved an arbitration award that had already been made. *Conn. Rec.*, 1:123.

the sugar was damnifyed and the plainteife hath bin attached sued and troubled by the owner of the said sugar."[41] No legal shorthand there.

Form was not entirely immaterial. Virtually every civil plaintiff labeled his action, even though there were no penalties for using an inappropriate label or no label at all. To be sure, plaintiffs did not adhere to the rigidities of the common law writ system. Until the end of the seventeenth century, all actions were debt, trespass, case, or some variation of the three. Imaginative combinations such as actions "of the case for debt" or actions "of the case for trespass" caution against imputing the distinctions of the common law categories to their colonial analogs.

Most civil actions in Connecticut were labeled actions on the case, which throughout the colonial period was an all-purpose form of action with little content and less consistency. However, many recitals cast as case closely resembled other forms of action at English common law. For example, William Keeney's suit against Elizabeth Gerrard in 1666, which he described as an "action of the case upon Accounts of freight for the vessell upon detaineing his due from him" —Keeney had been a partner with Gerrard's late husband in a shipping venture—in England would have been an action of account. Richard Ely's action on the case against John Robbins in 1674 "for unjust or unlawfull seizing and detaineing five yearelings" of Ely's resembled an action of replevin, even to the remedy—a jury verdict that Robbins should return the animals. John Gallop's suit against Deliverance Blackman, an "action of the case for non performance of a bill and agreement to provide two thousand of shingle," was a fair approximation of assumpsit or, depending on the nature of the bill, covenant.[42] These cases and others could have been cast as established English forms of action, but none of them was. The major categories of debt, trespass, and case adequately described the range of civil disputes, particularly with case as the residual category for grievances that might not fit either of the first two labels.

The key to the apparent lack of differentiation was that the labels were, until near the end of the century, descriptive rather than prescriptive. They did not prescribe a mode of procedure for the lawsuit that differed from one form of action to another. Nor did they deter-

---

41. Mugford v. Stalling, 3 NLCCR 58 (1673).

42. Keeney v. Gerrard, 1 NLCCR 81 (1666); Ely v. Robbins, 3 NLCCR 65 (1674); Gallop v. Blackman, 3 NLCCR 71 (1674).

mine what remedy would apply. Moreover, as long as defendants pleaded the general issue, there was no opportunity to object that the plaintiff had chosen the wrong form of action. The labels merely described the general nature of the plaintiff's complaint. What mattered was the substance of the complaint, not the form the plaintiff chose.

Nonetheless, litigants did recognize descriptive distinctions among the basic categories, although one should not assume rigor in their adherence to the distinctions. For example, actions to enforce rights in land in the latter half of the century generally took two forms—trespass and case. Compared to the elaborate scheme of land actions available in England, this represented an extraordinary simplification. Both the abundance of land in New England and the disinclination of the settlers to do so made it impossible to impose centuries of English property law on land that had not known more than a generation of English occupation. The Connecticut Code of 1650 borrowed a page —one of many—from the Massachusetts Body of Liberties of 1641 and abolished the restrictions and incidents that encumbered freehold interests in England.[43]

Simplification of land tenures, however, did not import clarity of content in the remaining land actions, at least not initially. In common law theory, trespass was available only to plaintiffs who had possession of the land at the time of the alleged incursion. Case was the proper action for claimants who did not have possession. This formal distinction between the two actions was not maintained clearly or

---

43. *Conn. Rec.*, 1:536–37. On the ample borrowing of the Code of 1650 from the Body of Liberties, see George L. Haskins and Samuel E. Ewing III, "The Spread of Massachusetts Law in the Seventeenth Century." For an excellent treatment of property law in England, see A. W. B. Simpson, *An Introduction to the History of the Land Law*.

Eighteenth-century lawyers recognized the difference between the formality of land titles in their time and the comparative informality of the previous century. As one such lawyer, William Samuel Johnson, observed in 1764, "the Title to these Lands is not fixed with precision but was left very Vague and indeterminate by the Charter which however is not infrequent in ancient Conveyances which past in the Infancy of the Colonies and at a time when Property was by no means so valuable or so well fixed as at Present. It would be very wrong in these Cases I think to apply with severity the present nice Rules of Law to such ancient loose transactions." William Samuel Johnson to Benjamin Kissam, 26 June 1764, William Samuel Johnson Papers, Letterbooks, 13:20–21.

consistently until the mid-1680s. There were intimations of the distinction in earlier actions, because only plaintiffs out of possession sued on case.[44] However, most other land actions were labeled "action of the case upon trespass" or "action of the case for trespass." Many involved plaintiffs in possession, but there were some in which possession was not clear.[45] Since there were also occasional actions of trespass in which the plaintiffs sued on their possession, the question of whether the hybrid actions were more case or more trespass is unclear.[46] It is also unimportant. If the form of the declaration had no bearing on either the pleadings or the evidence, whether an action should have been cast as trespass or case was immaterial. Litigants were doubtless generally aware of the distinction at common law. As long as the distinction had only descriptive value, however, there was no reason to apply it faithfully.

Beginning in the mid-1680s, the distinction between trespass and case on the point of the plaintiff's possession became one with a difference. John Leeds of New London, for example, recovered land from Joseph Latham in 1684 by suing him on case "for the improving and detayneing from him certain Land." The following year, when he had gained possession of the land, Leeds sued Latham in trespass for farming the land during the time Leeds was out of possession.[47] Regular observance of the possessory distinction between trespass and case came after the extensive efforts of Sir Edmund Andros in the late 1680s to conform colonial court procedure to English practice.[48] Thereafter, until the next change in pleading in the second decade of

44. Lester v. Williams, 1 NLCCR 45, 57, 61, 63 (1665) ("action of the case for siting downe upon his land and building and fenceing upon it without his leave and knowledge"); Lester v. Morgan, 1 NLCCR 81 (1666) ("Action of the case for unjustly takeing away his land and maintaining it to be another"); Parkes v. Parker, 3 NLCCR 70 (1674) ("action of the case for . . . Parker's denyeing or refuseing to give him possession and shew him the bounds of a certain lott of land").

45. Cotter v. Douglas, 1 NLCCR 82 (1666); Denison v. Richardson, 1 NLCCR 104 (1667); Lester v. Keeney, 1 NLCCR 81 (1666); Parkes v. Stark, 1 NLCCR 73 (1666); Richardson v. Babcock, 3 NLCCR 60 (1673).

46. Wheeler v. Bennett, 3 NLCCR 35, 45, 58 (1671–73).

47. Leeds v. Latham, 5 NLCCR 74 (1684); Leeds v. Latham, 5 NLCCR 119 (1685). The second action was known in England as the action of trespass for mesne profits.

48. David Konig notes a similar introduction of English practice under the Dominion in Massachusetts. David Thomas Konig, *Law and Society in Puritan Massachusetts: Essex County, 1629–1692*, pp. 160–64.

the eighteenth century, plaintiffs declared in trespass when they had possession and on case when they did not.

The hardening of the distinction between trespass and case was part of a general trend toward greater formality in legal practice and procedure that began with Andros's reforms and accelerated in Connecticut in the twenty years after his overthrow. The immediate impetus for the change is not hard to discern, although the consequences were more far-reaching and less obvious. It makes for a rather nice symmetry that, just as the bedrock of medieval English law was land law, the formal legal changes in Connecticut were prompted by competition for land.

The contours of the competition are well known.[49] In 1684 much of the colony east of the towns along the Connecticut River and north of the ones on Long Island Sound was in private hands. Whose hands was a matter of dispute. Until shortly after mid-century, the Mohegans had claimed the land as theirs. Then, by a series of grants ending in 1684, the Mohegan sachem, Uncas, and his two sons, Owaneco and Joshua, deeded the land to various prominent white colonists—among them John Winthrop, Jr., and, most importantly, James Fitch. Before 1675 the General Assembly had carefully supervised the laying out and settlement of new towns. It then changed its policy and simply confirmed the Indian deeds, leaving the grantees free to manage settlement of the land as they wished. The assembly did not impose residency requirements or regulate prices on sale of the new lands. Population increase and the shortage of available land in the settled parts of the colony had raised land values considerably, particularly in the east, which adjoined the principal sources of immigration from southeastern Massachusetts. Large profits were to be had by speculators, and the assembly was not averse to giving wealthier inhabitants free rein.

The imprecision of Indian land titles and the lack of supervision by the assembly combined to produce turmoil. Title disputes pervaded the region as the new proprietors sold competing deeds and struggled for supremacy. Popular factions formed around the opposing land barons, who waged legal war with one another, usually through their tenants and purchasers. Fitch, who claimed the most land, sold entire townships as well as smaller tracts, including land claimed by the Winthrops. Purchasers from both proprietors, as well as purchasers

---

49. The following discussion rests primarily on Richard L. Bushman, *From Puritan to Yankee: Character and the Social Order in Connecticut, 1690–1765*, pp. 83–103.

from lesser claimants, resold the land, thereby spreading ownership as well as contention.

Lurking behind the contention was a political struggle between Fitch, an ambitious man with a popular backwoods manner, and the Winthrops and their allies among the older, more conservative families of the colony. Law and politics merged. The General Assembly, which appointed the judges of the county courts, was itself the highest appellate court. The sympathies of the deputies and magistrates were thus crucial elements in the jockeying over land claims. Fitch narrowly missed gaining control of the assembly after the overthrow of Andros and the Dominion in 1689, but he remained dominant in New London County and continued to be a commanding presence in the assembly. As the elected assistant from New London County, Fitch was presiding magistrate of the county court there. He was also a shrewd legal tactician, evidently self-taught. Both as magistrate and lawyer, he was tireless in prosecuting trespassers, evicting tenants whose leases stemmed from the Winthrops, and defending his own titles and those of his allies. His skill raised the level of pleadings in land actions and forced the Winthrops to seek their own attorneys.

Fitch, for all his legal skill, was never able to transform his strong regional popularity into lasting political power. Popularity alone could not confer power in a society that was characterized by deference to conservative authority. Many of the reforms in court organization and procedure that the Winthrops and their allies secured in the closing years of the century trimmed the legal sails that had propelled Fitch's successes. In May 1697 the assembly barred appeals of civil actions from the court of assistants to the assembly. Eight months later, the assembly restructured the county courts. Whereas before, the courts had consisted of a presiding magistrate, who was an assistant resident in the county, and two or more commissioners, they were now constituted by three or more justices of the quorum and a presiding judge appointed by the assembly.[50] The justices of the quorum were justices of the peace—formerly titled commissioners—whose social position and experience qualified them for the county bench. The key change lay in the presiding judge, who no longer was automatically an assistant living in the county. Appointment of the judges, like all actions of the assembly, required the concurrence of the assistants and the deputies. The judges of the four county courts appointed in May 1698

50. *Conn. Rec.*, 4:200, 235–36.

included two assistants, the recently retired deputy governor, and the colony treasurer, but not James Fitch.[51] At the same session, Fitz-John Winthrop was elected governor, and Fitch failed to win reelection as an assistant for the first time since his initial election in 1681. The combined force of these orders stripped Fitch of his judicial authority. They assured that no matter how well Fitch fared in the county court, he would have no right of appeal beyond a court on which, even if reelected assistant, he would have only one vote among several.

One legacy of the legal and political contentions of the period was a deliberate shift to greater procedural regularity. Fitch's own sense of procedural propriety had long been apparent. At a county court in 1693 Fitch and his fellow judges had rejected a plea for a nonsuit by Alice Liveen and Nicholas Hallam, defendants in a book debt action. The parties had then joined issue, and the jury rendered a verdict for the plaintiff. The defendants reviewed the action to the next county court and renewed their plea for a nonsuit. Fitch knew that the plea was improper—the plea was available only to defendants, and Liveen and Hallam were now plaintiffs on review. Fitch argued to his colleagues that "it was contrary both to law reason and custome for plaintiffes to have an nonsuit," but he was outvoted. In a final attempt for accuracy, Fitch wanted the record to specify that the court had granted the nonsuit to the plaintiffs, rather than simply stating that it had granted a nonsuit, which normally referred to a plea by the defendant. Here, too, less formal minds carried the point, although the court of assistants ultimately agreed with Fitch.[52]

In the decade that followed, Fitch's success as a legal tactician impressed his adversaries. It particularly impressed Fitz-John Winthrop, who, although often on the losing end of Fitch's pleas, had an abiding admiration for English formality. One of the first legislative acts of Winthrop's governorship was an order that no member of the assembly could speak without first requesting and receiving permission from the governor—to prevent "all confusion and disorder in speaking to any matter that may be in agitation."[53] With such a penchant

51. Ibid., 4:261.

52. Steers v. Liveen and Hallam, 7 NLCCR 104, 105, 109, 2 CtAR 20r (1693); Memorandum of James Fitch, 22 Sept. 1693, SCF 174.

53. *Conn. Rec.*, 4:266. Richard Dunn discusses Fitz-John Winthrop's campaign for internal reform along English lines. *Puritans and Yankees*, pp. 321–22.

for order, similar restrictions on pleading seem in retrospect almost inevitable.

The assembly in 1704 took note of "disorderly pleading." It directed the courts to establish rules for "orderly pleading, and to oblige all parties concerned to speake one after another in their turnes," so that "there may not be clamours and noise to pervert justice." Orderly pleading also meant technical pleading. In further regulations adopted five years later, the assembly dealt with appeals from overruled pleas in abatement, joining issue after pleading in bar, demurrers, and the penalty for refusing to join issue.[54]

Pleading beyond the general issue overtook the courts rather suddenly. Judges, who for the most part were untutored in law, learned the intricacies of pleading from English custumals and from the example of the litigants before them. They did not become fluent in procedure overnight. The court of assistants in 1708 searched its records before deciding that it could allow a debtor to renew a plea in bar decided in the county court and that it could rule differently on it. The judges of the New Haven County Court in 1712 first granted a review from their abatement of a writ, then at their next session realized that pleas in abatement were not reviewable and, with some embarrassment, dismissed the case.[55] Different panels of judges could, and did, take opposite views of the same technical pleas.[56]

Litigants, too, required a period of adjustment. The assembly, for example, occasionally allowed litigants who had mistakenly joined the wrong issue to enter different pleas on rehearing, whereas normally they would be bound by admissions they had made in previous pleas.[57] Moreover, the colony had a liberal jeofailes statute, which excused "Circumstantial Errors or Mistakes" in pleading and summons "if the Person and the Cause be rightly understood and intended by the Court." In addition, a litigant who, in pleading to issue,

54. *Conn. Rec.*, 4:468, 5:106.

55. Gray v. Robe, 3 CtAR 81 (1708); Guy v. Tuttle, 2 NHCCR 482–83, 490 (1712).

56. For example, see Lyron v. Edwards and Sturgis, 2 NHCCR 443–44, 3 CtAR 189–90 (1710–11); Hoadly v. Johnson, 2 NHCCR 488, 3 CtAR 270 (1712–13).

57. See *Conn. Rec.*, 5:172; Petition of Nathaniel Johnson, 12 Oct. 1710, Conn. Arch., Priv. Controversies (1st ser.), 6:210. Courts sometimes allowed the same liberty to litigants with the consent of the other party. See Saltonstall v. Palmerlee, 1 SCR 286 (1717).

thought he had "missed the plea, . . . which would have saved him in his just cause," could offer a revised plea.[58]

These instances illustrate what the numbers confirmed earlier—that the second decade of the eighteenth century was a transitional period in the way people conducted their civil suits. Civil litigation was moving away from a communal model, in which the disputants argued their grievances under the general issue, to a sparring match controlled by technical rules that allowed the parties to narrow the range of relevant facts or to avoid them altogether and take issue on legal grounds. Under such a procedural scheme, the facts of a dispute were intrinsically worth less than how one pleaded them, which included not pleading them at all. This relative ordering of merit is readily apparent in what was, for Connecticut, a new phenomenon—defendants who resorted to pleading the merits of their cases only after their first line of defense, that of technical objections, had crumbled. If one can judge from the outcomes, defendants who pleaded thusly often had good reason to doubt the merits of their cases.[59] But the attraction of dilatory pleading was such that some defendants pleaded in abatement even though their cases were strong enough that they later won on the general issue.[60]

I I I

The suddenness of the transition in pleading, marked as it was by uncertainty on the part of judges and litigants, was in part traceable to the emergence of a group of professional lawyers. The concept of attorneyship, of standing in other people's shoes and speaking for

58. *Acts and Laws 1715*, p. 108; *Conn. Rec.*, 6:186. The draft pleadings in one case, an action on the case that arose from an alleged agreement to exchange currency, indicate that the defendants were prepared to plead that they "never owed unto the plaintiff any such money." The plaintiff's attorney pointed out that this was the wrong general issue for the action. The county court allowed the defendants to make a new plea, which is the only one formally entered in the records. Burroughs and Burroughs v. Rosewell and Hudson, 2 NHCCR 492, NHCCF 1 (1712–13).

59. Riggs v. Hotchkiss, 2 NHCCR 474–75, 3 CtAR 263–64, 274, 4 CtAR 105, 126 (1712–13); Johnson v. Blin, 3 NHCCR 9 (1713); Beecher v. Smith, 3 NHCCR 61 (1716); Noyes v. Bradley, 3 NHCCR 95, 2 SCR 15 (1718–19).

60. Collins v. Tuttle, 3 NHCCR 43, 3 CtAR 371, 1 SCR 17 (1715).

them, was commonplace. Initially, however, it referred to attorneys-in-fact rather than attorneys-at-law. Litigants who could not appear in court personally would execute a power of attorney to a friend, neighbor, or relative to appear in their stead and act for them.

In 1708 the assembly recognized the growing practice of people pleading for others. It ordered that no one should be allowed to plead for another person who had not first been approved by the court and taken an oath that followed the form for attorneys given in the English *Book of Oaths* of 1649. The clerk of the court that administered the oath was to record the event. The record would be proof of the taker's "admission as an atturney to the bar of the . . . court."[61] Within a year, eleven men had been admitted to the bar of the court of assistants.[62] None of the eleven was formally trained in law, and none treated legal practice as his principal occupation. But their own reading in law gave them greater knowledge and expertise than most litigants had and, for a time at least, more than most judges.[63]

For the next fifteen to twenty years, however, these lawyers argued

---

61. *Conn. Rec.*, 5:48. See also William Samuel Johnson, *The Superior Court Diary of William Samuel Johnson, 1772–1773*, p. liii n. 1. The only previous regulation had been in 1667, when the assembly established penalties for anyone who "shal take that boldnes to himselfe as to plead or speake in the behalfe of any person that is upon examination or tryal for delinquency, (except he speake directly to matter of law and with leave from the authority present)." *Conn. Rec.*, 2:59.

62. The eleven were Jeremiah Osborne, Jonathan Law, John Parker, Richard Edwards, James Rogers, Jr., John Read, Thomas Turnour, William Ely, James Bennett, Roger Wolcott, and Ebenezer Pumery. *Conn. Rec.*, 5:48 n. *.

63. Jeremiah Osborne, who was the first attorney licensed by the court of assistants in 1708, was suspended from pleading by the New Haven County Court in 1709 when he protested that a defendant's demurrer had been omitted from the record and described the omission as "a subverting of justice." In re Osborne, 2 NHCCR 418 (1709). The court did, however, amend the record. 2 NHCCR 413. Osborne was readmitted three months later after submitting a letter of apology in which he promised "for the future to behave myself with more care and moderation and consideration toward this Court." 2 NHCCR 431 (1710). Osborne, who was also a justice of the peace, was rather more learned, or perhaps only more ostentatious, than his judicial colleagues. In his records as justice, he headed pleadings "Coram Jeremiah Osborne Jus. Pac." and labeled attested copies of them "Copia vera." See copies in Miles v. Sperry, NHCCR 2 (1710).

more cases against laymen than they did against each other.[64] Attorneys-in-fact remained common.[65] Zachariah Baldwin's action in stepping off the jury to be sworn as an attorney for one of the parties in a case before the New Haven County Court was unusual, but it nicely symbolized the fact that most men, and the occasional woman, who appeared in court for others were, like jurors, "men of the neighborhood"—peers in a sense that licensed attorneys were not.[66] More commonly still, people pleaded their own cases, as the court of assistants recognized when it required that "all parties be prepared (by themselves or their attornys) to give in their pleas . . . fairly written to remain on file."[67]

The presence of lawyers nonetheless had a discernible effect on the conduct of lawsuits. At the beginning of the chapter we saw Stephen Perkins's outrage at the lawyer who quibbled about a complaint that to Perkins seemed perfectly adequate. Perkins was not the only plaintiff who lost his action because of a well-aimed technical plea by a lawyer. Benjamin Fairweather's writ, for example, was abated because he tried to bring an action of debt on an oral obligation rather than on a written one. Louis Lyron, who usually used attorneys but may not have here, saw his writ abated because he had not joined the husbands of two of the defendants.[68]

To be sure, the worm sometimes turned. Samuel Pond of Branford was not a lawyer, but he demolished a writ of attachment brought against him by a justice of the peace who was acting as attorney for a Boston merchant.[69] Pond's skill attested to the influence of lawyers on

64. A notable exception is Prout v. Langstaff, 3 CtAR 192 (1711), an appeal from a judgment on a *scire facias* that pit Jonathan Law against John Read.

65. See Samuel Bassett's power of attorney to his "trusty friend and well beloved Son in law," John Hitchcock, 5 Apr. 1715, Atwater v. Bassett, NHCCF 1 (1715); John Guy's to his "trusty frind," Daniel Collins, 21 Oct. 1712, Guy v. Collins, NHCCF 1 (1715); Thomas Sperry's to his brother, Nathaniel Sperry, Miles v. Sperry, NHCCF 2 (1710); and John Guy's to his wife, Anna Guy, 30 Apr. 1716, 3 NHCCR 69–70.

66. Guy v. Mallory, 3 NHCCR 73 (1716).

67. Memorandum of court procedure, 3 Oct. 1710, 4 CtAR 1.

68. Fairweather v. Lyron, 3 CtAR 190–91 (1711); Lyron v. Edwards et al., 2 NHCCR 475–76, 3 CtAR 271–72, 4 CtAR 102, 122 (1712–13).

69. Bradley v. Pond, 3 NHCCR 36 (1714) (Pond's pleas in abatement are in NHCCF 1).

pleadings. Pond was an exceptionally litigious character. Hardly a year passed that did not see him in court as plaintiff or defendant. His cases spanned the spectrum from misdemeanors to land claims. What galled his adversaries most was not his litigiousness, but his skill. When Pond brandished legal process or pleaded his own case, he won more often than he lost. He was, perhaps, more resourceful and determined than most people, but he was only using tactics that lawyers themselves used. Pond merely demonstrated that others, too, could play by the new, more formal rules and win.

The influence of lawyers on the conduct of lawsuits appeared not only in actions by people like Samuel Pond, who imitated lawyers for their own causes, but also in the activities of people like Joseph Tuttle of East Haven, who pleaded for clients as an unlicensed attorney. A cordwainer by trade, Tuttle handled cases on the side. He was once identified as an "attorney at Law" in a suit brought against him by a creditor from outside the colony who perhaps believed Tuttle's representations about himself.[70] Both Tuttle's cases and his clients, who included Indians and servants, tended to be small, even when measured by the limited standards of local litigation.[71] The most noticeable thing about Tuttle's unlicensed lawyering is that he was not very good at it. He lost cases, both his own and others, far more often than he won. His pleadings were often inappropriate or inarticulate. They give the impression of a man mouthing words he had heard others use but with little understanding of their proper context.[72] In one case Tuttle even admitted his mimicry. He offered as a plea something he had heard John Read, a skillful licensed attorney, say the night before and referred to Read by name as his authority. The borrowed plea did not quite fit Tuttle's case, and he lost.[73] It is a measure of the power lawyers had to shape litigation that others sought to imitate their ways.

The transitional nature of the period is underscored by the fact that

70. Carhart v. Tuttle, 3 NHCCR 44–45, 3 CtAR 372, 1 SCR 18 (1715) (the description of Tuttle is in the summons, 29 Oct. 1714, in NHCCF 1).

71. For example, see Johnson v. Toto, 2 NHCCR 445, 3 CtAR 191–92 (1710–11) (Indian); Guy v. Kirkham, 3 NHCCR 9, 17–18 (1713) (servant); Johnson v. John alias George, 3 NHCCR 55, 58 (1715) (Indian). Tuttle lost all three cases.

72. For example, see his pleas in Chittenden v. Tuttle, 3 NHCCR 55, NHCCF 1 (1715); and Collins v. Tuttle, 3 NHCCR 43 (1715).

73. Cooper v. Tuttle, 3 NHCCR 97, 2 SCR 58, NHCCF 1 (1718–19).

lawyers, too, required some adjustment to the new formality they had helped foster. The first licensed attorneys, all self-taught, did not burst on the scene spouting perfectly phrased pleadings. Like litigants and judges, they had much to learn. Consider, for example, John Read himself, a former minister who was among the first attorneys admitted to the bar of the court of assistants in 1708.

Read's legal career got off to an uneven start. Seven months after taking the attorney's oath he was suspended from pleading for "manifest contempt" of the court of assistants.[74] Read eventually emigrated to Boston, where he became attorney general of the province and, according to Thomas Hutchinson, "a very eminent lawyer and, which is more, a person of great integrity and firmness of mind."[75] Read's earliest efforts did not presage his later eminence. With occasional exceptions, his early pleading was not particularly skillful. His pleas in abatement rarely succeeded, but they were never so far off the mark as to suggest that Read was deliberately making a sham plea to facilitate appeal to the superior court.[76]

Nonetheless, Read did demonstrate flashes of procedural insight, particularly in formulaic matters such as whether the plaintiff had picked the right form of action or the defendant had made an appropriate plea. He knew, for example, that no appeal lay from a writ of *scire facias* issued on a prior judgment, that *nil debet* was not the proper general denial for an action on the case grounded on receipt of

---

74. *Conn. Rec.*, 5:48 n. *.

75. Thomas Hutchinson, *The History of the Colony and Province of Massachusetts Bay*, 2:285. On Read's legal career see David H. Flaherty, "Criminal Practice in Provincial Massachusetts," pp. 194–204, and Clifford K. Shipton, *Sibley's Harvard Graduates*, 4:369–78.

76. For some of Read's unsuccessful pleas in abatement, see Barker v. Page and Page, 2 NHCCR 446 (1710); Frisbie v. Thompson, 2 NHCCR 451 (1710); Treat et al. v. Bronson and Bronson, 2 NHCCR 435–36, 3 CtAR 153–54, 165–66, 185–86 (1710); Treat et al. v. Ferris, 2 NHCCR 436–37, 3 CtAR 154–55, 166, 186 (1710); Treat et al. v. Read, 2 NHCCR 427–28, 3 CtAR 155, 167, 186 (1710); Ely v. Lee, 8 NLCCR 2, 2 CtAR 217, SCF 178 (1711). Kinvin Wroth and Hiller Zobel noted the occasional practice of sham pleading in Massachusetts a half-century later. L. Kinvin Wroth and Hiller B. Zobel, eds., *Legal Papers of John Adams*, 1:xlvi. One of the rare instances of Read considering a sham plea at the beginning of his career is a plea in abatement that he drafted but did not make—that "the province Colony kingdom or county which the plaintiff lives in is not set forth only the town or parish Boston which is therefore uncertain there being severall Bostons."

money, and that a purchaser who lost land to a third party because his seller did not have good title should have vouched the seller to defend his title when it was challenged rather than wait and sue the seller on case. Read's pleas in this last case were sufficiently daunting—Connecticut courts in 1711 were not accustomed to hearing pleas such as "Action of the Case doth not ly against a Feoffor but voucher or Warrantia Chartae"—that the superior court had to continue the case to "further consider of the Pleas." Read's study of English legal texts continued. By 1717 he was able to lace his successful defense of a surgeon charged with murder with learned references to Hale, Coke, and Dalton, as well as to various English cases and scripture.[77]

Read's growing expertise was symptomatic of that of lawyers generally, at least the licensed ones. It did not, of course, mean that all lawyers became as adept. Some could not plead their way out of the procedural equivalent of a paper bag. James Peck, for example, advanced a plea in abatement in his own case that he thought had succeeded in another. He failed to recognize, however, that the plea he relied on was not the plea that had carried the day in the other case.[78] For clients of such attorneys, the only recourse was to appeal to the discretionary mercy of the assembly for a retrial, as John Arnold did after his lawyer lost his case by pleading to the wrong issue. Litigants in Arnold's position were vulnerable because, as he observed in his petition, "not being a Lawyer [he] did not understand the Rules of pleading."[79] Wittingly or unwittingly, Arnold captured the essence of the transformation. Pleading now had rules. More to the point, it had rules that were best understood by lawyers.

The transition in pleading was largely complete by 1720. Pleadings after then bear little resemblance to pleadings from the turn of the century. Despite occasional ameliorative statutes, pleading became more technical and formal. Thus, a plaintiff who sued in detinue when he should have sued in trespass, as John Andrews did in 1719,

---

Mico v. Arnold, 8 NLCCR 34, 2 CtAR 245 (1711–12) (draft pleadings in SCR 178).

77. Prout v. Langstaff, 2 NHCCR 449–50, 3 CtAR 192 (1710–11); Burroughs and Burroughs v. Rosewell and Hudson, 2 NHCCR 492, NHCCF 1 (1712–13); Fish v. Edgecomb, 2 CtAR 218, 251 (1711–12); R. v. Allin, 1 SCR 237, SCF 323 (1717).

78. Brockett v. Mather, 3 NHCCR 105, NHCCF 1 (1719).

79. Petition of John Arnold, Apr. 1722, Conn. Arch., Priv. Controversies (2d ser.), 1:129a.

could expect his writ to be abated, as Andrews's was, "for want of formality and surtainty."[80] The change was apparent at the lowest legal level. Records of proceedings before justices of the peace are scarce, particularly before mid-century, but occasional glimpses suggest the spread of technical pleas there as well. Thomas Yale, a justice of the peace in Wallingford of modest talents, had to adjourn court for a week in 1719 to consider how to rule on a plea in abatement in a replevin action.[81] Justice court records from Windsor in the 1720s and 1730s, which may be the earliest such records surviving, note pleas in abatement, pleas in bar, and demurrers as matters of course.[82]

The spread of technical pleading made lawyers essential to litigation. By the 1730s, pleadings had become duels between opposing lawyers. Statutorily prescribed attorneys' fees were a standard item in the victor's bill of costs. The General Assembly in 1730 attempted to limit the number of licensed attorneys in the colony to eleven—three in Hartford County and two in each of the four other counties— because "many persons of late have taken upon them to be attourneys at the bar, so that quarrels and lawsuits are multiplied, and the King's good subjects disturbed." It also restricted litigants to one lawyer each in non-land-title actions where the demand was not over ten pounds, and two each in actions where land title was concerned or where the demand exceeded ten pounds.[83]

The assembly rescinded its limitation on the total number of lawyers the following year, possibly under pressure from litigants left without counsel in large cases when their opponents engaged both lawyers allotted to the county. However, it retained the restriction on the number of attorneys a litigant could bring into court.[84] In practice, the restriction appears also to have been a minimum, judging by the number of cases in which attorneys pleaded two to a side. The growing dominance of lawyers did not, of course, prevent people from pleading their own cases. William Douglass's observation that, "particularly in New England, people are much addicted to quirks of the

---

80. Andrews v. Adams, 3 NHCCR 109, NHCCF 1 (1719).

81. Hough v. Johnson (1719), copy of proceedings in NHCCF 1.

82. See Windsor Inferior Court Records, 1719–34.

83. *Conn. Rec.*, 7:279–80. The statutory compilation of 1750 gives the amount in controversy separating the right to engage one and two attorneys as five pounds. *Acts and Laws 1750*, pp. 9–10.

84. *Conn. Rec.*, 7:358.

law," is amply supported by the frequency and skill of lay pleading.[85]
Lay skill notwithstanding, pride of place in pleading went to lawyers.

Amid the spectacle of lawyers arrogating control of pleadings to themselves, one should not overlook the fact that lawyers could spin their webs of technical pleas only in appropriate cases. Written credit instruments, for example, offered more opportunities for special or technical pleading than did book accounts. Their greater formality precluded pleading the general issue and arguing about the underlying debt. The fact that notes and bonds embodied the debt as perfectly as they did meant that, for the most part, whatever defenses the debtor might have could be raised only through technical pleas. The shift away from book accounts to promissory notes and conditioned bonds as the favored means of evidencing debt obligations provided a larger role for lawyers in collecting and defending debts. Lawyers themselves, however, had little, if anything, to do with bringing about the shift. Rather, it occurred, as we have seen, because of changes in the commercial life of the colony, changes which in turn created opportunities for the skills of attorneys.

These themes—the decline of the civil jury, the growing technical sophistication of pleading, the emerging dominance of lawyers—were part of the larger transformation of the legal system in the eighteenth century that is the subject of this book. Although the three occurred within roughly the same span of time and seem naturally related to one another, it would be misleading to try to fix the nature of their relationship too precisely. Causation is difficult to determine at such a remove. Moreover, as among the three phenomena studied here, establishing causation would not be a terribly useful exercise. The more important inquiry is to understand the social dimension of the changes—the dimension expressed in Stephen Perkins's plaintive cry. That inquiry, however, must wait until we have examined a few more of the elements of legal change.

85. William Douglass, *A Summary, Historical and Political, of the First Planting, Progressive Improvements and Present State of the British Settlements in North America*, quoted in Charles Warren, *A History of the American Bar*, p. 79.

4

THE FORMALIZATION OF

INFORMAL LAW

F O R Zephaniah Swift, arbitration was "an amicable and neighbourly mode of settling personal controversies." Arbitrators, he wrote, "are not tied down to the same strictness, formality and precision as courts of law. While they have greater latitude in the mode of proceeding than courts of law, they have ampler powers to do compleat and perfect justice between the parties in the decision of the matters in dispute."[1] Even as he sang its praises, however, Swift treated arbitration as an appendage to the legal system rather than as an integral part of it. He gave arbitration only eleven pages in his two-volume treatise, following self-defense and self-help.

Long before Swift wrote, arbitration played a significant role in resolving the disputes of people who preferred not to go to law. Unlike litigation, arbitration was inexpensive, expeditious, and private. Above all, it was, as Swift recognized, "neighbourly"—uniquely tied to and shaped by the communities in which it existed. The community ties were an essential part of arbitration. Without them, arbitration would not have been the popular and effective alternative to formal legal process that it was. As the bonds of community weakened, the legal system appropriated arbitration to itself and turned it into a formal process that differed little from legal adjudication.

I

Common law arbitration was sufficiently developed in England by the seventeenth century to merit part of a treatise.[2] Parties who decided to

1. Zephaniah Swift, *A System of the Laws of the State of Connecticut*, 2:7.
2. John March, *Actions for Slaunder . . . To which is added, Awards or*

submit their differences to arbitration rather than to law would select two or more men as arbitrators and instruct them on the task at hand.[3] The instructions took the form of an oral or written submission that set forth the nature and limits of the dispute and empowered the arbitrators to hear the parties and their evidence and to "make end" of their differences. The instructions, or "submissions," often stipulated a time limit within which the arbitrators had to make their decision and the form, whether written or oral, that the decision had to take. Submission of the dispute to arbitration was, of course, voluntary, at least in the sense that it was not compelled by legal authority.[4]

Voluntariness permeated the process. Executory oral contracts were unenforceable, which meant that either party to an oral submission could revoke the submission, and thus the authority of the arbitrators, with impunity.[5] To correct this problem, disputants framed the instructions in written instruments called deeds, which both parties signed. Submission by deed, however, did little to deter revocation. The aggrieved party whose opponent had revoked a written submission could bring an action of debt for nonperformance of the obligation in the deed. Courts, though, would award only nominal damages for the breach—after all, how much damage could a person sustain whose only "injury" was having to seek the king's justice by pursuing the original complaint at law?[6] Despite their coercive intent, deeds did little to impair the voluntariness of the process.

Arbitrements, pp. 149–241. Good historical studies of arbitration are few. The best one is also the oldest, Stewart Kyd, *A Treatise on the Law of Awards*. More recent treatments include William S. Holdsworth, *A History of English Law*, 14:187–98; William C. Jones, "An Inquiry into the History of the Adjudication of Mercantile Disputes in Great Britain and the United States"; and Paul L. Sayre, "Development of Commercial Arbitration Law." As the titles suggest, little has been written on noncommercial arbitration.

3. Stewart Kyd did write that "with us an unmarried woman may be an arbitratrix," but his statement was largely theoretical. Kyd, *Treatise on the Law of Awards*, pp. 70–71. The legal disability of women at least prevented the term "arbitratrix" from entering common usage.

4. One can, of course, imagine situations in which one party may feel compelled to submit to arbitration because of the superior bargaining power of the other party.

5. On the unenforceability of executory oral contracts at English law, see Holdsworth, *History of English Law*, 3:417–20.

6. Sayre, "Development of Commercial Arbitration Law," pp. 598–99.

The submission was not the only part of the process that relied on the continuing commitment of the parties. Even when the parties stood firm to the conclusion, there was no guarantee that they would abide by the award. For all practical purposes, arbitration awards were unenforceable. Arbitrators did not have legal process at their disposal to enforce their awards, nor could courts issue writs of execution on them.[7] If an award required one party to pay money, the party in whose favor the arbitrators had awarded could bring an action of debt or of assumpsit against his opponent.[8] Neither action, however, made the award itself enforceable. Moreover, each action was so hedged with procedural limitations that it was often simpler to sue on the underlying dispute. Successful arbitration rested on the good faith of the parties rather than on legal sanctions.

Unplighted good faith is thin assurance, however. To supply the necessary security for both submissions and awards, disputants took to submitting to arbitration on bonds that were written for a penal sum and conditioned on performing the award. The bonds did not make arbitration awards themselves enforceable, but they did raise the cost of ignoring them. People who refused to perform awards risked being sued on their bonds as well as on the underlying dispute. In fact, a person who revoked his submission was still liable on his bond, even if the arbitrators never made an award.[9] Important changes in both law and equity in the course of the seventeenth century undercut the efficacy of bonds in the English arbitration process, but they came after the first waves of migration to America and so belong to a later part of the story.

Such were the contours of arbitration in England on the eve of

---

7. Common law courts did not hold the party who failed to perform an arbitration award liable to pay damages until the end of the seventeenth century. Chancery would not grant specific performance on an award until the first half of the eighteenth century. Holdsworth, *History of English Law*, 14:193.

8. Kyd, *Treatise on the Law of Awards*, 277.

9. Vynior's Case, 77 Eng. Rep. 595 (K.B. 1609). A reference to *Vynior's Case* is a shibboleth of the arbitration literature, which usually cites it for the proposition that arbitration agreements were unenforceable at common law. Indeed, as one writer observed, "[m]ost articles on arbitration start with a violent poke at *Vynior's Case*." Philip G. Phillips, "Synthetic Courts—A General Introduction," p. 123. The best poke is probably Sayre, "Development of Commercial Arbitration Law," pp. 598–605.

colonization. Along with other legal traditions, arbitration was part of the cultural baggage of the transatlantic migration. The first two generations of settlers in Connecticut did not transplant all the practices used in contemporary English arbitration. Some elements, such as deeds and conditioned bonds, they left unused until a later time. The procedures they applied suited the communities they established, just as the ones they did not use reflected the society they had left behind.

II

Arbitration in Connecticut before 1700 was a community affair. So, for that matter, were all forms of dispute settlement. But the ties of arbitration to community were stronger. One measure of the communal qualities of book accounts, for example, was that as many as three-fifths of all book debt actions involved residents of the same town, as they did in Hartford County in 1700. By way of contrast, all arbitrations mentioned in petitions to the General Assembly before 1700 were between residents of the same town or members of the same family.[10]

10. "All" is a limited number. The petitions mention eleven arbitrations before 1700, all but two of which date from the last quarter of the century. One of the eleven does not contain complete identification of residence. Hillyard v. Reynolds and Preston, Conn. Arch., Priv. Controversies (1st ser.), 4:81 (1692). I have grouped together as intracommunity arbitrations those between members of the same family and those between inhabitants of the same town because each involved people who were bound in continuing relations with one another. Most of the intrafamily arbitrations were also intratown. The relative paucity of arbitrations mentioned in petitions before 1700 is, I think, a mark of the success of arbitration in processing disputes. See note 13. The sample after 1700 is better—seventy-eight arbitrations in petitions and a few others mentioned in county and superior court records.

The petitions referred to are gathered in the Private Controversies Series of the Connecticut Archives. They are from individuals who had taken their disputes to law after arbitration had failed to settle their differences and who were dissatisfied with the outcome of the litigation. The aggrieved party might then petition the General Assembly for equitable relief, which, if granted, usually consisted of a retrial in the superior court. The documents in the archives for each case consist primarily of the petition, which recounts the history of the dispute in great and self-serving detail, any reply made by the

The community nexus of arbitration should not surprise us. Arbitration was, after all, a consensual process. No one compelled disputants to submit their differences to the judgment of arbitrators, whose only authority came from the parties themselves. People did not sacrifice the compulsory process of law for the voluntariness of arbitration when they were strangers—the vagaries of the results could be too great. They chose arbitration over law when they knew one another and trusted each other to accept an award as final even though it was legally unenforceable. They also chose arbitration for its relative speed, inexpensiveness, and informality. Moreover, disputants came to arbitration together, rather than as plaintiff and defendant, without the heightened sense of being adversaries that such labels imply.

Court records contain only scattered references to arbitration before 1680. The paucity may be a measure of success. As early as 1645, the General Assembly recommended that many "unnessary tryalls by Jury . . . might be prevented if arbitrations were attended in a more privat way."[11] Both the assembly and the particular court encouraged litigants to resolve their differences privately. Each court, with the consent of the parties, referred cases to the determination of arbitrators whom the court chose from among the jurors present. Such references were rare, however.[12] Nonetheless, despite the lack of documentation, there is no reason to doubt that arbitration was an accepted form of adjudicating disputes in Connecticut before 1680. Arbitration was common in Massachusetts. When it first appears in the petitions

---

petitionee, and often copies of the written submission to arbitration, records from the subsequent litigation, and depositions.

The only arbitrations described in the petitions are ones that failed. Successful arbitrations did not leave tracks. Even when arbitrators made written awards, the awards disappeared with the trash of people who did not regard their personal papers as archives for posterity. This raises the question of the representativeness of the sources, and makes it difficult, although not impossible, to see a positive image in what was really a negative reflection. However, I am interested in the arbitration process rather than in the results of individual arbitrations. If the failed arbitrations reported in the petitions were aberrant, they would display different characteristics from what my model and other evidence of legal change would lead us to expect. They do not. I can only conclude that the arbitrations mentioned in the petitions are sufficiently representative to give us an accurate picture of the whole.

11. *Conn. Rec.*, 1:117.

12. See Chapter 3, n. 40.

to the assembly in Connecticut one does not get the impression of witnessing the discovery of fire.[13]

Arbitration did not exist in the shadows outside the legal system. Rather, it was an integral part of the legal structure. When the General Assembly recommended the use of arbitration, it did so in the preamble to a set of orders for regulating juries.[14] The juxtaposition of the two suggests that the assembly regarded arbitration and jury trial as complementary, coordinate elements of the legal structure.

Arbitration was less formal than legal adjudication, but it was a formal process nonetheless. Although "not tied to any formalities, or punctualities in Law," arbitrators operated within limits agreed upon by the parties and stipulated in the submission. An award had to be a final determination of all matters submitted. Arbitrators could decide only the questions that the parties submitted to them. They could not bind third parties who did not join the submission.[15] Courts could not review the substance of an arbitration award, but they could determine whether the award met the requirements of the submission, much as they could decide whether the terms of any other contract had been performed.

The formal validity of an award depended on whether it conformed to the submission. Awards that did not were void. Thus we see lawsuits on failed arbitrations where the defendant pleaded that "no award had been made"—by which he meant that the supposed award

13. David Konig has noted the extensive use of arbitration in Essex County. David Thomas Konig, *Law and Society in Puritan Massachusetts: Essex County, 1629–1692*, pp. 108–16. Kenneth Lockridge observed that the town covenant of Dedham directed the inhabitants to refer their differences to arbitrators. See Kenneth A. Lockridge, *A New England Town, The First Hundred Years: Dedham, Massachusetts, 1636–1736*, p. 6.
There are enough stray references to arbitration in Connecticut before 1680 to be certain of its existence. Moreover, it is improbable that a process that was widely used in Massachusetts would not also be popular in Connecticut, which was in large part populated by emigrants from Massachusetts. Because we can establish the existence of arbitration well before the end of the seventeenth century, the infrequent evidence of failed arbitrations in the court records must mean either that most disputants did in fact abide by the awards or that, when one party refused to perform the award, the other party was not sufficiently aggrieved to take the underlying dispute to law. The community context of arbitration and the litigiousness of seventeenth-century New Englanders suggest that the former conclusion is more likely.

14. *Conn. Rec.*, 1:117.
15. March, *Actions for Slander*, pp. 172–92 (quotation at p. 162).

did not conform to the submission and so was not legally an award. For example, two brothers, George and Christopher Sanders, were partners in a commercial venture to Jamaica and England. When they could not settle their accounts between themselves, they submitted their dispute to the arbitration of four men in 1677. Later, when one brother sued the other for not complying with the award, they exchanged lengthy pleas debating how the arbitration had been conducted, whether the arbitrators had exceeded the scope of the submission, and whether the arbitrators could make an award that conferred a benefit on a person who was not party to the submission.[16] These were technical questions that were appropriate to a formal process. It was within the authority of the courts to say whether the rules that the parties had agreed were necessary to a valid award had been met, even though the award itself was unenforceable.

Arbitration in Connecticut before 1700 was a formal process with mercifully few formalities. Its formal face consisted of the rules that specified the technical requirements for valid awards. It was its informal face, however, that made arbitration such a perfect expression of community structure. Communities in Connecticut in the seventeenth century were insular. Social relations within them were multifaceted and interdependent. Merely by virtue of living in the same community, disputants had a joint past and an expectation or necessity of a joint future. Their disputes had to be handled in a way that would enable them to resume their normal neighborly relations, even if only under a flag of truce.

Arbitration was well suited to the task of blurring the distinction between victor and vanquished so that the parties could continue their relations within the community. It was expeditious and inexpensive. It was less public and less adversarial than litigation. Most importantly, notions of compromise and reconciliation permeated arbitration, from the initial decision to submit to a voluntary process to the common law requirement that an arbitration award must be "mutual" to be valid.[17]

Everything about arbitration emphasized its ties to the community.

16. Submission to arbitration, 5 July 1677, Sanders v. Sanders, Conn. Arch., Priv. Controversies (1st ser.), 1:178 (1680); Reply of Christopher Sanders, n.d., ibid., 185; Argument of George Sanders, 14 Oct. 1680, ibid., 186; Pleas of George Sanders, 14 Oct. 1680, ibid., 187; Reply of George Sanders, 14 Oct. 1680, ibid., 188.

17. The requirement of "mutuality" in the award is an interesting one. "Mutuality" originally meant that each party had to receive something from

For example, we think of jurors as purveyors of community norms, and indeed they were, up to a point. However, jurors in seventeenth-century Connecticut were drawn from counties at a time when the community was the town. Arbitrators, on the other hand, tended to be from the same town as the disputants or from neighboring towns. As a consequence, arbitration offered disputants a method of resolving their differences that was intimately linked to the communities in which they lived.[18]

The bond between arbitration and community explains why the unenforceability of arbitration awards caused few problems in the first decades of settlement. The cohesiveness of the community, fostered by the necessity of living together in a physical and spiritual wilderness, gave adequate assurance that parties would abide by the awards of the arbitrators they had chosen. Obviously, people who did not trust one another would not submit to arbitration in the first place. Once they chose arbitration, however, the party that openly repudiated the award risked the disapproval of the community. As long as community sanctions sufficed, arbitration awards did not have to be legally enforceable.[19]

One reason arbitration merited such support was that it was not

---

the award. But it was quickly transmuted into the more familiar principle that the award should contain a final discharge of all future claims on the matters submitted by the party in whose favor the arbitrators decided. See Kyd, *Treatise on the Law of Awards*, pp. 218–20; Swift, *System of the Laws of the State of Connecticut*, 2:13–14. Nonetheless, awards in seventeenth-century Connecticut did sometimes require performance by both parties. For example, see Arbitration award, 15 Dec. 1679, Hall v. Hall, Conn. Arch., Priv. Controversies (1st ser.), 4:112 (1692).

18. A preference for local arbitrators, who would likely be familiar with the parties and the dispute, would not be surprising. It has been observed among groups as far removed from early New England as Sard shepherds. Julio L. Ruffini, "Disputing Over Livestock in Sardinia," p. 227. The value of community-based settlements was underscored by the fact that churches, which were themselves communities of believers, encouraged disputing members to resolve their differences without resorting to law by appointing other churchmembers to try to mediate a settlement. See Chapter 5.

19. David Underdown notes similar pressures to conform in English villages—close-knit, arable villages, in particular—in the sixteenth and seventeenth centuries and a consequent resort to mediation. David Underdown, *Revel, Riot, and Rebellion: Popular Politics and Culture in England, 1603–1660*, pp. 15–17.

subject to the procedural restraints of common law rules of pleading, evidence, and joinder of actions. Instead, arbitrators were free to consider all questions and evidence that the parties laid before them. For example, when the submission was general, arbitration was not limited by rules on joinder of actions, which at common law meant that separate claims could not be combined in one lawsuit. Because arbitrators could decide in one award matters that might have filled an entire docket at law, they were in a position to settle differences between the parties more completely than either a judge or a jury.

This freedom to join claims was appropriate to tightly knit communities, where disputes arose within complex webs of social relations rather than in isolation. In such communities, notions of what was relevant to understanding and resolving a dispute tended to be broad enough to place particular grievances in the context of the relationship between the parties, much as was the case with book debt actions. Arbitrators also had more discretion than common law judges did to fashion remedies to suit the grievance. Their greater discretion was a logical and fitting extension of the broadened inquiry that arbitration allowed. Disputants doubtless realized these advantages when they chose arbitration over litigation. By submitting to arbitration, they expressed a willingness to compromise that was absent from litigation, but which was consistent with a community-based form of processing disputes.[20]

The absence of evidentiary strictures, the power of the parties to define the scope of the inquiry, the availability of remedies that common law courts did not have, the spirit of compromise implicit in the submission, the ability to choose arbitrators, the mutuality of awards, the privacy of the process—these qualities made arbitration attractive in situations where the parties, for whatever reasons, had to be able to continue to deal with one another. In short, arbitration in seventeenth-century Connecticut was a uniquely community-based form of handling disputes and was well suited to the needs of the communities it served. Communities were not static, however. They grew and changed, often to the dismay of their inhabitants. When communities changed, as they inevitably did, arbitration changed, also. It was too closely identified with community not to.

---

20. For discussions of compromise as an element of arbitration, see Martin P. Golding, "The Nature of Compromise: A Preliminary Inquiry," pp. 20–21; Arthur Kuflik, "Morality and Compromise," p. 53.

III

The social landscape in Connecticut began to change near the turn of the century. Only six of the twenty-nine towns incorporated from 1686 to 1734 were settled by group migrations, compared with all twenty-five of the towns settled before then. Two of the six, Waterbury and Danbury, dated from the 1680s and were closer in time as well as in spirit to the towns settled in the first generation. The remaining towns owed their existence to land speculators rather than to groups of villagers or congregations of religious dissenters. They were settled by farmers whose primary interest was in making a living for themselves and their families.[21] The settlers doubtless expected to create stable communities, but, unlike their predecessors, they did not begin with communities already formed. The absence of a group-minded community meant that one of the conditions that encouraged voluntary arbitration was absent.

As new towns appeared, population growth and migration weakened the cohesiveness of the towns that were settled earlier. The population of the colony doubled in the thirty years between 1670 and 1700, and population density increased by half.[22] There was, in short, less land to go around. Fewer fathers in the second generation than in the first could endow all their sons with enough land to enable them to remain in the community. Landless sons migrated elsewhere or took up trades.[23] Population growth and the settlement of outlying areas within towns drew people away from the central common. As settlement within towns dispersed, outlying areas acquired the trappings of community and won incorporation as separate ecclesiastical societies, or parishes, with their own ministers and meeting-

21. Bruce C. Daniels, *The Connecticut Town: Growth and Development, 1635–1790*, pp. 17–27.

22. The population grew from 15,799 in 1670 to 31,502 in 1700. During the same period, density increased from 6.39 to 9.52 persons per square mile. See Daniels, *Connecticut Town*, pp. 47, 50.

23. See Philip J. Greven, Jr., *Four Generations: Population, Land, and Family in Colonial Andover, Massachusetts*, pp. 125–72. Historians are beginning to see settlement and dispersal as elements of a continual process. See Bernard Bailyn, *The Peopling of British North America: An Introduction* and *Voyagers to the West: A Passage in the Peopling of America on the Eve of the Revolution*.

houses.[24] Town populations were swelled by people who did not nec-essarily share the communitarian ideals of the first inhabitants. Towns became less insular. People still had continuing relationships that they wished to preserve, but those relationships increasingly crossed town boundaries.

Given the dependence of arbitration on community, it is not sur-prising that, as communities changed, so did arbitration. In the half-century after 1700, the proportion of arbitrations that paired dispu-tants from the same town or the same family dropped to 57 percent.[25] People continued to use arbitration. But as the bonds of community weakened, it became harder to rely on community sanctions to assure voluntary compliance with awards. The legal unenforceability of arbi-tration awards, once of little consequence, now became a serious de-fect. In response, disputants adopted various devices that in time changed the nature of arbitration itself.

The first such device was submitting to arbitration by deed. The practice was novel in Connecticut in the last quarter of the seven-teenth century, but it had been common in England a century earlier. At common law in England deeds were documents under seal that extended the range of questions that could be submitted to arbitra-tion.[26] In Connecticut, deeds took the form of a written submission signed by both parties that contained a promise that either person who failed to perform the award would forfeit a penalty sum.

Arbitration deeds marked a transition, both in arbitration and in the underlying communities. Disputants turned to deeds when oral promises alone no longer sufficed. Unfortunately, deeds did little to advance the enforceability of arbitration awards. If one party failed to perform an award, the other could bring an action on the case for breach of the promises in the deed. However, deeds were not conclu-sive evidence of the promises they contained. The plaintiff needed additional evidence. If the mere existence of a deed did not assure recovery, deeds could not be predictable guarantors of arbitration awards. For example, when Joseph Latham and John Leeds of New

24. Daniels, *Connecticut Town*, pp. 95–97; Richard L. Bushman, *From Puritan to Yankee: Character and the Social Order in Connecticut, 1690–1765*, pp. 54–72.

25. The exact figures are four of seven for the period 1700–1725 and twelve of twenty-one for the period 1726–53.

26. March, *Actions for Slaunder*, pp. 154–55.

London executed a deed of submission in 1684, they bound themselves "enterchangably etch to other in the fforfiture of one hundred
pounds currant money of New England" to stand to the award. Leeds
later renounced the award, which was not to his liking, so Latham
sued him on the deed in an action on the case for the full amount—
and lost. The deed, which they had properly executed, proved ineffectual.[27]

To make matters worse, deeds undercut the arbitration process by
opening a line of collateral attack on arbitration awards. Before deeds
entered the process, the only legal redress for a party who was un-
happy with the decision of arbitrators was to question the formal
sufficiency of the award. With deeds, however, disgruntled disputants
could, in the course of their actions for breach of the promises in the
deed, relitigate before a jury points lost in arbitration. Deeds thus
suffered the double disadvantage of presupposing the absence of the
trust necessary for oral submissions without adding significantly to
the enforceability of arbitration awards. An action on the case for
breach of promises made in a deed of submission was not a sufficiently predictable method of assuring compliance with an award that
one party was inclined to ignore.

A second device, submitting to arbitration on conditioned bonds,
followed as a consequence of the weakness of deeds. The shift from
deeds to bonds coincided with the shift in the residence patterns of
parties to arbitration at the turn of the century. The parties would
execute bonds in each other's favor for a penal amount conditioned
on nonperformance of any award granted by the arbitrators named in
the bonds. They would then exchange the bonds and proceed to arbitration. Conditioned bonds had long been a mainstay of bilateral
contracts at English law and had been commonplace in arbitration
since the medieval period.[28] As used in arbitration, bonds raised the
cost of ignoring an award by creating an enforceable debt obligation.

A person who refused to perform an award risked being sued for
the full penal sum of his bond. The bond so completely embodied the

27. Submission to arbitration, 28 Nov. 1684, Leeds v. Latham, Conn.
Arch., Priv. Controversies (1st ser.), 3:35; Copy of New London County
Court record, 2 June 1685, ibid., 38.

28. Holdsworth, *History of English Law*, 14:189; A. W. B. Simpson, *A
History of the Common Law of Contract: The Rise of the Action of Assumpsit*, pp. 173–74. For a discussion of conditioned bonds at English common
law, see Simpson, *History of the Common Law of Contract*, pp. 88–125.

debtor's obligation to pay the penalty that an obligee could put the bond in suit in an action of debt without further proof of the debt. The obligor in such actions had few options. He could plead *non est factum*, that the bond was "not his deed" but had been altered in some material fashion. Or he could plead performance of the condition, that is, that he had performed the award. These pleas, however, were inappropriate if the obligor refused to accept an award that was not to his liking. When that was the case, the obligor who defaulted on his arbitration bond could only plead that there had been "no award."[29] That plea put in issue not the correctness of the arbitrators' judgment, but the formal sufficiency of the award—that is, whether it conformed to the limits set in the submission. Liability on the bond thus turned not on the merits of the dispute, but on the technical adequacy of the arbitration. One who felt wronged by a formally correct award had no choice but to perform the award or to lose judgment for the penal amount of the bond.

By the time conditioned bonds became common in arbitrations in Connecticut, their utility in England had already diminished. Early in the seventeenth century, Chancery began to refuse to enforce obligations on bonds for amounts greater than the damages actually proved.[30] Once equity turned against penalties, it was only a matter of time before law followed. That time came in 1697, when Parliament enacted the Statute of Fines and Penalties, which precluded recovery of the face value of a conditioned bond unless the actual damages justified the full amount.[31] The statute impaired the value of conditioned bonds in arbitration by neutralizing their *in terrorem* effect. In Connecticut, however, there was nothing to prevent courts from enforcing conditioned bonds to their full penal amount. Parliamentary statutes did not automatically apply to the colonies. Moreover, Connecticut had no courts with chancery jurisdiction, although the assembly did have broad equity powers, which it occasionally invested in lower courts in carefully restricted amounts.[32]

The reign of conditioned bonds in arbitration did not last long in

---

29. See Kyd, *Treatise on the Law of Awards*, pp. 280–311.

30. See Simpson, *History of the Common Law of Contract*, pp. 118–19.

31. An Act for the Better Preventing of Frivolous and Vexatious Suites, 8 & 9 Will. 3, ch. 11 (1697).

32. Barbara Black has examined a similar doling out of equity powers in Massachusetts. Barbara A. Black, "The Judicial Power and the General Court in Early Massachusetts, 1634–1686," pp. 151–62.

Connecticut. They appear to have been used as early as the 1680s.[33] By 1730, they had been replaced by promissory notes, which the parties executed in favor of each other and deposited with the arbitrators as pledges to perform the award. After making the award, the arbitrators could either return the notes to their makers or turn them both over to the party in whose favor they had decided. The reason for the shift from bonds to notes is not entirely clear. It was not an emulation of English practice—English arbitration treatises mention nothing similar. Submission to arbitration on promissory notes appears to have been a colonial invention, although promissory notes themselves were not.[34] The most likely explanation for the shift is that early in the eighteenth century Connecticut courts began to entertain motions to chancer bonds after judgment, as Chancery had done in England a century earlier.[35] This meant that obligees could no longer exact the penal amounts of bonds. Instead, they had to settle for their actual damages, which reflected only the negligible injury of having to go to law to litigate the dispute that arbitration had failed to resolve.

Promissory notes offered several advantages over the now-emasculated conditioned bonds. First, they were simple enough for parties to draft without the aid of a scrivener. Second, unlike conditioned bonds, they were absolute in form, which, at least initially, made them even more difficult to defend.[36] Third, and most importantly, promis-

33. For example, see Disbrough v. Bloomer (1680), in Norbert B. Lacy, ed., "Records of the Court of Assistants of Connecticut, 1665–1701," p. 87; Packer v. Estate of Latham, 5 NLCCR 84 (1684).

34. See Holdsworth, *History of English Law*, 8:170–76; William Cranch, "Promissory Notes Before and After Lord Holt."

35. See Simpson, *History of the Common Law of Contract*, pp. 118–19. In 1708, the General Assembly empowered the New Haven County Court and the court of assistants to chancer the arbitration bond of William Hoadly in a dispute with Dugall MacKenzie, "taking for their direction therein the record of the court where judgment on said bond was recovered, shewing the value of the said bond and the sum, which by the award of the arbitrators specified, the said MacKenzie was to pay to the said Hoadly." *Conn. Rec.*, 5:79. Shortly afterwards, in 1709, there is mention of the court of assistants considering and rejecting a motion to chancer an arbitration bond. Copy of court of assistants record, 4 Oct. 1709, Estate of Andrews, Conn. Arch., Priv. Controversies (1st ser.), 6:158 (1710).

36. This particular advantage of promissory notes was quickly tempered. Shortly after notes supplanted conditioned bonds in arbitration, courts began

sory notes gave arbitrators a means of securing compliance with their awards. This last point was crucial.

When arbitration was conducted on deeds or conditioned bonds, the only means arbitrators had of securing compliance with their awards was persuasion. Conditioned bonds were more effective than deeds in assuring that parties would perform the awards, but they did not give the arbitrators themselves a role in that assurance. Disputants who submitted to arbitration by conditioned bonds exchanged their bonds with one another directly. The arbitrators had neither possession nor control of the bonds. When people submitted to arbitration by depositing promissory notes, however, they conferred novel powers on the arbitrators. Notes, unlike conditioned bonds, were absolute promises to pay the face amount. Because they were unconditional, the obligee who had possession of his obligor's note could sue on it and win with relative ease. The case of James Peck and Stephen Howell of New Haven, who submitted a dispute over fencing rails to arbitration in 1744, illustrates the importance of possession of the notes.[37]

Peck and Howell executed notes and deposited them with Jeremiah Osborne, one of the arbitrators. During an adjournment in the arbitration, Howell visited Osborne. Under the pretext of examining papers relating to the controversy, Howell snatched up his note and refused to return it. With Howell in possession of his own note, nothing remained to secure his compliance with an award. When Peck learned what had happened, he understandably "appeared very un-

---

to allow the promisor who was sued on his note to plead the submission as a parol condition of the note. The transition appears to have taken place between 1732 and 1734. Compare Petition of John Parker, 26 Sept. 1732, Parker v. Bellamy, Conn. Arch., Priv. Controversies (2d ser.), 21:20b (1732), which complained that the court had sustained a demurrer to Parker's plea that submission to arbitration had been a parol condition of his note, with Petition of Isaac Bennett, 28 Aug. 1734, Bennett v. Dixon, Conn. Arch., Priv. Controversies (2d ser.), 3:52a (1734), which recited that the plaintiff had traversed a similar plea and the issue had gone to the jury. Despite this development, promissory notes remained the preferred mode of submission because of their comparative simplicity and the power they conferred on arbitrators.

37. The following account is based on the records and files of Peck v. Howell, 4 NHCCR 207, NHCCF 16, 8 SCR 246, 297 (1744); Peck v. Osborne, 4 NHCCR 316, NHCCF 18, 9 SCR 322, SCR 327 (1748).

easy," as one of the other arbitrators observed. To smooth things over, Osborne substituted his own note for Howell's to guarantee that Peck would receive whatever the arbitrators might award him. Osborne was now, at least constructively, a party to the dispute and so could not continue as an arbitrator. His two colleagues resumed their deliberations and made an award in favor of Peck. They endorsed Osborne's note down to the amount of the award and delivered it to Peck.[38] Peck then sued Osborne on the note that Osborne had substituted for Howell's, while Howell stood by, bemused and unsuable.

Similarly, in an earlier case, Timothy Hosford of Litchfield recognized the importance of possession of the notes when he "craftily and knavishly" tried to get the notes from the executor of an arbitrator's estate that he and Nathan Gillette had deposited five years earlier. At first Hosford did not succeed. However, his son later acquired the notes from the surviving arbitrators, to whom the executor had delivered them. Hosford then sued Gillette on his note.[39]

Possession of the notes allowed arbitrators to compel compliance with their awards. Arbitrators could return the notes to their makers or give both notes to the person in whose favor they had awarded. They could turn the loser's note over to the winner immediately, or, if they were of a mind to give him time to perform the award, they could wait.[40] They could endorse the loser's note down to the amount of the award before delivering it to the winner for collection, or they could deliver it unendorsed and thereby enable the victor to sue for the full face amount. These powers amounted to private enforcement of arbitration awards.

Promissory notes also gave arbitrators a source of power that was independent of whatever personal prestige they might have. Before the shift to promissory notes, arbitrators had only their social authority in

38. When arbitrators endorsed a promissory note down to the amount of the award, they simply reduced the face value of the note. In substance, this was very much like the action of chancellors who peered behind conditioned bonds and issued a decree of specific performance to surrender the bond in exchange for part payment in the amount of the actual damages.

39. Petition of Nathan Gillette, 6 May 1735, Gillette v. Hosford, Conn. Arch., Priv. Controversies (2d ser.), 12:37 (1735).

40. The arbitrators in a dispute between John Soper and Enoch Drake refused Soper's request of a two- or three-day delay before they delivered his note to Drake. Petition of John Soper, 28 Apr. 1748, Soper v. Drake, Conn. Arch., Priv. Controversies (2d ser.), 26:50a–50b (1748).

the community to persuade disputants to accept their awards. Notes gave them a means of legal compulsion. Jonathan Rogers of New London recognized this power when he signed a promissory note proffered by his arbitrators, "whome it behooved him then not to displease," even though he later claimed that they had not let him read it. Rogers's signature on the note bound him. None of his subsequent pleas that the note was not his deed because of his fear of the arbitrators were to any avail.[41]

By the same token, arbitrators who did not overawe disputants could rely on the power conferred by possession of the notes. For example, Eleazer Kilborn and Josiah Griswold of Wethersfield selected Daniel Hovey and Joseph Herrick, two strangers whom Kilborn had met on the highway, to arbitrate their dispute over a slave in 1748. Hovey and Herrick awarded title of the slave to Griswold and "took much pains and used many arguments with ... Kilborn to persuade him to comply with [their] judgment" voluntarily. As strangers, however, Hovey and Herrick had no personal authority, only the power implicit in custody of the notes. When they could not persuade Kilborn to comply with their award voluntarily, they had no alternative but to deliver his note to Griswold, who promptly put it in suit.[42]

Arbitration was once a voluntary process from beginning to end. With notes, it became voluntary only in its beginning—in the decision to submit to arbitration. By the 1730s, its end was coercive.

IV

The changes in arbitration discussed thus far—shifts in the residence patterns of the parties and in the forms of submission—were essentially external changes. To understand the position of arbitration in the larger legal structure and how that position changed, we must look at why people chose arbitration in the first place and whether it fulfilled their expectations.

Although litigation occasionally afforded some of the social benefits of arbitration, people who chose arbitration rather than law seemed to believe that arbitration offered advantages that they could not ob-

41. Rogers v. Rogers, 17 NLCCR (June 1730) no. 60, NLCCF 199, 5 ½ SCR 41, 93, SCF 9 (1730–31).

42. Deposition of Daniel Hovey, 6 Apr. 1750, Kilborn v. Griswold, Conn. Arch., Priv. Controversies (2d ser.), 16:103 (1750).

tain elsewhere. People tried arbitration "for the avoiding of future troble and lawsuits," "to settle peace between the parties, so as that no further disputes, debates, or lawsuits might arise," "for the freindly ending and appeasing of difference and controvercies," "to the end that justice may be don . . . and that controvercy may be prevented," "hoping and expectinge the difference wolde in love and utmoste frindship be settled," "to prevent cost and troble in the law."[43] They wanted an end to disputing, not simply a resolution of a particular dispute.

We can see the hope and belief that arbitration could achieve what law could not in the example of two brothers who turned to arbitration after litigation had failed to end their differences. When James Rogers died in New London in 1688, he left extensive land-holdings and a will that directed that "[i]f any differance should arise about my land here willed . . . my will is that there shall be no lawing among my children before earthly judges but that the controversy be ended by lott." The stakes, however, proved too high and the family too disputatious. Two of Rogers's sons contested title to part of the land through several trials and appeals. Then, "findeing they are not likely to come at a sattisfyeing issue in the case by ordinary process of law," they submitted to arbitration to settle the matter "according to the rules of righteousnes."[44]

43. Plea of Samuel Wells and Thomas Wells, 8 May 1699, Estate of Wells, Conn. Arch., Priv. Controversies (1st ser.), 5:121a (1699); Summons, 30 May 1720, Babcock v. Palmer, NLCCF 188 (1720); Arbitration award, 14 May 1733, Gillette v. Hosford, Conn. Arch., Priv. Controversies (2d ser.), 12:39 (1735); Petition of Charles Hazelton, 2 Oct. 1740, Hazelton v. Fancher, ibid., 13:175c (1740); Petition of James Enos, April 1745, Enos v. Enos, ibid., 10:108c (1745); Petition of Richard Ely, 20 Apr. 1748, Ely v. Ely, ibid., 10:78a (1754).

44. Will of James Rogers, 11 Nov. 1683, Estate of Rogers, Conn. Arch., Priv. Controversies (1st ser.), 5:93 (1699); Submission to arbitration, 17 Oct. 1693, ibid., 91. Thomas Thrall of Windsor and his son-in-law, William Thrall, evidently had similar hopes when, despite a jury verdict in their dispute, they submitted to arbitration, persuaded by "[s]om frinds who desired the peace of the fameleys." William's wife, Hannah, had taken their daughter and sought refuge with her father, Thomas, after unspecified "domestic controversies." William refused a reconciliation and sued Thomas for keeping his child from him. The jury did not think William much damaged and awarded him one shilling. It was after that verdict that Thomas and William submitted to arbitration. Petition of Thomas Thrall, 25 Sept. 1734, Thrall v. Thrall, Conn. Arch., Priv. Controversies (2d ser.), 27:161 (1734).

The fact that Joseph and Jonathan Rogers submitted their dispute to arbitration attests to the power of the belief that arbitration could restore peace between disputing parties—a belief that in this instance was misplaced. The arbitrators did make an award, but Joseph claimed that Jonathan had procured it on false evidence and pressed his suit at law.[45] What made their belief inappropriate was that the dispute was not one that could be compromised by each brother receiving something.

The brothers were contesting title to a piece of land. A Solomonlike division of the land would have been outside the limits of the submission. Title had to rest in one brother or the other. Without the possibility of compromise, arbitration had nothing to offer. The brothers had already sacrificed the other advantages of arbitration—speed, cheapness, and privacy—when they chose first to go to law. Yet they evidently believed that arbitration was worthwhile. Each one sacrificed some advantage to leave law for arbitration. Joseph withdrew an appeal, which he could later renew only with special leave from the assembly. Jonathan risked losing the benefit of the two court judgments he had won.[46] Their hope that arbitration could perform its traditional function of restoring peace between the parties blinded them to the limits to what arbitration could accomplish.[47]

45. Arbitration award, 27 Nov. 1693, Estate of Rogers, Conn. Arch., Priv. Controversies (1st ser.), 5:91 (1699); Plea of Jonathan Rogers, Oct. 1699, ibid., 108; *Conn. Rec.*, 4:210.

46. *Conn. Rec.*, 4:108, 231–32; see Rogers v. Rogers, 7 NLCCR 105, 2 CtAR 20 (1693).

47. Anthropologists have noted that compromise may not be appropriate even in continuing relationships when disputes involve a finite resource such as land that is a source of status or power. See June Starr and Barbara Yngvesson, "Scarcity and Disputing: Zeroing-In on Compromise Decisions."

Groups of land proprietors encouraged arbitration to settle disputes over land divisions, but they probably did so to prevent proprietary matters from being aired in court. The proprietors of the common and undivided land in Guilford, for example, established a formal arbitration procedure that included notice periods and time limitations, although they also submitted to more traditionally structured arbitration. See Guilford Proprietors Records, 1:96r (31 Mar. 1730), 106v (15 Sept. 1741), 108r (20 Sept. 1742). The proprietors of two adjoining common fields in Guilford, the Great Oxpasture and Long Cove Meadows, submitted their dispute over the boundary line between them to arbitration. "The Record of the Votes and Doings of the Proprietors of the Common field in Guilford called the Great Oxpasture," pp. 19–22 (10 Mar., 14 Apr. 1735).

One source of the belief that arbitration could achieve what law could not was that arbitration awards could, in fact, offer remedies that legal judgments could not. Early arbitration awards sometimes resembled decrees in equity, with instructions that amounted to injunctive relief. For example, in 1679 the arbitrators in a long and bitter dispute between Francis Hall of Stratford and his son, Isaac, confirmed Isaac in the possession of land he then held, fixed the rent he should pay to his father for it, directed Francis to confirm the reversion of the land to Isaac so that title would pass to Isaac when Francis died, ordered the cancellation of all accounts between them (except an account for cattle, which Isaac was to repay within three years), and directed Isaac to return to Francis the jointure under which he had claimed additional land belonging to Francis.[48]

Similarly, arbitrators made a seven-part award in another dispute forty years later between a father and son, Thomas and William Hancox of Farmington. They directed Thomas to execute and deliver to William an "assurance" of certain lands, assessed Thomas damages for taking hay that belonged to William, confirmed William in the peaceable enjoyment of a lease from his brother "without molestation" by his father, balanced their book accounts, directed the parties to perform a "former bargin" by which one had agreed to supply the materials and the other the labor for work on a house, instructed William to return a deed to his father and to release his right in the land to him, and voided a lease of land and stock from Thomas to William.[49]

Arbitration thus appears to have been an important source of equity within the legal structure. This aspect of arbitration is worth noting, because the colonists of the seventeenth century had reason to distrust equity jurisdiction. They left England at a time when the less benign facets of equity were identified with the very abuses of prerogative power they sought to escape. Nonetheless, they appreciated the substantive advantages of equity. In New England, they created sources of equitable relief without conferring formal equity jurisdic-

---

48. Arbitration award, 15 Dec. 1679, Hall v. Hall, Conn. Arch., Priv. Controversies (1st ser.), 4:112 (1692). A later award in 1692 in the same protracted dispute included an instruction that Isaac's brother, Samuel, should return Isaac's bible. Arbitration award, 4 Apr. 1692, Hall v. Hall and Hall, Conn. Arch., Priv. Controversies (2d ser.), 13:15b (1692).

49. Arbitration award, Oct. 1719, Hancox v. Hancox, Conn. Arch., Priv. Controversies (2d ser.), 13:86 (1721).

tion. They could create one without the other in part because the relative informality of pleading and procedure in seventeenth-century New England mitigated the rigors of the common law for which formal equity jurisdiction provided relief. Rather than establish separate courts of equity, the settlers gave broad equity authority to their assemblies, which could then grant equitable relief on private petitions or confer limited equity powers on lower courts.[50] Within this scheme, arbitration was an alternate source of equity. Like equity, arbitration rested on the substantively rational norms of the community.

In the eighteenth century, however, arbitration lost its ability to do equity. The omnibus awards that made arbitration so effective in addressing disputes in all their ramifications became infrequent after the first quarter of the century. With them disappeared the injunctions to perform or to refrain from performing various acts that had given early arbitration awards their equitable character. They were replaced by purely monetary awards, which partook more of damages awarded at law than of remedies tailored to the social circumstances of individual disputes.

Why this shift to monetary awards occurred is unclear. In all likelihood, it was a consequence of the use of written debt obligations. Promissory notes, unlike the forms of submission that were popular before 1730, gave arbitrators the power to coerce compliance with their awards. In theory, of course, the notes were pledges for performance of the awards. There was no intrinsic reason why they should have become substitutes for performance. However, the fact that arbitrators could endorse the losing party's note down to the amount of the award before delivering it to the victor permitted arbitrators to use the notes as devices for the payment of damages. Notes were, after all, the one part of the process that arbitrators could control completely. Whether consciously or not, arbitrators began to tailor their awards so that they could be satisfied by delivery of the loser's note. Hence the shift to monetary awards. Arbitrators became, in effect, judges who awarded damages that were satisfied by the loser's note.

50. See T. F. T. Plucknett, *A Concise History of the Common Law*, pp. 191–98; George L. Haskins, *Law and Authority in Early Massachusetts: A Study in Tradition and Design*, pp. 130, 182, 212–18; Stanley N. Katz, "The Politics of Law in Colonial America: Controversies over Chancery Courts and Equity Law in the Eighteenth Century," p. 263; Konig, *Law and Society in Puritan Massachusetts*, pp. 58–60; Black, "The Judicial Power and the General Court in Early Massachusetts," pp. 151–62.

The growing prominence of monetary awards in the eighteenth century also reflected the declining community basis of arbitration. The large proportion of arbitrations between disputants from different towns after 1700 indicated the geographic dispersal and consequent attenuation of the underlying social relations. Disputes in such circumstances tended not to be played out against a complex range of relations between the parties. Instead, they focused rather narrowly on the individual transactions in question. When the social relations of the parties comprehended more than the dispute at hand, the omnibus awards of early arbitration offered compromise by their very comprehensiveness and flexibility. The monetary awards of later arbitration, on the other hand, were appropriate for the more precisely defined disputes that arose from instrumental relations.[51]

Arbitration became more lawlike by the middle of the eighteenth century. As if to emphasize the change, there was some indication that arbitration was becoming a public event, much like court days. By mid-century, petitions came to the assembly with depositions by people who were present at the arbitration, not as parties or as arbitrators or even as witnesses, but evidently as spectators.[52] When arbitration

---

51. The correlation between the complexity of social relationships and the adequacy of remedies is a difficult question. Richard Abel has discussed the changes in remedies that accompany the rationalization of legal process. In particular, he notes the shift to remedies that require single acts rather than courses of conduct, that substitute the transfer of property for the performance of an act, and that rely on fungible property—money—rather than on unique property. See Richard L. Abel, "A Comparative Theory of Dispute Institutions in Society," pp. 282–83. Although in theory it might be possible to attach a monetary value to each item of dispute, add them up, direct the loser to pay the balance to the winner, and still call the outcome a compromise, one must question whether it is psychologically possible. When both parties have to perform reciprocal acts, even though one has to perform more than the other, each has extracted something from the other. But when all items of dispute are reduced to monetary terms, like a balance sheet, only one party pays the final balance. The symbolism of one party paying the balance to the other is enough to prevent the parties from regarding the award as a compromise of their differences. Instead, the award becomes a judgment that one party has won and the other has lost. It may be, then, that monetary damages preclude compromise. The question is a large and difficult one and requires further inquiry.

52. For example, see Lyon v. Brush, Conn. Arch., Priv. Controversies (2d ser.), 17:143, 146, 148, 150, 152, 155, 169 (1741). For discussions of the

went public, it lost the privacy that had enabled arbitrators to settle disputes fully and quietly. At that point, the qualities that distinguished arbitration from formal adjudication were few.

V

Arbitration in Connecticut underwent one final change before the Revolution. The most visible sign of the change was a statute enacted in 1753 that, for the first time, created a formal legal framework for arbitration.[53] In a larger sense, the statute was simply an extension of the longstanding effort to secure compliance with arbitration awards. It completed the formalization of what had once been a rather neighborly way of handling disputes.

There is little formal evidence of commercial arbitration in Connecticut before 1750. Only six commercial arbitrations, two of which arose in family contexts, figured in petitions to the General Assembly before 1700. In the next half-century there were only three more.[54] The paucity of commercial arbitrations in the petitions can hardly mean that merchants and traders in Connecticut did not resort to arbitration. The few that we do see depict arbitration as a standard method of settling disagreements between merchants. In all likelihood, so few traces of commercial arbitration appear in the court records because, by and large, commercial arbitration succeeded.

Merchants traditionally formed communities defined by common interests, common goals, trade usages and the like. Like all professionals, lawyers included, merchants developed shorthand styles of ordering their world—styles that doubtless seemed obscure to outsid-

---

importance of court day rituals, see Rhys Isaac, *The Transformation of Virginia, 1740–1790*, pp. 88–94; A. G. Roeber, *Faithful Magistrates and Republican Lawyers: Creators of Virginia Legal Culture, 1680–1810*, pp. 73–95.

53. An Act for the More Easy and Effectually Finishing of Controversies by Arbitration, *Conn. Rec.*, 10:201–2. Connecticut was the first colony to adopt such an act.

54. See Ely v. Ely, Conn. Arch., Priv. Controversies (1st ser.), 1:23 (1666); Sanders v. Sanders, ibid., 1:178 (1680); Lord v. Blackleach, ibid., 2:34 (1682); Willis v. Lord, ibid., 3:213 (1687); Arnold v. Weed, ibid., 4:70 (1690); Hillyard v. Reynolds, ibid., 4:81 (1692); Curtis v. Kilborn, Conn. Arch., Priv. Controversies (2d ser.), 7:149 (1738); Downer v. Berry, ibid., 9:46 (1738); Denison v. Richardson, ibid., 8:79 (1743).

ers, but which streamlined and rationalized merchants' dealings among themselves. In England, a separate body of law, the law merchant, grew from the recognition that merchants had special needs which the populace at large did not share and which the common law did not serve. As one seventeenth-century observer wrote, the "commonwealth of merchants hath always had a peculiar and proper law to rule and govern it."[55]

Part of the strength of the law merchant was that it left the adjudication of mercantile questions to merchants. Arbitration, which allowed parties to choose their own judges, offered the same advantage. Gerard Malynes, a merchant who published a treatise on the law merchant in 1622, recognized the importance of arbitration to merchants when he ranked it as the second of four means "to end the questions and controversies arising between Merchants." Wyndham Beawes later recommended that merchants include arbitration provisions in their partnership agreements, noting that doing so "might prevent many suits at law."[56]

Merchants in the American colonies, like their counterparts in England, needed ways to settle disputes that would not delay them in their business of making money. But the institutions and special jurisdictions that supported the law merchant in England did not cross the Atlantic. Instead, colonial merchants were left largely to their own devices. Arbitration was a readily available substitute. The only authority arbitrators needed to settle disputes was that conferred by the parties in their submission. Moreover, until the middle of the eighteenth century, the mercantile community retained enough community of interest that procedural mechanisms for enforcing arbitration awards were both unnecessary and inappropriate.

Merchants who bought and sold goods in distant markets tended to do business with traders with whom they had dealt before. It was simpler and safer to deal with people from whom they knew what to expect. Some merchants solved the problem of whom to entrust with their goods by installing family members as their agents in distant

55. John Davies, *The Question Concerning Impositions* (1656), 10, quoted in Leon E. Trakman, "The Evolution of the Law Merchant: Our Commercial Heritage," p. 1. On the law merchant generally, see Holdsworth, *History of English Law*, 5:60–154.

56. Gerard de Malynes, *Consuetudo, vel, Lex Mercatoria: Or, The Ancient Law-Merchant*, p. 305; Wyndham Beawes, *Lex Mercatoria: Or, a Complete Code of Commercial Law*, p. 498.

ports. Others cultivated contacts.[57] The fact that merchants shipped goods on consignment made trustworthy representatives crucial. One can sense both the hopefulness and the urgency in a letter from an aspiring young merchant in Boston, John Ellery, to a potential consignee in Charleston, South Carolina: "Sir, From the Recommendation of Mr. Foster and Mr. Randell I'm induced to make you this consignment, which if I've sutable incouragment, may serve but as a prelude to a following course of Trade . . . If, Sir, it might happen in my power to serve you or any young gentlemen of your acquaintance, in the way of Trade each opportunity would with pleasure be embraced."[58] Ellery did not succeed. He moved to Hartford, tried to continue in trade there, and died in 1746 at the age of thirty-four. The merchants who did succeed developed over time a stake in the continuation of their trading relationships that diminished the significance of differences over individual transactions. Merchants could no more afford to disrupt a trading relationship than towns could afford rifts in the multilayered relations that bound their inhabitants together. For that reason, merchants tended to act with restraint in their dealings with one another.[59]

When merchants could no longer forbear disputing, the compromise implicit in arbitration suited their needs. For merchants as for nonmerchants, arbitration enabled disputing parties to continue their relations within the community. Richard Lord and John Blackleach, for example, partners in the *Hartford Merchant* and its cargo to the West Indies in 1678, recognized the importance of the larger enterprise when they argued during loading over a missing barrel of tar. Loading resumed and the ship sailed after Blackleach gave Lord his written promise to submit the matter to arbitration upon their return.[60]

If courses of dealing were more important than individual transactions in mercantile relations, their significance would be a factor in

57. Bernard Bailyn, *The New England Merchants in the Seventeenth Century*, pp. 34–35, 87–91.

58. John Ellery, Jr., to Philip Brioleau, 23 Apr. 1735, Letterbook of John Ellery, Jr., 13.

59. The same pattern appears among modern businessmen. See Stewart Macaulay, "Non-Contractual Relations in Business: A Preliminary Study," pp. 61, 63–65.

60. Memorandum by John Blackleach, 16 Mar. 1678, Lord v. Blackleach, Conn. Arch., Priv. Controversies (2d ser.), 2:37 (1682).

why so few commercial arbitrations appear in the court records before 1750. The economic consequences of losing a trading partner could be great. Merchants might not wish to risk future gain for temporary advantage. Self-interest encouraged merchants to compromise their differences. Merchants' preferences for handling their disputes within the mercantile community—preferences shaped by the fact that law offered no satisfactory alternative—not only predisposed them toward arbitration, but also discouraged them from going to law if arbitration failed. With the support that commercial arbitration enjoyed in the mercantile community, the comparative absence of commercial arbitration from the records would appear to be a measure of its success.[61]

Toward the middle of the eighteenth century, however, the mercantile community began to change as Connecticut became a society of commercial producers. Relatively steady economic growth accelerated after 1740. The price of foodstuffs, the main export of the colony, increased fivefold relative to other goods. Merchants and farmers increased their exports accordingly. As trade expanded, so did the ranks of merchants, whose numbers by mid-century were increasing both absolutely and relative to other occupational groups.[62]

The commercialization of the economy not only meant that more people were engaged in trade, but also that more traders were newcomers who did not appreciate the norms of the business community. At the same time, the increased opportunity for business-related disputes made commercial arbitration all the more desirable for its speed and choice of judges. New traders and established merchants, however, did not necessarily share the community of interest that enabled commercial arbitration to function as smoothly as it had when merchants were a more homogeneous group. The changes in the business community may help explain the sharp increase in the number of failed commercial arbitrations after mid-century. Whereas only two commercial arbitrations appear in the petitions between 1700 and 1753, twenty-five appear between 1754 and 1774.

It was thus against a context of discord that merchants urged the

61. Morton Horwitz has also noted merchants' avoidance of common law settlements at a later period. Morton J. Horwitz, *The Transformation of American Law, 1780–1860*, pp. 145–48.

62. Daniels, *Connecticut Town*, pp. 140–41, 147–49, 152–54; Bruce C. Daniels, "Economic Development in Colonial and Revolutionary Connecticut: An Overview," pp. 435, 437.

General Assembly to enact an arbitration statute in 1753.[63] The Connecticut law was a variant of the English Arbitration Act, which Parliament enacted in 1698 to soothe merchant outrage over the statute of the previous year that barred recovery of the face value of conditioned bonds unless justified by the actual damages. Although in form the English act applied to all disputes, it particularly addressed the need of the mercantile community for arbitration that rested on something more than the good faith of the parties.[64]

The English arbitration statute enabled disputants to have their submission to arbitration made a rule of court. A party that revoked the submission or failed to abide by the award could then be punished for contempt of court. The statute codified the earlier practice of referring disputes to arbitration under a rule of *nisi prius* with the consent of the parties. Long after the act, English judges regarded submission under a rule of court with some suspicion, as they were wont to regard many innovations. As Stewart Kyd observed in his treatise on awards, "in more instances than one a judge is stated to have said, that these references were but newly introduced, and he never knew any good to arise from them."[65] However, backed as it was by contempt process, submission by rule of court offered too many advantages not to be accepted.

The Connecticut arbitration act permitted parties to have their submission to arbitration made a rule of court. Disputants who did so were then under court order to submit to arbitration and to abide by

63. Horwitz discusses a similar arbitration act passed in New York in 1791 as part of a "process ... of accommodation by which merchants were induced to submit to formal legal regulation in return for a major transformation of substantive legal rules governing commercial disputes." His explanation presupposes the existence of both a professionalized commercial bar and a cohesive merchant class. Horwitz, *Transformation of American Law*, pp. 145–55 (quotation at p. 154). Connecticut in 1753 had neither. There was not yet a commercial bar, and, although one might speak of a merchant class, Connecticut merchants in 1753 were far behind their New York brethren of 1791 in terms of wealth and power.

64. An Act for Determining Differences by Arbitration, 9 & 10 Will. 3, ch. 15 (1698).

65. Kyd, *Treatise on the Law of Awards*, p. 21. On the earlier English practices, see J. S. Cockburn, *A History of English Assizes, 1558–1714*, pp. 135–36; Holdsworth, *History of English Law*, 14:189; Kyd, *Treatise on the Law of Awards*, p. 21; John H. Langbein, Review of J. S. Cockburn, *A History of English Assizes, 1558–1714*, pp. 91–92.

the award. Failure to do either was punishable by contempt process. More importantly, when parties made their submission a rule of court, the statute empowered the arbitrators to file a return of their award with the county court, which could then grant a writ of execution to collect the award "in case of disobedience of either party."

The availability of execution process distinguished the Connecticut statute from its English counterpart. With writs of execution, arbitration awards were directly enforceable by legal process. Executory promises to arbitrate were still unenforceable, but disputants who invoked the statute and submitted to arbitration under a rule of court lost the power to change their minds. Some people learned this the hard way. Andrew McKenzie of New London, for example, tried to revoke the authority of the arbitrators to whom he and Joseph Chew had submitted a dispute under a rule of court in 1757. The arbitrators ignored McKenzie's attempted revocation and proceeded to make their award. Both the superior court and the assembly rejected McKenzie's argument that he had a legal right to revoke the authority of the arbitrators.[66]

Not all disputants, however, invoked the statute. Fewer than one-fifth of the noncommercial arbitrations and two-fifths of the commercial arbitrations mentioned in petitions to the assembly between 1753 and 1775 were under a rule of court.[67] This does not mean that the statute was ineffectual. On the contrary, it spurred the development of yet another form of submission—one that took the salient features of submission by rule of court and improved upon them. In the new form, disputants would execute promissory notes, confess judgment on the notes before a justice of the peace, and take out writs of execution on the judgments. They then deposited the writs of execution with the arbitrators. When the arbitrators made their award, they would endorse the execution against the loser down to the amount of the award and deliver it to the victor.[68]

66. Petition of Andrew McKenzie, 5 Oct. 1758, McKenzie v. Chew, Conn. Arch., Priv. Controversies (2d ser.), 18:25a (1758).

67. Five of the twenty-seven noncommercial arbitrations in which the form of submission could be determined and four of the ten commercial arbitrations in which the form could be determined were under a rule of court.

68. For example, see Petition of Allen Sage, 1 May 1769, Sage v. Richards, Conn. Arch., Priv. Controversies (2d ser.), 24:132b (1769); Petition of Noah Wadhams, 2 May 1769, Wadhams v. Sheldon, ibid., 29:19a (1769). Kyd mentioned that on references at *nisi prius* it was "not unusual for the plaintiff to

Pledging executions had the same practical effect as submission by rule of court. Both made execution process available on the award. Pledging executions, however, was more convenient. Parties could confess judgment and take out executions before a local justice of the peace without having to wait for a regular court session to bless the submission. In fact, if one of the arbitrators was a justice of the peace, the disputants could confess judgment before him and receive the writs of execution from him, then immediately return the writs to him to hold as one of the arbitrators.[69] Moreover, a party who received the execution against his opponent from the arbitrators could have it served immediately. By way of contrast, when the parties had submitted under a rule of court, the arbitrators had to file a return of their award with the appropriate court, which would hold a hearing on any objections to the award before deciding whether to accept it and grant execution on it. Comparatively few noncommercial disputants availed themselves of the statute. The new practice of pleading executions, however, extended and, at least in terms of efficiency, improved upon the statutory principle of enforcing arbitration awards by execution process.[70]

Other significant changes in arbitration also occurred after 1753. For example, parties began naming justices of the peace as arbitrators. Using honorifics as a rough identifier, 40 percent of all arbitrations (41 percent of the noncommercial arbitrations and 36 percent of the commercial arbitrations) in the petitions after 1754 included one or more justices of the peace as arbitrators. Until then, justices of the peace had appeared only rarely.

The presence of a sworn judicial officer, even one who in theory was not acting in his official capacity, gave the proceedings a more formal, legalistic tone. After 1753, one finds for the first time parties testifying under oath at arbitration hearings, lawyers participating as

---

take a verdict by consent for security," although it would still be necessary to take out execution after the award. Kyd, *Treatise on the Law of Awards*, p. 314.

69. For example, see Petition of Nathaniel Barnes, Jr., 12 Sept. 1764, Barnes v. Cook, Conn. Arch., Priv. Controversies (2d ser.), 2:176a (1764).

70. Pledged executions resembled recognizances, which medieval creditors commonly used to bind their debtors. See Simpson, *History of the Common Law of Contract*, pp. 126–35. Despite this commercial background, none of the commercial arbitrations in the petitions for which I can identify the mode of submission was conducted on pledged executions.

counsel to the disputants, and even lawyers conducting arbitrations on depositions in their clients' absence.[71] In one instance, an arbitrator, who was a justice of the peace, issued writs of summons in his capacity as justice for witnesses to appear before the arbitrators.[72] He did not seem to distinguish between his two roles. To him, and evidently to everyone else, arbitration was a judicial proceeding, and there was nothing anomalous about using legal process to facilitate it.

After 1753, disputants submitted to arbitration with increasingly legalistic expectations. For example, before Barnabas Baldwin of New Haven agreed to submit a land dispute to arbitration in 1761, he consulted a lawyer for advice on what "in equity or reason he ought to pay" to redeem the land, which he had mortgaged several years earlier. The amount he later tendered in satisfaction of the award was the amount recommended by the attorney, even though it was less than the arbitrators had awarded. Similarly, many people ceased to regard arbitration as sufficiently different from law to warrant greater procedural flexibility. Simeon Minor, Jr., of Stonington lost his suit on an arbitration bond in 1767 on the obligor's plea that the arbitrators had taken evidence "out of the view of the parties without giving them an opportunity of crosexaming the witnesses." In 1768, two attorneys persuaded the superior court to overturn an award against their client by pointing out an irregularity in the submission. When the losing party petitioned to reinstate the award, the General Assembly was not swayed by his argument that "a favourable and benign construction ought to be made to support the award of arbitrators, which is much favoured in law, in order to finish controversy."[73]

71. For example, see Deposition of Timothy Swan and William Wheeler, 10 Oct. 1767, Minor v. Hewitt, Conn. Arch., Priv. Controversies (2d ser.), 19:64a (1768); Petition of Ezekiel Pierce, 15 Apr. 1771, Pierce v. Stuart, ibid., 22:18b (1773); Petition of Samuel Minor, 7 Oct. 1765, Minor v. Minor and Minor, ibid., 19:55c–55d (1765); Petition of Seth Wales, 29 May 1770, Wales v. Smith, ibid., 29:80c–80d (1771); William Samuel Johnson to John Smith, 23 July 1763, William Samuel Johnson Papers, Letterbooks, 12.

72. See Summons, 19 Jan. 1757, Beecher v. Perkins, 5 NHCCR 119, NHCCF 21 (1757).

73. Petition of Barnabas Baldwin, 6 May 1761, Baldwin v. Jones, Conn. Arch., Priv. Controversies (2d ser.), 2:77e–77f (1761); Petition of Simeon Minor, Jr., 28 Sept. 1767, Minor v. Hewitt, ibid., 19:56a (1768); Petition of Eliphalet Beecher, 28 Apr. 1769, Beecher v. Sabin, ibid., 3:18d–18e (1769).

Glimpses such as these suggest an arbitration process that was increasingly bound by procedural niceties.

The new enforceability of arbitration awards made procedural formalization inevitable. The enforceability of awards and the freedom of arbitrators to decide without reference to rules of law were inversely related. Arbitrators had greater discretion when their awards were not readily enforceable. Under those circumstances, their discretion was bounded only by the parties' perceptions of the fairness of the award. When an award was unenforceable, people who believed it to be unjust could choose to ignore it. But when awards became more like legal judgments, as they did with the extension of execution process, the community required that they be governed by similar legal standards. Procedural regularity became important.[74]

The factors that led to the procedural formalization of arbitration also produced a substantive formalization of arbitration awards. The trend toward exclusively monetary awards was now complete. None of the awards in the petitions after 1753 displayed the variety or complexity of the awards from earlier in the century. There was none of the joinder of claims or mixture of remedies that characterized early awards. When arbitration awards became legally enforceable, arbitrators lost the discretion to fashion remedies that differed from what was available at common law. Because executions were levied for money rather than for specific articles, arbitration backed by execution process favored monetary awards. Disputants still spoke of submitting to arbitration to achieve "an equitable settlement" or a resolution "according to the rules of equity and justice," but it is clear that little equity remained in the process, at least in the remedies that arbitrators applied.[75] A process that once directed parties to perform executory contracts now offered only monetary judgments, much like any court of law. After the statute, the persistence of the rhetoric of equity indicated, as James Henretta observed in a related context, "little more than futile calls to a vanished past."[76]

74. See E. J. Cohn, "Commercial Arbitration and the Rules of Law: A Comparative Study," pp. 8–9.

75. Petition of Samuel Tyler, 7 May 1761, Tyler v. Barnes, Conn. Arch., Priv. Controversies (2d ser.), 28:200a (1761); Petition of Nathaniel Eells and Edward Eells, 18 Sept. 1769, Eells and Eells v. Baldwin, ibid., 9:164a (1769).

76. James A. Henretta, "The Morphology of New England Society in the Colonial Period," p. 395.

The transformation of arbitration awards into legal judgments permitted a measure of direct enforcement that arbitration had never before enjoyed. The newfound legalization of arbitration was not without a price, however. Arbitration, which had always been adjudicatory in nature, now became downright legalistic. Not only were the awards different, but the hearing process itself had changed. After the statute, arbitrators looked more like judges than they did before. Indeed, many of them were judges. They presided over proceedings that resembled formal hearings with examinations of witnesses and maneuverings that imitated pleadings. The process still went by the name arbitration, but it was no longer what the name once implied. In the course of becoming legally enforceable, a community-bound form of handling disputes lost its simplicity, and thus its uniqueness. Arbitration changed because the communities that shaped it changed. Once severed from the communities it had served, arbitration, at least insofar as it rested on rules of court or pledged executions, differed little from formal legal adjudication. It no longer occupied a special niche in the legal structure.

VI

Formalization limited the ability of arbitrators to dispense substantive justice, to do equity between the parties. But the equitable functions that arbitration had served did not disappear. They were taken up elsewhere in the legal system. The assembly, for example, had the power to grant equitable relief on private petitions. It could appoint a committee of three of its members and give them chancery authority to inquire into the matters alleged in a petition. The committee would then conduct hearings and report its findings and recommendations to the assembly, which usually accepted them.

The committees, which the assembly used only sparingly before 1753, echoed the earlier English practice of prerogative arbitrations commissioned by Chancery and the Privy Council. Prerogative arbitrations grew from the Chancery practice of using panels of laymen to examine witnesses outside London. Although commissioned to take testimony, the examiners were in a position to suggest compromise resolutions to the parties, in part because Chancery tended to appoint men who enjoyed a measure of prestige in their communities. By the middle of the sixteenth century, commissions that conferred authority to "hear and end [disputes] according to equity and good conscience" were frequent. Merchants benefited from the Chancery custom of commissioning arbitration panels of merchants to hear mercantile disputes. The Privy Council first commissioned merchants as arbitrators in disputes that involved foreign merchants, where the process appears to have been a concession to the need to facilitate foreign trade.[77]

To be sure, the committees appointed by the Connecticut assembly operated more formally than arbitration process did. For one thing, the disputants did not select the members of their committee. For another, the committees could compel witnesses to appear and testify under oath. Moreover, disputants before a committee did not play undifferentiated roles, as they did in arbitration. They stood as petitioner and petitionee, as one party who was sufficiently aggrieved to seek redress and another who was summoned to appear. In arbitration, the mutuality of the submission meant that there was no moving or complaining party—rather, the disputants came to the process together.[78]

Despite these differences, there were strong similarities between the committees and arbitration in its early, community-based form. The assembly endorsed the resemblance on occasion when it appointed committees of the same men who had sat earlier as arbitrators in the same dispute.[79] The resolutions by which the assembly empowered committees often evoked the spirit of compromise that characterized early arbitrations, as when the assembly instructed the committee first to "endeavour an amicable agreement and accommodation among the parties."[80]

The most important similarity between the committees and early arbitrations lay in what they gave the disputants. The remedies that

77. John P. Dawson, *A History of Lay Judges* pp. 163–65, 167–68. The Privy Council soon extended the same privilege to English merchants, in whose hands the arbitration commissions could sometimes apply principles that were well ahead of common law doctrines of the period. See John P. Dawson, "The Privy Council and Private Law in the Tudor and Stuart Periods," p. 409.

78. Richard Abel includes the demarcation of the roles of plaintiff and defendant as one of his indices of processual legal change. Abel, "A Comparative Theory of Dispute Institutions in Society," p. 273.

79. For example, see Pease v. Easty, Conn. Arch., Priv. Controversies (2d ser.), 21:73b, 75 (1753); Beecher v. Keeney, ibid., 3:25 (1764).

80. *Conn. Rec.*, 6:391.

committees proposed to the assembly resembled early arbitration awards in their flexibility and in their attempt to do justice. One committee recommended that a man should be held to his promise to pay for the loss of a sloop, even though his promise "might not be so express as to oblige him by the strict rules of the common law." Another recommended that an estate should reimburse the petitioner, who had stood surety for the decedent, even though it was legally immune from liability.[81]

The ability of committees to render equitable awards may explain why the use of committees burgeoned after 1753. In the thirty years before the arbitration act, the assembly appointed twenty-three committees on petitions. In the twenty years after the statute, it appointed 164. There were no changes in the equity power of the assembly that would account for the increase. The sudden popularity of the committees did, however, coincide with the statutory formalization of arbitration. It may be that disputants petitioned the assembly to appoint committees when the only remedy they could receive from arbitration was monetary awards. Through use of the committees, the assembly assumed some of the equitable functions once performed by arbitration. Substantive justice remained served, albeit perhaps not as well.

VII

Arbitration in Connecticut underwent considerable change in the hundred years or so before the Revolution. So, for that matter, did the entire legal system. What is important, however, is not the fact of the change but why it occurred and what it tells us about the nature of legal change.

The key lies in the community nexus of arbitration. Arbitration in Connecticut before the end of the seventeenth century was deeply rooted in the communities it served. The absence of evidentiary strictures, the power of the parties to define the scope of the inquiry, the spirit of compromise implicit in the submission, the ability of the parties to choose their arbitrators, the mutuality of awards, the privacy of the process, the discretion of the arbitrators—all made arbitra-

81. Committee report, 27 Apr. 1739, Trowbridge v. Cobb, Conn. Arch., Priv. Controversies (2d ser.), 28:139c (1739); Committee report, May 1756, Lockwood v. Rundel, ibid., 18:76c (1756).

tion useful in preserving the interdependent relations that contributed to the stability of insular communities.

What worked for members of the same community, however, did not necessarily work for others. The social context of disputing changed as population growth and migration weakened the cohesiveness of existing towns and as new towns were settled by individuals rather than by groups. Arbitration remained an attractive alternative to litigation, even for lawyers. William Samuel Johnson, for example, once expressed "great pleasure" upon learning that a client had agreed to arbitration, "in which Method they may certainly be settled with less Expence and more effectual justice may be done to all concerned than in the endless Litigation of the Law."[82] However, the disintegration of group-minded communities meant that the community norms that had excused the lack of sanctions in arbitration no longer existed. If people wished to continue to use arbitration, as they manifestly did, they had to resort to artificial means of assuring compliance with awards—compliance once given freely and voluntarily because the community expected it. Disputants resorted first to deeds, then to conditioned bonds and promissory notes to supply the need for enforceability. To a certain extent, they succeeded.

The gains in enforceability were not without a price. The social changes that prompted the shift to secured submissions also led to the rise of simple monetary awards in place of the omnibus awards of early arbitration. The multifaceted nature of the early awards had allowed arbitrators to address the full range of differences between the parties. But when the social relations between the disputants became sufficiently attenuated, their differences could more easily be reduced to monetary terms. When that occurred, arbitration no longer offered the parties remedies that they could not obtain at law. It did not matter that in individual cases disputants might in fact stand in a traditional relationship and need a traditional award. When arbitration changed for the many, it also changed for the few.

The statutory formalization of arbitration in 1753 ratified and accelerated these changes. The statute represented the culmination of earlier efforts to secure the performance of arbitration awards, this time by merchants who demanded legislative relief when their community—the community of merchants—could no longer assure per-

---

82. William Samuel Johnson to Thomas Wright, 28 Sept. 1764, William Samuel Johnson Papers, Letterbooks, 13:43–44.

formance informally. After the statute, arbitration resembled a legal proceeding with lawyers, judges, sworn witnesses, depositions, and technical objections. It was, as Zephaniah Swift later wrote, "a court created, constituted, and appointed by the parties."[83]

There are limits to how much some things can change before they become transformed. The statute made arbitration awards enforceable at law, which had been the goal of secured submissions. But the changes set in motion by the search for enforceability transformed arbitration from a voluntary, communal process into a pale imitation of legal adjudication.

83. Swift, *System of the Laws of the State of Connecticut*, 2:7.

5

CHURCHES, EQUITY,

AND LEGALISM

Two very different proceedings in 1716 and 1717—one ecclesiastical, the other equitable—illustrate complementary elements of disputing in the shadow of the legal system. One, a church proceeding, was part of a system of ecclesiastical discipline that, like arbitration, grew more legalistic in the eighteenth century. The other, a special court of equity, was a dead end, an experiment which might have answered recurring demands for formal equity jurisdiction but which was never repeated. In 1717, however, it was not clear what lay ahead for either kind of proceeding.

The church action began early in 1716, when Samuel Webb of Windham complained to the church in Mansfield that one of its deacons, Thomas Huntington, "had taken a false oath in an account he had layed" before arbitrators. The two men had submitted a dispute over various business transactions to arbitration, and Huntington had won. The church appointed three of its members to meet with a delegation from the church in Windham and investigate the complaint. It specifically instructed the committee "not to regard or mind, anything of controversy with respect to a civil right but what is a breach of any gospel rule." The evidence, however, was murky and contradictory. The churchmembers found it too difficult to consider the allegation of perjury apart from the legal requirements for how creditors prove their accounts.

To advise the committee, the Mansfield church turned to two prominent ministers and a colony assistant—Timothy Edwards, Timothy Woodbridge, and William Pitkin. These three men heard the evidence and tried to determine what Huntington had sworn to and whether the accounts to which he had sworn were accurate. They decided in Huntington's favor on every issue. In the course of their report to the church, they remarked that "not only the Rule of Law and Practise upon it is to show that Private Contracts shall be proved by the oath of the person who receives benefit by them but also this is a known and allowed practice among Christians." Their linking of legal procedure and church procedure is instructive. The three advisers recognized the similarity between the two and did not think it inappropriate to apply a legal standard to a church proceeding. The connection was hardly unnatural. Oaths at common law drew their evidentiary force from their religious significance. But the incident reveals a potential for legalism that was fully realized in church proceedings within a few decades.[1]

The proceedings in equity were more curious. The General Assembly created a court of equity in October 1715 at the petition and expense of one Nathaniel Clark. The sole purpose of the court was to adjudicate some fifty debts allegedly due to the estate of René Grignon, a Huguenot trader and goldsmith who settled in Norwich, grew wealthy, and died there in 1715. Clark married Grignon's principal beneficiary and moved into Grignon's house, which then burned down. Lost with the house were Grignon's bills, bonds, and account book—the evidence of every debt owed to him. Without that evidence, Grignon's debtors could not be sued in a court of law. Clark petitioned the assembly "for relief," which it granted by creating the court and allowing Clark to prove the debts by their listings in the estate inventory and by his oath.[2]

The action of the assembly in establishing a tribunal to enable one creditor to recover debts that were legally unenforceable was unusual, to say the least. In fact, it was unique. In the early 1680s, the assembly had considered a bill to establish a court of chancery, but the proposal died without a vote. Twenty years later, the assembly received a petition for a court of chancery that claimed that "there have been discoures and expectations a long time in the Contry of such a court."[3] The "discoures and expectations" were genuine, but the closest Con-

---

1. Mansfield, First Congregational Church Records, 1710–88, A:50–54 (27 Feb. 1716, 21 June, 15 Aug. 1717).

2. Conn. Arch., Miscellaneous (1st ser.), 2:140–41; Conn. Rec., 5:533, 538–39. The Court of Equity records are bound in 3 ½ SCR. On Grignon, see Frances M. Caulkins, History of Norwich, Connecticut: From Its Possession by the Indians, to the Year 1866, pp. 288–89.

3. Bill, n.d. (but before 1683), Conn. Arch., Civil Officers (1st ser.), 1:62; Petition, 8 Oct. 1702, ibid., 1:83b.

necticut ever came to having a chancery court was the court of equity convened for Grignon's estate. The failure to establish a formal equity jurisdiction and the changes in church disciplinary proceedings were two sides of the same phenomenon—a growing acceptance of law as the standard by which all forms of disputing were measured.

I

Early puritanism defined the relationship between God and the individual as contractual in nature, embodied in the covenant of grace that God made with Abraham. God offered salvation in return for belief that Christ would come and, later, that Jesus was God. Federal theologians in the early seventeenth century analyzed the covenant in explicitly contractual terms. They wrote of offer and acceptance, consideration, breach, performance, even of suing God for the promised salvation. For them, the language of law was a natural medium. It aided them in wrestling with the dilemma of how to make an inscrutable God scrutable, of how to render the mysterious workings of an omnipotent deity susceptible to comprehension by human reason. God remained omnipotent and unknowable, but he had consented to be bound by the covenant. That concession made it possible to regard the relationship between God and each individual as little different from more routine social relations in which the rights and obligations of each party were subject to legal analysis. The language of law was so deeply embedded in the way people thought about their relations with one another and with the state that its absence from theological inquiry would have been more remarkable than its presence.[4]

The legalism of covenant theology had far-reaching consequences in seventeenth-century New England. There, the religious covenant between God and individual believers was the model for social covenants that linked individuals in communities and communities to God. Church covenants and town covenants bound their subscribers in communities of mutual obligations, among which was the obliga-

---

4. Perry Miller asserted the legalism of puritan theology most clearly in "The Marrow of Puritan Divinity." Recent historians, however, have argued that Miller overstated the case. See Norman Pettit, *The Heart Prepared: Grace and Conversion in Puritan Spiritual Life*; Michael McGiffert, "American Puritan Studies in the 1960's," pp. 47–50.

tion of the community—however defined—to watch and correct the behavior of its members. The imperative behind such watch and care was that transgressions of individual members, if left uncorrected, imperiled the community at large in its covenanted relationship with God. Correction could not be summary, however. Church disciplinary actions followed procedural rules that governed how the churches should deal with their "delinquent" members. The basic procedures were those authorized by the Cambridge Platform of 1648 and described first by Thomas Hooker and later by Cotton Mather.[5]

The procedures were particularly notable in their distinction between public offenses and private offenses. The question of what things are public and what private is a vexing one that does not admit of clear or constant answer.[6] In church disciplinary proceedings the distinction was double. On one level, the classification of an offense as public or private was determined by the number of witnesses to the act. Hooker and Mather both distinguished instances where, in Mather's words, "a Scandalous Transgression is known only to One or Two" from those where, according to Hooker, "the offense be Famous and Notorious At The First Practice Of It." Thus, when the Reverend Samuel Hooker of Farmington raised with his congregation the question of "what was truly to bee accounted a publique and what a private offence," he did so in best lawyerly fashion by posing a hypothetical case—is an offense public or private if it "is committed

---

5. *A Platform of Church Discipline*; Thomas Hooker, *A Survey of the Summe of Church-Discipline*; Cotton Mather, *Ratio Disciplinae Fratrum Nov-Anglorum: A Faithful Account of the Discipline Professed and Practised; in the Churches of New-England*. The text of the Cambridge Platform is also printed in Williston Walker, *The Creeds and Platforms of Congregationalism*, pp. 194–237. Previous studies of church discipline have focused on matters of morality, doctrine, attendance at worship, and, less frequently, questions of debt, contract, land title, and business ethics. See Emil Oberholzer, Jr., *Delinquent Saints: Disciplinary Action in the Early Congregational Churches of Massachusetts*, pp. 43–163, 186–215; William E. Nelson, *Dispute and Conflict Resolution in Plymouth County, Massachusetts, 1725–1825*, pp. 30–34. For present purposes, however, the most pertinent aspect of church discipline is not its subject matter, but its procedure.

6. The question continues to vex. See the papers from the University of Pennsylvania Law Review Symposium on The Public/Private Distinction, 23 Jan. 1982, 1289ff.

not in a corner but in the open street in the audience, and observation of diverse . . . famelyes, and so . . . cometh to bee in the mouthes of many."[7]

On another, but not entirely separate, level, the distinction between public and private offenses was measured by the nature of the injury, which in turn rested at least in part on the substantive nature of the offense. Behavior that injured individuals rather than the community at large gave private, rather than public, offense. Such behavior tended to arise from relations between individuals—debt, contract, and fraud, for example. In that respect, it differed from drunkenness, profanity, sabbath breach, and the like, which most people regarded as matters of public offense even if observed by only one or two witnesses. The distinction between the two was largely situational. Fornication and adultery were public offenses even though they arose from relations between individuals. Slander and defamation, on the other hand, could be public or private offenses depending on the circulation of the slander, even though the injury was distinctly personal.

The classification of offenses as public or private was a matter of more than taxonomic interest. Much like the common law writ system, the classification of the act determined the procedure. Persons aggrieved by private offenses were to follow the procedure directed in the eighteenth chapter of Matthew. They first had to meet privately with the offender "and seriously endeavour[ ] to bring him to Repentance." Hooker counseled caution at this stage. Individuals should understand the imperfections of human nature and not presume to give private correction without evidence of the offense. Such precautions could prevent "the many offences committed amongst Brethren, while they come to reform one offence given." If the offender remained obstinate, the aggrieved person was supposed to redouble his efforts with the assistance of one or two fellow churchmembers. Only when that failed was it proper for the injured party to complain to the minister, who, as Mather explained, would "pursue[ ] the Designs of Humiliation on the Soul of the Offender." The pastor would then deal with the offender privately if he relented in his obstinacy or with the assistance of the church if he did not. Even repentant offenders might

7. Mather, *Ratio Disciplinae*, p. 148; Hooker, *Summe of Church-Discipline*, p. 35; Farmington, First Church of Christ (Congregational) Records, 1652–1938, 1:91 (21 Oct. 1677).

have to face the church if "the Matter have so taken Air, as to be a Matter of common Fame, and the Talk of the People."[8]

Proceedings on public offenses, on the other hand, dispensed with the preliminary attempts at private correction. Instead, they began with an examination of the offender by the minister, usually with the assistance of the elders. The examination served as a kind of probable cause hearing. The complaining party had to be prepared to prove his accusation. For their part, the elders were to focus on the case at hand and not, as Hooker cautioned, "suffer [the parties] to darken the truth, disturb the proceedings, and bring confusion to the whole debate." If the delinquent maintained "that hardness of Heart, that bespeaks for him a publick Admonition," or if the nature of the offense required it, the pastor would refer the matter to the hearing and determination of the church, which would recommend admonition, censure, excommunication, or, occasionally, acquittal.[9]

The difference between the two procedures was not simply a matter of starting the disciplinary process at different points. The requirement that disputants in private offenses first deal with one another privately laid a conciliatory foundation that was absent from the inquisitorial proceedings on public offenses. To be sure, conciliation often fell victim to obstinacy and recrimination. But the hope that private dealing could forestall formal discipline was an essential article of faith in covenanted communities.

Churches not only inquired whether complainants had followed "the gospel rule" of Matthew, they also examined the complainant's substantive compliance with the scriptural injunction, much in the spirit of the maxim that one who seeks equity must first do equity. For example, when Jacob Bacon of Voluntown charged in 1725 that Thomas Welsh had never dealt with him privately "according to the rules of the scripture" before complaining to the minister, the church "enquire[d] into the method Welsh had taken with his brother Bacon, and found that he had spoken to Mr. Bacon before two of the Brethren and privately by himself but not in that christian, serious and sober manner or regular way which he ought."[10]

---

8. Mather, *Ratio Disciplinae*, pp. 148–49; Hooker, *Survey of Church-Discipline*, pp. 34–35. See Matthew 18:15–17.

9. Hooker, *Summe of Church-Discipline*, pp. 36–38; Mather, *Ratio Disciplinae*, pp. 144–46.

10. Voluntown and Sterling, Congregational Church Records, 1723–1914, 1:29 (14 Apr. 1725).

Even when private dealing failed, churches still urged disputants to settle their differences themselves. The first church of Middletown, for example, deferred hearing Joseph Kirby's complaint against John Sage for over a year, then accepted with alacrity an agreement offered by the two men "wherein they declared that they were come to a very peaceable compliance one with another." When three members of the Voluntown church complained against Thomas Cole, the church initially leaned toward not considering the complaint at all, "thinking so it would contribute to peace." However, "understanding that the parties concerned would not thereby be peaceable nor satisfied," the church referred the matter to its next meeting in what proved to be a vain hope that the parties would reconcile their differences. The same church deferred formal action on Robert Parke's complaint against John Smith and was able to drop the matter altogether when Parke and Smith agreed "to burn the papers on all sides and to make no more noise about them."[11]

Perhaps the clearest affirmation of the value placed on conciliation through private dealing was a unanimous resolution of the Voluntown church in 1726. A person who "does not take the scripture rule," yet who later settled his complaint after "occasioning the calling of a church meeting" and "finding he could not make his charge good," was "guilty of a scandal." Moreover, it was "scandalous in the church not to censure such proceedings." The church affirmed that conciliation was something that private disputants should seek from the beginning and not resort to only when harsher redress failed.[12]

The undercurrent of conciliation is missing from later proceedings, private as well as public. This is not to say that private dealing ceased to be the starting point in the disciplinary process for private offenses, only that it no longer set the tone for the procedure. As early as the 1720s, but more particularly from the 1740s, church disciplinary proceedings began to adopt the rhetoric and procedures of secular courts. This is no indication that they did so deliberately, although there is often a self-consciousness to the rhetoric that gives one pause.

For example, the records of a proceeding in 1725 against a deacon of the church in Voluntown who was accused of lying about a case that had recently been tried before a local justice of the peace, in-

11. Middletown, First Congregational Church Records, 1668–1871, 1:33 (7 Feb. 1710), 34 (4 Apr., 2 May 1710), 35 (4 Apr. 1711); Voluntown Church Rec., 1:33 (17 Jan. 1726), 1:34 (21 Mar., 2 May 1726).

12. Voluntown Church Rec., 1:27–28 (1 Jan. 1725).

cluded a written complaint to the pastor, written interrogatories answered and signed by the deacon, two depositions in legal form, written pleadings that attacked not the merits but the procedure of the
complaint and which the records note "are too tedious and long to be
here inserted but are ready upon file," and an issue "drawn up" for
the church to determine "[a]fter hearing both parties." The written
complaint was probably not unusual—one finds it elsewhere at least
as early as 1710. The other documents, however, do not appear in any
recorded disciplinary proceedings in Connecticut before 1725.[13] Yet
within a few years afterward, disputants used them often enough to
make church disciplinary proceedings resemble civil trials in virtually
every important respect—except, of course, that of the available
remedies.

From roughly 1740 onward, individuals who were called before
their churches to answer complaints, whether public or private, did
not simply appear to discuss the allegations, they appeared and
pleaded. David Wallis, complained against by a deacon of the church
in Woodstock in 1739 "for censurable falshood," pleaded not guilty
"and put the Church to prove the Charge against him." Joseph Park
of Kent, accused of drunkenness by Samuel Bates in 1741, pleaded in
the alternative that he was "not guilty of matter of fact and further
supposing said fact to be true yet said complaint was unjust because
he had even offered gospel satisfaction unto him." Nathaniel Hunt,
summoned before the church in Mansfield in 1747 to answer a charge
of fornication, "offered a plea in Barr of the Church's Proceeding."[14]

"Summoned" is the correct description of how offenders were notified of the proceedings. Citations to appear before the church were
nearly identical to writs of summons issued by justices of the peace.
They directed the recipients to appear before the church at a specified

13. Ibid., 1:28–30 (14 Apr. 1725). The complaint and the depositions bear
the same date, 19 Mar. 1725. Thomas Welch, the complainant, evidently
submitted the depositions, which supported his allegations, to the pastor
along with the complaint. The earliest written complaint I found was that of
Joseph Kirby against Edward Shepard on 3 Oct. 1710. Middletown Church
Rec., 1:34 (2 Jan. 1711).

14. North Woodstock [orig. Woodstock First Church], Congregational
Church Records, 1727–1900, 1:31 (3 Apr. 1739); Kent, Congregational
Church Records, 1739–1823, 17 (2 Oct. 1741); Mansfield, First Congregational Church Records, 1710–88, A:95 (5 Mar. or 5 Apr. 1747, date uncertain).

time and place "to hear and answer" the complaint laid against them. A brief recitation of the complaint followed. Church citations differed from writs of summons only in that they were signed by the minister rather than a justice of the peace, they appointed a churchmember rather than a constable to make service and return, and they were issued not in the name of the king but on rather different authority, "in the Name of our Lord Jesus Christ." These differences merely emphasized the formal similarity of church citations and legal writs of summons, a similarity deepened by citations to witnesses that also tracked the legal forms for summoning witnesses to testify in civil proceedings.[15]

By the 1750s, churches had begun to address questions of procedure explicitly rather than treating them as incidental to individual cases. The church in Kent voted in 1748 that disputants and their witnesses should withdraw "after the Publick hearing of the evidences and Pleas" while the church deliberated in private. The first church in Plainfield and the fourth in Hartford each passed resolutions in the 1750s that no process could issue to begin disciplinary proceedings without a written complaint to the minister that specified the allegations and listed the witnesses who could substantiate them. Churches also began to entertain motions from alleged offenders that the proceedings be adjourned to allow them time to prepare their defenses— motions that, when denied, could be denied in strikingly legalistic terms.[16]

15. Citations and other papers in folder marked "Norwich, Conn. 1st Cong. Church. Church Discipline, 1756, 1760–61, 1766," Norwich, First Congregational Church Records, 1699–1917. There is also the notation that Ebenezer Peck of Kent "did not appear to answer the said complaint tho' cited by the Pastor and a copy of the complaint left Timely at the Place of his abode." Kent Church Rec., 42–43 (15 Dec. 1773).

16. Kent Church Rec., 27 (1 Sept. 1748); Plainfield, First Congregational Church Records, 1747–1899, 1:18 (5 July 1754); West Hartford [orig. Hartford Fourth Church], Congregational Church Records, 1713–1924, 1:168 (16 June 1758). The fourth church in Hartford rejected a motion to adjourn with the words "which motion was overruled by the Church and the Parties ordered to proceed to Trial." West Hartford Church Rec., 1:169 (25 July 1757). For other motions to adjourn, see Scotland [orig. Windham Third Church], Congregational Church Records, 1732–1915, 2:49 (21 Oct. 1756); East Haddam, First Congregational Church and Ecclesiastical Society Records, 1702–1927, 1:115 (4 Jan 1774).

In the face of such procedural niceties, it is not surprising that church disciplinary proceedings came to resemble civil trials, even to the appearance of legal counsel. A case in point, although admittedly a bit extreme, was the trial of Joshua White, Jr., in 1756 by the third church in Windham for breach of the ninth commandment, which proscribes perjury.[17]

White, it appears, had given a quantity of beef and tallow in 1755 to Captain James Brewster to sell for him in Rhode Island. If one can believe the many people who testified against White at the church trial, Brewster was to sell the beef as his own because White feared that one of his uncles would seize the beef if he shipped it under his own name. Brewster, however, had the bad grace to die before he completed the transaction, the apparent owner of everything in his possession. Given the secret nature of the deal, White would have been hard-pressed to prove that the beef had been his. So he did the next best thing—he lied. In sworn testimony, White told two different sets of auditors who were appointed to determine Brewster's estate that he had sold the beef and tallow to Brewster before Brewster sailed from Norwich. According to what White later admitted to the church, he thought that lying under oath would save him the expense of litigating ownership of the beef "if his oath might be admitted for truth."

In August 1756, a few weeks after White's second meeting with the auditors, the church took note of "a Publick rumour" that White had perjured himself. It appointed a committee of three men, two of them deacons, to investigate the reports "and if they find Cause of Action to Prepare a complaint" against White. Two months later the church summoned White by written citation to appear before it and answer the charge that he had committed "a Heinous Breach of the Ninth Command in the moral Law."

White appeared as directed. The meeting opened with a reading of the complaint and a prayer. White then requested an adjournment "that he might have opportunity to get such council as he desired and which he could not then obtain." The church granted his request and adjourned for three weeks. When it reconvened, White appeared with his "counsel." The church records do not identify the man, and there is no way to determine if he was a licensed attorney. Whether or not

17. The following account is drawn from the Scotland Church Rec., 2:49–52 (26 Aug., 21 Oct., 12 Nov. 1756, 2, 16 Jan., 9 Oct. 1757).

he was a lawyer, however, is less important than the fact that he acted like one.

The "counsel" appeared before the church and argued White's defense—not very well, perhaps, but argued nonetheless. The trial featured a virtual parade of witnesses, eight of whom testified in person and two by written depositions—one given by a local justice of the peace "solemnly engaged to speak the Truth and the whole Truth before proper ecclesiastical authority" and the other by a witness in Rhode Island "engaged according to Law." All but one witness, White's son, testified against White. White's counsel attacked the credibility of the witnesses and argued for a more benign interpretation of his client's oath to the auditors, but the church found White guilty "almost unanimously."

One can read the record of Joshua White's trial and almost forget that it was a church proceeding, not a civil one. The procedure and the language in which it was couched mimicked common law practices so closely that references to "prayer" or "the church" are what seem anomalous. Yet the trial did not represent the farthest advance of legalism in church disciplinary proceedings. In the decade or so afterward, several churches appointed permanent committees to supervise the administration of church discipline.

The structure and functions of the committees varied. The first church of East Hartford agreed in 1763 "to chose seven or eight of their number to be elders . . . who shall be designed to have a more special watch over the Lives of Professors." The elders would try "to heal and make up private differences," "give private reproofs," and advise the pastor in cases that required "an ecclesiastical tryal." The fourth church of Hartford resolved in 1765 that there should be a committee chosen "as often as the Church thinks fit" to inquire into allegations of "flagrant" or "scandalous" immorality and, "if they find upon enquiry such evidence as will support in their judgment a strong suspicion of . . . guilt," to attempt private discipline under the rule of Matthew 18 and make a formal complaint should that fail. In 1769, the church in Redding appointed a committee of five men, two of them deacons, "Desiring them in cases which call for it to take the steps of the gospel Rule concerning Discipline with offending Brethren." In 1772, the first church in East Haddam appointed a committee of five men—again, two of them deacons—"to stand during the churche's pleasure" to act with the minister in hearing and determining "cases of difficulty." Offenders whom the committee censured were to present their cases to the church for determination, but church members could also bring before the church cases of people whom the committee had cleared.[18]

The establishment of formally constituted committees to oversee the preliminary stages of church discipline—stages that in many instances would doubtless also resolve the matter—was striking in itself. Even more striking, however, were the reasons why churches turned to more formal mechanisms. The church in East Hartford made the obligatory noises about the declining purity of the church and the growth of "error, looseness and impiety" among its members. But it seemed most concerned about the administrative difficulty posed by "the intricacy and perplexity of matters of scandal, and ecclesiastical causes; to get a right and true understanding whereof tis scarce possible for the body of the church to allow themselves time and Leisure." The fourth church in Hartford acted because "there seems to be no propriety in a Minister's being an informing officer to the Church, but various Mischiefs will accrue if he must not only preside and execute but inform also." The church in Redding attributed "a neglect of discipline" to members who "are ready to think that it is no more incumbent on them to prosecute an offending Brother than it is on others."[19]

These statements in part reflect the reassertion of ministerial authority and congregational autonomy. They also reflect the beginning of a trend that reached its conclusion after the Revolution, as churches gradually removed themselves from the business of discipline. The retreat was not so much a collective decision as it was the consequence of fewer people bringing private disputes to the church and of lesser willingness to invoke church process in matters of public offense. Churches were losing their authority at the same time as they were attempting to shore it up with increasingly formal rules of procedure.[20]

18. East Hartford, First Congregational Church and Ecclesiastical Society Records, 1699–1913, 1:5 (1 Aug. 1763); West Hartford Church Rec., 1:175 (26 June 1765); Redding, Congregational Church and Ecclesiastical Society Records, 1729–1882, 1:81 (9 Nov. 1769); East Haddam Church Rec., 1:113 (28 Aug. 1772). The East Hartford resolution matches verbatim one adopted by the first church in Lebanon in 1735. Lebanon, First Ecclesiastical Society and Congregational Church Records, 1700–1883, 4:76 (16 June 1735).

19. East Hartford Church Rec., 1:5 (2 Aug. 1763); West Hartford Church Rec., 1:175 (26 June 1765); Redding Church Rec., 1:8 (9 Nov. 1769).

20. On the use of ruling elders and church disciplinary committees to enhance the authority of the minister and to assert the autonomy of the indi-

In that respect, the growing formalization of church process resembled similar, contemporaneous changes in arbitration. The distinction drawn by the fourth church in Hartford—that it was improper for a minister to preside over proceedings on complaints he had initiated—recognized a sophisticated differentiation of legal function. Once churches reached that level of legalistic discrimination in their disciplinary proceedings, they, like arbitration, no longer offered a means of addressing private disputes or offenses that differed procedurally from what was available in the civil courts, only one that was less satisfactory.

The growing legalism of church proceedings was a negation of the communalism that infused earlier disciplinary actions. Although not up to the procedural standards implicit in Grant Gilmore's description of hell as a place where "due process will be meticulously observed," the increasing procedural rigor of church hearings reflected a declining acceptance of the values that permitted such nonlegal hearings to function in the first place.[21] The turn to greater procedural formality almost seemed an attempt to compensate for a weakening consensus on the authority of church hearings. If the transformation had an air of inexorability about it, the impression stemmed not from any imagined inevitability of legal rationalization but rather from the association of the change with dissension and controversy in local churches.

The first recorded committee to handle disciplinary matters was in Voluntown in 1726. The church there established the committee "as the best expedient to remove the present difficulties in this place and

---

vidual congregation in Massachusetts, see [John Wise,] *The Churches Quarrel Espoused*, and the controversy between the Reverend Samuel Fiske and his church in Salem, related in the following pamphlets: *Letter Relating to the Divisions in the First Church*; *Remarks on some Contents of a Letter relating to the Divisions of the first Church in Salem*; *A Just and Impartial Narrative of the Controversy Between The Rev. Mr. Samuel Fisk the Pastor, and A Number of the Brethren of the First Church of Christ in Salem*. William Nelson observed the declining frequency of church disciplinary actions in Plymouth County, Massachusetts, in his *Dispute and Conflict Resolution in Plymouth*. The loss of clerical authority has been noted before. Edmund Morgan stated it most succinctly when he wrote that "[i]n 1740 America's leading intellectuals were clergymen and thought about theology; in 1790 they were statesmen and thought about politics." Edmund S. Morgan, "The American Revolution Considered as an Intellectual Movement," in Arthur M. Schlesinger, Jr. and Morton White, eds., *Paths of American Thought*, p. 11.

21. Grant Gilmore, *The Ages of American Law*, p. 111.

to prevent further controversies in this church." It gave a self-perpetuating committee of eleven men plus the minister full authority to receive, hear, determine, and judge "all complaints proper for ecclesiastical consideration . . . without a previous reference of them to the church."[22] The committee apparently did not function long. By 1730 the entire church was hearing complaints again. However, the idea of the committee as a device to impose agreement where none existed without it indicated the conditions that elicited legalist solutions.

An important part of the same transformation was the growing legalism of the ecclesiastical councils that exercised a measure of quasi-appellate authority over the proceedings of individual churches. Similar councils were common in the seventeenth century. They were gatherings of ministers or, later, ministers and elders summoned by a neighboring church to help resolve disputes that the church could not resolve itself. Their authority was moral and persuasive, rather than coercive and binding.

Churches could call councils on any matter of disagreement, from differences on points of discipline to disputes on calling or retaining a minister. Individuals could also request councils in instances where, as Cotton Mather put it, "a Person may be oppressed by unjust Passion and Prejudice, and have a Censure unjustly passed upon him." In those instances the council, "(chosen with mutual Satisfaction,) to judge of the Proceedings," reviewed the actions of the church in a public hearing. It considered evidence submitted by the aggrieved member and the church and rendered its recommendations in writing, "wherein they first Report what they find, and then advise what they would have to be done."[23]

After the ministers of the first generation of settlement passed from the scene, ministerial councils trod a fine, and not always clear, line between congregational and presbyterian principles. The difference between the two lay, in part, in the nature of clerical authority. Some congregations resisted the suggestion that councils of ministers could have any supervisory authority over individual congregations. Such authority was antithetical to traditional tenets of congregational independence. Many ministers, on the other hand, looked to meetings with their fellow clerics as a source of intellectual stimulation and support that ameliorated their often-confining dependence on their congregations. Toward the end of the seventeenth century, some of the

22. Voluntown Church Rec., 1:35–36 (6 June 1726).
23. Mather, *Ratio Disciplinae*, pp. 158–60.

meetings grew into informal, county-wide associations of ministers who met regularly and discussed, among other things, matters of church discipline.[24]

The move to turn these meetings into formal organizations gathered strength after the turn of the century, when ministers adopted the association idea as a platform from which to reassert their authority. The movement foundered in Massachusetts, but it quickened in Connecticut with the election of Gurdon Saltonstall, minister of the first church in New London, as governor in 1707. At Saltonstall's urging, the General Assembly issued a call to the churches in May 1708 to send their ministers and lay representatives to meet in the several county towns "to consider and agree upon ... methods and rules for the management of ecclesiastical discipline." Delegates from the county meetings were then to meet in Saybrook and draft a single platform of church discipline to present to the assembly.[25]

The Saybrook Platform, which the assembly accepted and recommended to the churches in October 1708, erected a formal structure of ecclesiastical organization where none existed before. The platform called for a general council or association that would meet annually to discuss problems common to the churches, although it would have no substantive powers to enforce its recommendations. The platform also established county-wide associations of ministers to license and regulate the clergy and to "consider and resolve Questions and Cases of Importance which shall be offered by any amoung themselves or others." Most significantly, it created county consociations of ministers and lay delegates called messengers, with quasi-appellate authority in cases of church discipline and disputes.[26]

---

24. For general discussions of the early association movement, see Perry Miller, *The New England Mind: From Colony to Province*, pp. 209–68; David D. Hall, *The Faithful Shepherd: A History of the New England Ministry in the Seventeenth Century*, pp. 218–22; Paul R. Lucas, *Valley of Discord: Church and Society along the Connecticut River, 1636–1725*, pp. 144–45; Benjamin Trumbull, *A Complete History of Connecticut, Civil and Ecclesiastical*, 1:406–9.

25. *Conn. Rec.*, 5:51–52. On the failure of the association movement in Massachusetts, see Lucas, *Valley of Discord*, pp. 146–84; Walker, *Creeds and Platforms*, pp. 465–94.

26. *Conn. Rec.*, 5:87. The text of the Saybrook Platform is printed in Trumbull, *Complete History of Connecticut*, 1:410–14, and Walker, *Creeds and Platforms*, pp. 502–6.

Not all churches accepted the Saybrook Platform. Some that did placed restrictions on their associations and consociations.[27] Nonetheless, the juridical impulses of the Saybrook Platform transformed the structure of ecclesiastical discipline and created an environment in which legalism could, and did, flourish.

A concern for procedural regularity surfaced early in the several consociations and associations. At the first meeting of the consociation of New Haven county, the ministers and lay representatives debated the disciplinary articles of the Saybrook Platform and voted on how they would construe and apply each provision. The ministers of the North Association of Hartford County in 1719 discussed whether witnesses who had been properly summoned in ecclesiastical cases could refuse to testify without incurring censure and whether testimony could be taken although "not sworn by Civill authority." One of the first acts of the new Fairfield East Consociation after the division of the Fairfield County Consociation into eastern and western halves was to adopt eleven "overtures," which dealt primarily with procedural and jurisdictional matters. Three of the articles prescribed procedures for summoning parties and witnesses that closely paralleled the requirements for service of civil summons.[28]

The Fairfield East Consociation displayed a striking sense of procedural propriety in its hearings on a complaint against the perennially troubled first church of Stratford in 1738. When the principal complainant, Edmund Lewis, a justice of the peace and quorum for Fairfield County, objected against the moderator of the consociation for "being prejudg'd, with respect to the . . . complaint," the consociation chose another moderator "in his Roam pro ista vice" without comment or argument. The minister of the Stratford church then pleaded in bar of the complaint that he and the church had not been "orderly notified." The consociation ruled that it could not "without manifest

27. See Richard L. Bushman, *From Puritan to Yankee: Character and the Social Order in Connecticut, 1690–1760*, pp. 151–55; Lucas, *Valley of Discord*, pp. 189–93.

28. New Haven East Consociation Records, 1731–1893, A:1072m–1072n (meeting of the association, 27 Sept. 1748, at which the association ordered an account of the consociation meeting of 13 Apr. 1709 entered into the records); "A register of the Rules and Resolves of the North Association of the County of Hartford [1708–1800]," 10 (19 Aug. 1719); "A Book of Records for the Venerable the Eastern Consociation of the County of Fairfield [1736–1813]," 3–4 (17 Oct. 1738).

irregularity proceed to the Consideration of said caus or a judgment upon it" and dismissed the complaint because Lewis had not notified the Stratford church, "a Party nearly concerned in said Complaint," according to the rules established by the consociation. However, the consociation noted that it stood ready "as soon as may be to look into and judge upon such Case, when orderly brought before us, and all Persons duly notified according to our Constitution."[29]

For all their procedural formality, ecclesiastical councils had no means to compel compliance with their judgments other than the *in terrorem* effect of their exhortations. Thus, although legalism was latent in the conciliar apparatus itself, so were the limits to how far it could develop. Ironically, the ultimate unenforceability of ecclesiastical judgments may have contributed to the self-consciously legal character of council proceedings.

The use of legal language and procedure was a way to invoke the appearance of authority. That it was only the appearance, and not the substance, could be painfully clear. For example, in 1732 the first church of Guilford pleaded to the jurisdiction of a council by submitting "a paper denying the authority of the Council and declaring they thought it their duty not to submit that case to their determination." The council, with its best judicial demeanor, "overruled that plea and asserted their authority, and ordered the case to go forward." The church, however, refused to proceed. While the church remained adamant, the council could do nothing but sputter and issue a toothless judgment.[30]

Although often ineffectual, the invocation of legal formality was also natural. The language of law suited religion well. Both appealed to higher authority and spoke through rituals that excluded the uninitiated except as supplicants. As systems of authority, law and religion in the eighteenth century were no longer coequal as they had

29. Fairfield East Consoc. Rec., 6–8 (7–9 Oct. 1740).

30. Proceedings of council at Guilford, 21 Nov. 1732, Conn. Arch., Ecclesiastical Affairs (1st ser.), 4:200. The council was one of six that met in the course of a protracted and bitter dispute over settlement of a minister. The controversy eventually split the parish and led to the creation of the first poll parish within a territorial parish. For full accounts, see Bernard C. Steiner, *A History of the Plantation of Menunkatuck and of the Original Town of Guilford, Connecticut*, pp. 301–28; Trumbull, *Complete History of Connecticut*, 2:85–103; Bruce H. Mann, "Parishes, Law, and Community in Connecticut, 1700–1760," pp. 151–93.

been in the seventeenth. The formalization of ecclesiastical proceed-ings along legal lines implicitly acknowledged that inequality. In adopting the vocabulary and procedures of the civil law, churches and ecclesiastical councils conceded the authority of the formal legal sys-tem by paying it the compliment of trying to copy it.

With the spread of written complaints, dilatory pleadings, written testimony, and the like, it should not surprise us to see occasional, direct links between the worlds of secular law and ecclesiastical adju-dication. For example, an earlier council of eleven ministers and nine lay messengers in the Guilford dispute noted above rested its decision largely on an erroneous interpretation of two civil statutes enacted by the assembly to govern ecclesiastical affairs. The anomaly did not go unnoticed. The losing party complained to the assembly—thus ironi-cally invoking secular authority itself—that the council "have got a little beyond their own province" in determining "the meaning of the statutes of the land."[31]

Similarly, the ministers of the associations sometimes solicited advi-sory opinions from secular judges, which then became the basis for subsequent association decisions in like cases. For example, when James Moger's sister-in-law, the widow of his dead brother, took a civil oath charging him as the father of her bastard child, the church at New Fairfield thought "that Measures ought to be taken." Moger steadfastly maintained his innocence to the church, which in 1764 sought the advice of the Fairfield East Association. The association in turn solicited the advice of the county court, because "the Merits of the Case seem much to depend upon the Meaning of the Law of the Colony how much Weight is to be laid upon a Womans Oath in such a case" and "the Civil judges" are "the best capable of construing their own Laws." The judges of the Fairfield County Court concluded that the mother's oath alone, unsupported by other evidence, was insuffi-cient to prove a man guilty of fornication. Moger and the church then laid the case before the consociation, which considered the report of the judges and recommended that the church readmit Moger to communion.[32]

31. Council at Guilford, 10 Mar. 1731, Ezra Stiles Papers; Steiner, *History of Guilford*, p. 316. The petition itself is nowhere to be found in the Connecti-cut Archives, and there is no indication that the assembly ever acted on it.

32. Sherman [orig. New Fairfield North Church], North Congregational Church Records, 1744–1921, 1:23–24 (27 Mar., 10 Apr. 1764, 6 June 1765); "A Book of Records for the Reverend the East Association in the County of

Two years later, the same question came before the East Association of New Haven County, which adopted the same rule on its own, without consulting civil judges.[33] There was no reason for the second association to repeat the procedure of the first. Word of the Moger case would have circulated among the ministers at the annual meeting of the General Association in Hartford. Thus, when the problem arose in New Haven, the ministers there doubtless knew how their colleagues elsewhere had resolved it. The opinion of the judges became, in effect, law for the associations. The subordination of religion to law in matters of adjudication was complete.

II

René Grignon made his will on 20 March 1715, in his last illness. With the exception of four minor bequests, he gave everything, including "all Debts due to me from any person by book, bill, bond, or otherwise," to Mary Vrinne, a single woman who lived with him and whom he described as "my dear and well beloved friend." Grignon died a few days later. The estate inventory listed real and personal property appraised at slightly more than £1600. It also listed seventeen debts owed to Grignon on bills and bonds by eighteen men from nine towns in amounts which ranged from £2 9s. to £60, nearly £300 in all. The list of debts ends with the appraisers' notation that "What is due to him upon Book we cannot yet Come at."[34]

Mary Vrinne did not remain single for long. She married Nathaniel Clark of Saybrook, who quickly moved into Grignon's house and began casting the accounts in Grignon's book to determine who owed what. He had not completed the task when Grignon's house burned on 2 August 1715. The bills and bonds were lost, and the account book was charred beyond use.

The normal role of an executor in administering an estate included

---

Fairfield [1734–1813]," 70 (Oct. 1764) (reverse of volume of Fairfield East Consoc. Rec.); Fairfield East Consoc. Rec., 79 (May 1765).

33. New Haven East Consoc. Rec., 4:45–46 (26 May 1767).

34. Will of René Grignon and Inventory, Estate of René Grignon, Town of Norwich, New London Probate District, 1715, File No. 2317. There is no list of debts owed by the estate other than funeral and appraisal charges. Caulkins, however, remarked that there were many debts to be paid "and the residue was small." Caulkins, *History of Norwich*, p. 289.

collecting whatever debts may be due, by lawsuit if necessary. To sue, however, a creditor needed the evidence of the debt—a bill, bond, or book, depending on the nature of the debt. Richard Bushnell, executor of Grignon's estate, had none of these. Before the fire, however, Clark had compiled a list of forty-three debtors with the amounts that, by his reckoning, they owed on book—nearly £260 altogether. This list, and the list of bills and bonds contained in the estate inventory, encouraged Clark to petition the assembly for relief.[35]

Clark's petition has not survived, so it is not clear whether he made a specific request of the assembly or simply recited his tale of woe and prayed for whatever assistance they could grant. Later in the century, Zephaniah Swift wrote that if bonds or notes "are burnt, destroyed, or lost by any accident, equity may grant relief," but authority for such relief at the beginning of the century is uncertain. The assembly considered a bill in October 1715 that would have allowed Clark to sue in the county court on the bills, bonds, and book at law "as if [they] ware extant," proving the debts by the estate inventory or by swearing to the list he had made. That, however, would have abrogated the rules of evidence in a court of law, a move that gave the assembly pause. Instead, the assembly endorsed a proposal that "a sutable number of persons be commishanated to looke into the matter with full power to call persons before them, sware parties and evidences, and make decree or decrees Refering to such debt or debts." It named six men as commissioners and instructed the governor to issue their commission.[36]

The commission from the governor, Gurdon Saltonstall, contained the first reference to a court of equity. It stipulated the number for a quorum and authorized the commissioners to appoint a register or clerk to keep the files and records and issue writs of summons or attachment and execution. The commissioners were to proceed "according to the Rules of good Reason and Equity." The commission did not include any provision for appeal. Disappointed parties could have one review in the court from any decree upon "giving special bail as is

35. Bushnell may have urged Clark to petition. In addition to being a justice of the peace and a member of the New London County Court, Bushnell had been speaker of the lower house of the assembly in its most recent session.

36. Zephaniah Swift, *A System of the Laws of the State of Connecticut*, 2:461; Draft bill, Conn. Arch., Miscellaneous (1st ser.), 2:140; Committee bill, ibid., 2:141 (1715); *Conn. Rec.*, 5:533, 538–39. A committee representing both houses of the assembly made the compromise proposal.

usuall in other Courts in this Colony." To cover unforeseen contingencies, the commission made a general grant of "all such further and more ample power and authority . . . as shall be necessary according to the proceedings and Course of a Court of Equity."[37]

The novelty of the Grignon court of equity doubtless accounted for its organization and personnel. The rules in the governor's commission that dealt with summoning and examining parties and witnesses, keeping records, review, special bail, and the like, were patterned on similar rules in the county courts. The deliberateness of the pattern appears in the direction to the clerk to take an oath of office "in form of the oath of a County Clerk Mutatis mutandis."

The county court rules were a natural point of reference. The governor, who drafted the commission in consultation with his council, was a skillful lawyer. Moreover, the six commissioners chosen by the assembly exuded legal knowledge as well as personal authority. Five were assistants, and the sixth was elected an assistant the following year. Four were judges of the superior court, three were presiding judges of the county courts in their respective counties, two were probate judges for their counties. By experience and prestige, they were qualified for the "more Especiall trust and Confidence in your wisdom and integrity" that the governor invoked in his commission.[38]

The court first met in New London on 27 March 1716. It appointed a clerk and adjourned without further business. When it reconvened in Norwich on 15 August, the clerk read the enabling act and the governor's commission, whereupon the court adjourned to the next morning. Business the next day consisted entirely of Nathaniel Clark presenting bills of complaint to the commissioners on Bushnell's behalf, each bill reciting Clark's grievous loss and asking the court to summon the named debtor. The clerk issued the requested writs, and the court again adjourned to the next morning, Friday, 17 August.

At the adjourned session, thirty of the debtors, led by Colonel John Livingston and Captain Peter Mason, submitted a plea that challenged

37. Commission from Gurdon Saltonstall, 26 Oct. 1715, SCF 2.

38. *Conn. Rec.*, 5:491, 508–9, 547. The six commissioners were Peter Burr, Richard Christophers, Samuel Eells, Jonathan Law, William Pitkin, and Joseph Talcott. The following account is based on the records of the Court of Equity (no pagination, bound with 3 ½ SCR) and the papers of the court found in SCF 2, which include the pleas made and depositions taken in the various cases.

the legitimacy of the court and its proceedings. They asserted that there could be no court of chancery without either a royal commission or a special enabling clause in the charter, "both which are too apparentley wanting," and alleged various technical inadequacies in the rules and procedures of the court. The court, which was not inclined to deny its legitimacy, overruled the pleas. Clark had filed a lengthy reply that denied each assertion made by the debtors, but the legitimacy of the court and its procedures did not turn on questions of technical sufficiency. Clark recognized this himself when, near the end of his reply, he remarked, "I humbly Conceive this honorable Court is not bound [by] all the Rules in the Chauncery in England close att the heels any more than the Common pleas of this Colony [are by] the Common pleas in England."

After the court overruled the debtors' plea, three of the debtors who had signed the plea reached a settlement with Clark and Bushnell. The remaining debtors protested that Clark had not filed the bills of complaint in time to allow them to prepare their defenses. The court agreed that one day was rather short notice and continued their cases to November. Some of the debtors settled with Bushnell and Clark within a day, including Peter Mason, one of the principal instigators of the joint plea. Others went directly to trial with further pleadings and witnesses. Two debtors did not appear at all, and the court ordered writs of capias issued for their arrest.

Of the forty-four debtors initially summoned, twenty-five eventually settled with Clark and Bushnell, two never appeared, and one had his case continued to a session that may never have met. Of the sixteen cases that were tried, Clark and Bushnell recovered their full demand in only seven. At trial, Clark would state on oath that he had cast the debtor's account from Grignon's book before the fire and entered "the true balance" on the list presented in court. Six debtors swore that they had made payments that Grignon apparently had not recorded. In each instance the court accepted their sworn testimony as true, which for two of them meant that they owed nothing at all. None of the seven against whom Clark recovered the full amount he demanded testified on oath. Only nine of the forty-four debtors—the seven found to owe all and the two found to owe none of what Clark had claimed was due—denied that they had owed Grignon anything. For the rest, the only question was how much.

The same pattern applied to the ten debtors who were first summoned to the fourth session of the court, held in Norwich on 2 April 1717. None of the ten appear on the list Clark made before the fire and relied upon as evidence afterward. It seems, however, that Clark had been compiling a second list, which burned in the fire. The court allowed Clark to swear to what he remembered the balances to be. Seven of the actions, however, were captioned "sum uncertain." Of the ten cases, four of the debtors reached a settlement with Clark and Bushnell, three were able to prove that they owed nothing, and one successfully swore to partial payment of the debt. The remaining two cases were continued.

At the close of its session on 3 April 1717, the court adjourned to the following August. The adjournment is the last entry in the record —the remaining eleven pages are blank. Five cases had been reviewed or continued to the announced August session, but there is no indication that the court ever met again.[39]

III

The most curious aspect of the court of equity is that, after the initial joint plea with the thirty signatures, all of the debtors but one accepted the legitimacy of the court. The sole exception was John Livingston of New London, the prime mover of the joint plea. Despite a barrage of pleadings and evidence from Livingston, the court ruled against him for the full £11 11s. that Clark and Bushnell demanded. On 3 April 1717, Livingston addressed a letter to "the Court of Eq-

39. Two cases in the record note that writs of execution were granted in July and December 1717 and returned unlevied. Those entries may mean only that the clerk of the court, Christopher Christophers, still had the record book and authority to issue writs of execution. The files contain several writs of summons and attachment against one James Poison, who was listed in the estate inventory as Grignon's largest debtor, on a bond for sixty pounds. Poison never appeared in court at the sessions covered by the record book. The last writ of attachment on file is one issued by Christophers against Poison on 2 May 1721, returnable to the court of equity to be held that month in Hartford. The sheriff's return reported that he had attached Poison's body on 15 May and taken bond for his appearance. The court may have met then. The assembly had just adjourned, and all six of the original commissioners were in Hartford. In all probability, however, Clark was simply making a last effort to collect the largest outstanding debt. It is unlikely that the court met again after its last recorded session. See Writ of attachment, 2 May 1721, Bushnell v. Poison, SCF 2. Another file in SCF 3 contains Clark's prosecution bond, dated 2 May 1721, for that action.

uity (so called)" that referred to the adverse judgment and concluded, "Yet being under the happie Liberties of a Subject of the Crown of England and accounting myselfe hardly dealt withall in being denied the Libertie of a Jury, If still, I must be denied that privilidge I do appeal to the General Assembly to be holden at Hartford in May next."[40]

Livingston, however, never appealed to the assembly. Nor did any of the other debtors, even though the legitimacy of the court was doubtful, at best. Why did the debtors acquiesce without so much as a protest to the assembly? Perhaps they did so because in over three-quarters of the cases the question was not whether the debtor owed anything, merely how much. Most of the debtors were willing to concede that they owed something. Under those circumstances, the willingness of the court to accept any evidence of payment or offset to which the debtor would swear defused much of the opposition to the court.

Livingston's persistent antagonism suggests a further explanation. His insistence upon a jury strikes a modern note in its concern for the niceties of common law procedure. None of the other debtors felt similarly aggrieved, at least not so much that they joined Livingston in continued protest. For them, oaths still mattered. The court of equity provided a procedure that, though irregular, seemed fair enough. If the debtors did not object to a nonlegal mode of procedure, it may be that they did not yet accept the formal legal system as the sole model for handling private disputes.

As late as the beginning of the eighteenth century, disputing was a rather pluralist affair in terms of the procedural options that were available. Common law courts were not the only legitimate tribunals, and common law procedures were not the only legitimate rules. This is not to suggest that the alternatives were necessarily informal or that they offered only substantively irrational justice. Rather, their formality was not determined solely by reference to the legal system. Early arbitration, church disciplinary proceedings, and the Grignon court of equity were all, in their own ways, formal processes. Each had its own standard of procedural regularity that the participants recognized, accepted, and expected. The different tribunals and procedures suited the different disputes and disputants.

40. John Livingston to the Court of Equity, 3 Apr. 1717, Bushnell v. Livingston, SCF 2.

Within a short time, however, Livingston's position became the dominant one. The formal legal system became the standard for adjudicating disputes. The language and procedures of the common law insinuated themselves into arbitration and church proceedings and transformed them from distinctive alternatives to litigation to pale imitations of legal adjudication. The issue of a court of equity did not arise again in Connecticut until 1770, when the assembly rejected a bill to establish one.[41] Long before then, the formal legal system had established its hegemony over the ways people chose to settle their disputes. The notion of law, formally applied, prevailed.

41. Conn. Arch., Civil Officers (2d ser.), 1:81. The assembly allowed a similar bill to die in 1772. Conn. Arch., Miscellaneous (1st ser.), 3:308.

6

NEIGHBORS AND STRANGERS

In 1718, John Guy sued John Chidsey for a small book debt and won. The two men were from neighboring parishes in New Haven. A local justice of the peace rendered the judgment. Chidsey appealed to the county court. There, his attorney, Micah Palmer, asked to see Guy's book. Guy produced the account, whereupon Palmer pleaded "that it was the account of A Stranger and not Sufficient Evidence to Maintain the action" against Chidsey. Guy was taken aback by the plea. In a line worthy of vaudeville, he replied that "the account is not brought against a stranger but against the wife of said Chidsey." And so it was. She had incurred the debt before she married Chidsey, upon which blessed event he, like all husbands, became liable for his wife's previous debts. That, however, was not what Guy had alleged. He had claimed that it was Chidsey who owed him the money on book. Chidsey was, to be sure, liable, but not because it was his book. He was liable because it was his wife's debt. Still somewhat confused as to why that should make a difference, but nonetheless acknowledging the distinction, Guy withdrew his reply and pleaded instead "that allthough the account was at the time of making . . . the account of a stranger yet now that stranger is . . . the wife of the said Chidsey and by his marying her it became his debt and an action well lyeth against him for it." Chidsey admitted that all this was true, but argued that that was not what Guy had said in his writ. The judges agreed and ruled that Guy had no action on the writ.[1]

What is striking about the story is Guy's confusion, so palpable in the draft pleadings, over the word "stranger." Chidsey and his attorney used it as a legal term of art to denote a person who was not a party to the alleged dealings between Guy and Chidsey. Guy, on the other hand, initially understood the term in its lay sense. He could not fathom how a man's wife could be a stranger. She certainly was no

1. Guy v. Chidsey, 3 NHCCR 105–6, NHCCF 1 (1719).

stranger to Guy. They had traded on book and lived in the same town. In that sense, they were neighbors. And yet, as Guy had pleaded his case, they were unquestionably strangers, at least insofar as the law was concerned.

Guy's confusion captures a moment of equipoise in the legal and social history of Connecticut. Guy was a frequent, although not terribly skilled, litigator. He was a trader who appeared in court regularly to sue for his debts, which he often lost because of some procedural misstep. Legal formality was not his strong suit. Yet, as his revised plea indicated, with a little prodding he knew enough of the rules to play the game. The game, however, was an unnatural one. It could turn neighbors into strangers, regardless of where they lived or how well they knew one another, simply by applying a formal test of legal relevance that did not depend on subjective criteria. That test, in time, superseded an older test that had made relevance a function of the social context of the dispute, as broad or as narrow as the relations between the litigants required. The shift from one test to the other reflected deeper changes in social and economic relations and, ultimately, in the nature of community.

One cannot, of course, explain every legal development in social terms. The fit between law and society is imperfect at best. Yet one sometimes finds convergences. The communal elements of law and disputing in the seventeenth century are inescapable. Whether people pleaded their cases in court, submitted them to arbitration, or took them before the church, the forms and procedures they used did not place artificial constraints on their ability to address their grievances. The breadth of relevant evidence in book debt actions or in actions submitted to the jury under the general issue allowed litigants to air their differences as fully as they thought necessary. The discretion of arbitrators to tailor individual awards and the liberty of disputants to define the scope of their submission made arbitration a popular and effective alternative to formal legal process. Church disciplinary proceedings were the purest form of communal adjudication—judgments by communities of believers of their fellow members. Each of these ways of disputing offered the potential of helping people reconcile their differences in a manner that allowed them to resume their sometimes quarrelsome, but mutually dependent, neighborly relations.

"Neighborly" in this context did not mean a soft glow of vague good feelings. Rather, it referred to the obligations and interdependencies that defined community in seventeenth-century Connecticut. By necessity as well as by ideal, neighbors had to live together, if not in peace, then at least in a truce. How they settled their disputes reflected that reality. Rather than transplant the common law in all its rigorous glory, they adopted practices and procedures that treated disputes individually within a community context. Breaches in social relations were inevitable. But, if handled properly, they did not have to become permanent—unless, of course, that was what the parties wanted.

Disputing changed dramatically in the eighteenth century. Little that was legal or lawlike remained untouched. The formal legal system grew more formalistic, less accommodating to the vagaries and eccentricities of individual disputes. The "informal" legal system, if one may call it that, of arbitration and church proceedings became a denatured shell of its seventeenth-century self, waxing formalistic while waning in significance. The component strands of these changes were several, and their causes were diverse, but they tended in the same direction and were part of the same general process.

In the large area of debt litigation, the changes were closely tied to commercialization of the economy and to the changing social context of economic relations. In the equally large area of pleading and procedure, formalization was a largely autonomous development that owed less to shifts in economy or society and more to the tendency of lawyers to treat law as normative fact. Lawyers in the common law tradition are bound by acquired habits of thought that determine how they define and address legal problems. Although lawyers themselves may be creatures of their surroundings, the way they think about law is not so bound. That detachment, which can be professionally self-serving, is what allows legal reasoning and the procedures that embody it to become as much ends in themselves as means to the resolution of disputes.[2] In the seventeenth century, the means mattered. There were neighborly and unneighborly ways of disputing. The blurring of that

2. Max Weber discussed the relationship between legal training and legal thinking in *Economy and Society: An Outline of Interpretive Sociology*, 2:775–76, 784–802. Alan Watson has described the relationship pithily: "There is a lawyer's way to approach a problem. This mode of thinking inoculates them from too much concern with the demands of the society." Alan Watson, *The Evolution of Law*, p. 42. William Samuel Johnson, a prominent attorney and later a judge, stated the detachment well when he advised a client that the law was against him, "yet If you think proper to imploy me I have no objection against bringing the matter for you to a fair Trial and indeavouring to support the Sale by the best arguments I can devise for Lawyers are not obliged never to say anything against their own opinions

distinction in the eighteenth century epitomized the changing relationship between law and community.

Other elements contributed to the new face of disputing as well. Technical pleadings, which defined issues in legal terms rather than factual ones, sharply limited the use and discretion of the jury. Moreover, the fact that pleading now had rules that were best understood by lawyers effectively introduced a third party into litigation. Lawyers were not disinterested parties, nor were their clients' interests wholly congruent with their own. When lawyers arrogated control of pleading to themselves, civil litigation moved away from a communal model in which the disputants had argued their grievances themselves under the general issue and laid their differences before the jury with little regard for niceties of legal form. Instead, litigation became sparring matches controlled by technical rules in which lawyers were the actors, the nominal litigants were mute spectators, and facts were intrinsically worth less than how one pleaded them. The recreational qualities of litigation now seemed more for the entertainment of the lawyers than of the litigants.

The changes in pleading and the use of juries—which were not primarily social or economic in origin—dovetailed with the changes in debt litigation—which were—to transform the nature of local litigation. The social contexts of disputes became increasingly irrelevant, at least insofar as the formal legal system was concerned. The decline of the civil jury, the use of pleadings that framed generalizable legal issues rather than individualized factual ones, the spread of instruments that were adjudicated on formal rather than substantive criteria, the ascendance of lawyers for whom law was a business rather than a means of securing redress, and, above all, the appearance of these changes within towns as well as without—all point to the conclusion that law became less responsive to individual communities.

The significance of law becoming less communal in the eighteenth century lay in the fact that community changed as well. The ideal of community persisted.[3] But the reality was different. Population

---

both because they are fallible and their opinions may be and often are wrong and because free dispute and candid Examination are the glory of Englishmen and of English Tribunals." William Samuel Johnson to John Provoost, 20 Dec. 1762, William Samuel Johnson Papers, Letterbooks, 12.

3. On the continued appeal of the norms and values of community, see James A. Henretta, "The Morphology of New England Society in the Colo-

growth, migration, commercialization, economic stratification, war, and religious revival had swept over individual towns, leaving behind people who could not forget what they had seen and experienced. Many things, of course, remained the same. Life for most people was still agrarian. Whatever changes did occur were superimposed on a society that was fundamentally traditional. Nonetheless, there were changes. In the seventeenth century the town had been the focus of community. In the eighteenth century it was not. Towns fell victim to increasing size and, more importantly, internal diversity. Not that they faded into obsolescence, but they ceased to be the primary community to which people belonged.

As changes in economy and society drew people outside their towns, traditional patterns of social relations gave way in part to patterns that were organized on different principles. For example, the persistence of book debt in intratown debt transactions in urban towns suggests a community defined by commercial relations. Merchants, shopkeepers, artisans, and their customers traded with one another in concentrated business districts. They developed courses of dealing that were regular, mutually beneficial, and worth preserving. Book accounts facilitated these local exchanges and provided a link between the former town community and the newer community of the marketplace.

Similarly, church disciplinary proceedings remained communal, but their community was no longer that of the town. The multiplication of parishes and dissenting congregations meant that most townspeople lay outside the jurisdiction of any single church. Asa Merrills illustrated this boldly when, after the fourth church in Hartford ordered him to make gospel satisfaction for defaming the minister, he converted to Anglicanism and declared to his former brethren that he "had nothing further to do with the Church."[4]

Of the new kinds of community, the one that most closely approximated the town was the parish. Parish inhabitants gathered in parish meeting to elect officers, appoint committees, discuss repairs to the meetinghouse, levy taxes to support the minister and other parish

---

nial Period"; Kenneth A. Lockridge, "Social Change and the Meaning of the American Revolution"; and James A. Henretta, "Families and Farms: *Mentalité* in Pre-Industrial America."

4. West Hartford [orig. Hartford Fourth Church], Congregational Church Records, 1713–1924, 1:169 (2 Aug. 1759).

responsibilities, hire a schoolmaster, debate the investment of parish funds, and worry over lawsuits brought by or against the parish—activities they had formerly attended to in town meeting.[5] Nonetheless, the parish was too small to be the complete, all-encompassing community that the town had been. In an increasingly commercial economy, parishes could not replicate the economic insularity of seventeenth-century towns. Nor could they be as socially or politically self-contained as towns had been. Parish inhabitants continued to participate in town affairs. Traders, itinerant preachers, court days, markets, and the like served as continual reminders of the world beyond the parish or town.

The eclipse of the town as the primary focus of community did not necessarily mean that community declined. On the contrary, petitions to the assembly for parish privileges were affirmations of community. Each petition was a collective act by neighbors who shared more of the indicia of community with one another than they did with more distant fellow townsmen.[6] But the community thus affirmed was not that of the town. By the 1770s more than half the towns in the colony contained parishes that crossed town lines and covered adjoining parts of two or more towns.[7] The boundaries of community were natural, not artificial. They were drawn around networks of social interactions, which in the eighteenth century could not be contained within town limits.

Law became less communal in part because community itself changed. Law and community diverged, as law became more general

5. For a discussion of the emergence of the parish as a legal entity, see Bruce H. Mann, "Parishes, Law, and Community in Connecticut, 1700–1760," pp. 102–50.

6. Gregory Nobles advances a similar argument with respect to town divisions in western Massachusetts. See Gregory H. Nobles, *Divisions throughout the Whole: Politics and Society in Hampshire County, Massachusetts, 1740–1775*, pp. 132–54. Richard Bushman discusses the proliferation of parishes in a somewhat different light as more of a fragmentation of community. Richard L. Bushman, *From Puritan to Yankee: Character and the Social Order in Connecticut, 1690–1765*, pp. 54–72. Parish divisions could be handled amicably, as Christine Heyrman found in Gloucester. Christine Leigh Heyrman, *Commerce and Culture: The Maritime Communities of Massachusetts, 1690–1750*, pp. 52–95.

7. Bruce C. Daniels, *The Connecticut Town: Growth and Development, 1635–1790*, p. 98.

and community more particular. The gains in certainty, predictability, and uniformity that accompanied the formalization of legal practice and procedure allowed people from different communities to deal with one another within the common framework of an integrated legal system. They also allowed people to treat their neighbors as they did strangers, at least in terms of their legal relations.

One consequence of the divergence of law and community was that the formal legal system became the standard for all forms of disputing. The changes in arbitration and church disciplinary procedure—two quintessentially communal forms of disputing—demonstrated the growing hegemony of the formal legal system over the ways in which people resolved their differences. That hegemony marked both an end and a beginning. It was the end of a time when communities of people tied together in multilayered relations could, in effect, create their own law through flexible means of keeping accounts, liberal use of juries and pleadings, arbitration, and the like. Such communities did not, of course, disappear, but they no longer predominated. Smaller, more specialized units such as the parish, however effective they were in recreating elements of community, could not create their own law in any general sense.

The hegemony of the formal legal system was also a beginning. The growing formalism of nonlegal forms of disputing suggests the emergence of a new consensus on the proper role of law in society, a role that had to be larger than individual communities if communities, however defined, were to coexist in society. It may be that the development of a legalist paradigm, with its emphasis on generalizable, predictable rules and results rather than on individualized inquiries and remedies, was an essential part of the development of a revolutionary ideology that transcended particular communities and united the several colonies into a new nation. Whether it was or not, it seems clear that law by the middle of the eighteenth century had become less identified with community and more with society.

The redefinition of the relationship between law and society was not a process that ended with the Revolution, nor did it continue uninterrupted in a single direction, as crude modernization theory would suggest. It was a dynamic relationship, not a static one. But the legal changes discussed here marked a divide. Law afterward partook more of states than of communities. The distinction was never absolute, but the course was clear. Informal, neighborly ways of disputing continued. Once, however, they had been the rule. Now they were the exceptions to a norm defined by the formal legal system. It may be that, like people and their faces, societies get the law they deserve. For the people who sensed the divergence of law and community in the eighteenth century, we now understand better what they saw in the mirror.

APPENDIX

Debt Actions in the Hartford County Court, 1700–1760
(in Percentages)

Decade[a]	Book	Bond	Note[b]	Total	N
1700	82.9	2.9	14.3	100	35
1710	65.5	21.8	12.6	100	87
1720	29.7	49.3	20.9	100	296
1730	19.5	16.2	64.3	100	653
1740	20.9	9.7	69.4	100	900
1750	17.0	3.8	79.1	100	599
1760	25.6	1.9	72.5	100	313

[a] "Decade" in this and subsequent tables denotes aggregated data from two court sessions in the listed year and two sessions from five years later. For example, *1700* includes data from *1700* and *1705*. The sole exception is *1760*, which includes data from two court sessions in that year only.

[b] The category of "note" here includes promissory notes and the far less numerous bills obligatory.

TABLE 2

Contested and Uncontested Debt Actions in the Hartford County Court,
1700–1760 (in Percentages)

Decade	1700	1710	1720	1730	1740	1750	1760
Book							
Contested	64.3	42.6	49.4	26.0	24.0	34.0	28.0
Uncontested	35.7	57.4	50.6	74.0	76.0	66.0	72.0
N	29	54	83	123	183	100	75
Bond							
Contested	0	42.1	31.2	10.5	10.3	36.4	16.7
Uncontested	0	57.9	68.8	89.5	89.7	63.6	83.3
N	0	19	141	105	87	22	6
Note							
Contested	50.0	57.1	21.0	2.7	5.8	8.1	6.3
Uncontested	50.0	42.9	79.0	97.3	94.2	91.9	93.7
N	6[a]	11[a]	61	415	619	471	224
Total Written							
Instruments							
Contested	40.0	40.0	29.2	4.4	6.4	9.3	6.5
Uncontested	60.0	60.0	70.8	95.6	93.6	90.7	93.5
N	6	30	202	520	706	493	230

[a] All of the instruments reported here as notes were bills obligatory.

TABLE 3

Intratown Debt Actions in Country Towns in the Hartford County Court, 1710–1760 (in Percentages)

Decade	Book	Bond	Note	Total	N
1710	77.8	22.2	0	100	9
1720	14.3	71.4	14.3	100	42
1730	7.1	15.3	77.6	100	98
1740	7.9	5.2	86.9	100	229
1750	12.9	0.6	86.5	100	163
1760	21.3	1.1	77.7	100	94

TABLE 4

*Intratown Debt Actions in Secondary Towns in the Hartford County Court,
1710–1760* (in Percentages)

Decade	Book	Bond	Note	Total	N
1710	66.7	33.3	0	100	15
1720	26.7	61.9	11.4	100	105
1730	20.5	15.4	64.2	100	254
1740	18.3	6.3	75.4	100	284
1750	17.5	1.3	81.2	100	154
1760	30.9	0	69.1	100	81

TABLE 5

Intratown Debt Actions in Urban Towns in the Hartford County Court,
1710–1760 (in Percentages)

Decade	Book	Bond	Note	Total	N
1710	76.0	22.0	2.0	100	50
1720	39.1	35.5	25.4	100	138
1730	23.1	16.6	60.3	100	290
1740	31.6	14.5	53.9	100	373
1750	19.7	6.2	74.1	100	274
1760	26.8	3.9	69.3	100	127

TABLE 6

Distance and Rates of Contest in Debt Actions in the Hartford County Court, 1715–1760 (in Percentages)

	1715–1735	1740–1760
Book		
Intratown	34.7	43.0
Intertown	65.3	57.0
Total	100.0	100.0
Contested	36.7	28.2
Uncontested	63.3	71.8
Total	100.0	100.0
N	248	351
Written Instruments		
Intratown	42.7	39.6
Intertown	57.3	60.4
Total	100.0	100.0
Contested	12.0	7.4
Uncontested	88.0	92.6
Total	100.0	100.0
N	724	1364

TABLE 7

Intratown/Intertown Comparison of Contested and Uncontested Debt Actions in the Hartford County Court, 1715–1760 (in Percentages)

	1715–1735	1740–1760
Book		
Contested		
Intratown	37.4	47.5
Intertown	62.6	52.5
Total	100.0	100.0
N	91	99
Uncontested		
Intratown	33.1	41.3
Intertown	66.9	58.7
Total	100.0	100.0
N	157	252
Written Instruments		
Contested		
Intratown	43.7	35.6
Intertown	56.3	64.4
Total	100.0	100.0
N	87	101
Uncontested		
Intratown	42.5	39.9
Intertown	57.5	60.1
Total	100.0	100.0
N	637	1263

TABLE 8

Residence of Debtors in Debt Actions in the Hartford County Court,
1720–1760 (in Percentages)

Decade		Book			
	Urban town	Secondary town	Country town	Total	N
1720	37.8	46.3	15.9	100	82
1730	23.0	52.5	24.6	100	122
1740	37.9	29.1	33.0	100	179
1750	37.8	26.5	35.7	100	98
1760	32.4	35.1	32.4	100	74
		Written Instruments			
	Urban town	Secondary town	Country town	Total	N
1720	32.5	45.2	22.3	100	197
1730	38.5	37.5	24.0	100	509
1740	27.0	35.6	37.4	100	682
1750	37.0	28.9	34.0	100	470
1760	27.4	35.8	36.8	100	212

TABLE 9

Residence of Debtors in Intertown Debt Actions in the Hartford County Court, 1720–1760 (in Percentages)

| Decade | Book | | | | |
	Urban town	Secondary town	Country town	Total	N
1720	25.5	49.0	25.5	100	51
1730	18.3	47.6	34.1	100	82
1740	14.7	34.3	51.0	100	102
1750	19.6	35.3	45.1	100	51
1760	23.4	38.3	38.3	100	47

| | Written Instruments | | | | |
	Urban town	Secondary town	Country town	Total	N
1720	27.5	45.8	26.7	100	120
1730	32.7	34.9	32.4	100	281
1740	20.2	33.7	46.1	100	371
1750	29.2	32.0	38.9	100	319
1760	20.1	35.1	44.8	100	134

TABLE 10
Rates of Contest among Urban and Rural Debtors in the Hartford County Court, 1720–1760 (in Percentages)

	1720	1730	1740	1750	1760
Book (Intratown)					
Urban debtors					
Contested	66.7	15.4	24.5	37.0	30.8
Uncontested	33.3	84.6	75.5	63.0	69.2
N	18	13	53	27	13
Rural debtors					
Contested	0	0	28.6	50.0	33.3
Uncontested	0	100.0	71.4	50.0	66.7
N	0	12	7	12	6
Book (Intertown)					
Urban debtors					
Contested	61.5	33.3	26.7	21.4	18.2
Uncontested	38.5	66.7	73.3	78.6	81.8
N	13	15	15	14	11
Rural debtors					
Contested	46.2	21.4	21.2	30.8	22.2
Uncontested	53.8	78.6	78.8	69.2	77.8
N	13	28	52	26	18
Written Instruments					
(Intratown)					
Urban debtors					
Contested	38.7	3.8	2.8	4.9	0
Uncontested	61.3	96.2	97.2	95.1	100.0
N	31	104	109	81	31
Rural debtors					
Contested	25.0	0	6.0	11.1	22.2
Uncontested	75.0	100.0	94.0	88.9	77.8
N	12	31	84	36	18
Written Instruments					
(Intertown)					
Urban debtors					
Contested	33.3	3.3	8.0	8.6	3.7
Uncontested	66.7	96.7	92.0	91.4	96.3
N	33	92	75	93	27
Rural debtors					
Contested	18.2	4.4	6.4	7.3	10.0
Uncontested	81.8	95.6	93.6	92.7	90.0
N	32	91	171	124	60

TABLE II

Rates of Contest in Intratown and Intertown Debt Actions in the Hartford County Court, 1710–1760 (in Percentages)

	1710	1720	1730	1740	1750	1760
Book						
Intratown						
Contested	44.4	54.8	27.5	27.3	36.2	33.3
Uncontested	55.6	45.2	72.5	72.7	63.8	66.7
N	18	31	40	77	47	27
Intertown						
Contested	40.6	47.1	25.6	22.5	33.3	25.3
Uncontested	59.4	52.9	74.4	77.5	66.7	74.7
N	32	51	82	102	51	47
Written Instruments						
Intratown						
Contested	50.0	31.2	4.8	6.1	7.3	7.7
Uncontested	50.0	68.8	95.2	93.9	92.7	92.3
N	10	77	228	311	151	78
Intertown						
Contested	38.9	29.2	3.2	7.0	9.4	6.7
Uncontested	61.1	70.8	96.8	93.0	90.6	93.3
N	18	120	281	371	319	134

TABLE 12

Jury Verdicts and Bench Judgments in Contested Civil Actions and Contested Debt Actions (Intratown and Intertown) in the Hartford County Court, 1710–1760 (in Percentages)

Decade	All Civil Actions							
	Intratown				Intertown			
	Jury	Bench	Total	N	Jury	Bench	Total	N
1710	51.4	48.6	100	37	40.5	59.5	100	37
1720	33.9	66.1	100	62	25.0	75.0	100	80
1730	31.6	68.4	100	57	21.0	79.0	100	62
1740	20.9	79.1	100	67	9.7	90.3	100	72
1750	22.2	77.8	100	63	12.5	87.5	100	72
1760	17.2	82.8	100	29	5.6	94.4	100	36

Decade	Debt Actions Only							
	Intratown				Intertown			
	Jury	Bench	Total	N	Jury	Bench	Total	N
1710	35.7	64.3	100	14	45.5	54.5	100	22
1720	24.4	75.6	100	41	22.2	77.8	100	63
1730	23.8	76.2	100	21	20.6	79.4	100	34
1740	25.0	75.0	100	40	8.2	91.8	100	49
1750	14.3	85.7	100	28	10.0	90.0	100	50
1760	6.7	93.3	100	15	8.7	91.3	100	23

TABLE 13

Jury Verdicts and Bench Judgments in Contested Civil Actions in the
Hartford County Court, 1710–1760 (in Percentages)

Decade	Debt Actions Only [a]				Other Civil Actions			
	Jury	Bench	Total	N	Jury	Bench	Total	N
1710	42.1	57.9	100	38	55.2	44.8	100	58
1720	23.0	77.0	100	100	39.0	61.0	100	77
1730	22.8	77.2	100	57	27.8	72.2	100	126
1740	15.5	84.5	100	84	24.2	75.8	100	99
1750	11.1	88.9	100	81	34.7	65.3	100	124
1760	7.9	92.1	100	38	40.8	59.2	100	71

	All Civil Actions			
	Jury	Bench	Total	N
1710	50.0	50.0	100	96
1720	29.4	70.6	100	177
1730	26.2	73.8	100	183
1740	20.2	79.8	100	183
1750	25.4	74.6	100	205
1760	29.4	70.6	100	109

[a] I counted the occasional special verdict as a jury verdict because in both instances the litigants submitted the issue to the jury for decision, regardless of what the jury then did with it. I counted rulings that sustained pleas in abatement as bench judgments unless the plaintiff amended his writ or appealed the ruling because such rulings effectively ended the litigation by judicial action.

TABLE 14

Jury Verdicts and Bench Judgments in Contested Debt Actions in the Hartford County Court, 1710–1760 (in Percentages)

	Book Actions Only				Written Instruments Only			
	Jury	Bench	Total	N	Jury	Bench	Total	N
1710	52.2	47.8	100	23	25.0	75.0	100	12
1720	41.5	58.5	100	41	10.2	89.8	100	59
1730	26.7	73.3	100	30	17.4	82.6	100	23
1740	16.3	83.7	100	43	14.6	85.4	100	41
1750	11.8	88.2	100	34	10.9	89.1	100	46
1760	0	100.0	100	21	20.0	80.0	100	15

	All Debt Actions[a]			
	Jury	Bench	Total	N
1710	42.1	57.9	100	38
1720	23.0	77.0	100	100
1730	22.8	77.2	100	57
1740	15.5	84.5	100	84
1750	11.1	88.9	100	81
1760	7.9	92.1	100	38

[a] The figures for all contested debt actions include a very small number of actions of debt grounded on oral promises rather than on book accounts or written instruments.

TABLE 15

Defendant's Initial Plea in Contested Civil Actions in the Hartford County Court, 1710–1760 (in Percentages)

	Denial	Bar	Abate-ment	Demur-rer	Total	N
1710	25.0	35.0	40.0	0	100	20
1715	29.4	15.7	52.9	2.0	100	51
1720	7.7	7.7	74.4	10.3	100	39
1725	25.8	7.2	12.4	54.6	100	97
1730	15.6	7.8	15.6	60.9	100	64
1735	22.8	14.0	21.1	42.1	100	57
1740	9.2	4.6	24.6	61.5	100	65
1745	7.2	18.8	17.4	56.5	100	69
1750	23.6	12.7	12.7	50.9	100	55
1755	6.7	9.3	14.7	69.3	100	75
1760	8.3	10.0	5.0	76.7	100	60

TABLE 16

Defendant's Initial Plea in Contested Civil Actions in the Hartford County Court, 1710–1760—Summary (in Percentages)

	Factual Pleas	Legal Pleas	Total	N
1710	60.0	40.0	100	20
1715	45.1	54.9	100	51
1720	15.4	84.6	100	39
1725	33.0	67.0	100	97
1730	23.4	76.6	100	64
1735	36.8	63.2	100	57
1740	13.9	86.2	100	65
1745	26.1	73.9	100	69
1750	36.4	63.6	100	55
1755	16.0	84.0	100	75
1760	18.3	81.7	100	60

BIBLIOGRAPHY

MANUSCRIPT SOURCES

Congregational House, Hartford

"A Book of Records for the Reverend the East Association in the County of Fairfield [1734–1813]"

"A Book of Records for the Venerable the Eastern Consociation of the County of Fairfield [1736–1813]"

New Haven East Consociation Records, 1731–1893

New London County Association Records, 1709–1788

"A register of the Rules and Resolves of the North Association of the County of Hartford [1708–1800]"

"The South Association of Hartford County Book of Records [1744–1822]"

Connecticut Historical Society, Hartford

William Samuel Johnson Papers

Jonathan Law Papers

Farmington Inferior Court Records, 1770–1773

Farmington, Justice Court Records, 1741–1750 [Thomas Hart, J.P.]

Glastonbury Inferior Court Records, 1753–1765

Windham, Justice Court Records, 1754–1761: "First Record Book of Samuel Gray, Esq., of Windham, from June 6, 1754 to April 2, 1761"

Windsor Inferior Court Records, 1719–1734

Connecticut State Library, Hartford

Court and Assembly Records

    Connecticut Archives (Civil Officers, Ecclesiastical Affairs, Miscellaneous, Private Controversies)

    Court of Assistants Records, 1665–1711

    Hartford County Court Records, 1666–1855 (records for 1677–1706 are in Records of the Hartford County Probate Court), and Files, 1713–1855

New Haven County Court Records, 1666–1855, and Files, 1700–1855
New London County Court Records, 1665–1834, and Files, 1691–1855
New London Justice Court Records, 1739–1774
Superior Court Records, 1711–1798, and Files, 1712–1760

Church Records

East Haddam, First Congregational Church and Ecclesiastical Society Records, 1702–1927

East Hartford, First Congregational Church and Ecclesiastical Society Records, 1699–1913

Farmington, First Church of Christ (Congregational) Records, 1652–1938

Kent, Congregational Church Records, 1729–1823

Lebanon, First Ecclesiastical Society and Congregational Church Records, 1700–1883

Mansfield, First Congregational Church Records, 1710–1788

Middletown, First Congregational Church Records, 1668–1871

North Woodstock [orig. Woodstock First Church], Congregational Church Records, 1727–1900

Norwich, First Congregational Church Records, 1699–1917

Plainfield, First Congregational Church Records, 1747–1899

Putnam [orig. North Killingly Church], First Congregational Church Records, 1715–1904

Redding, Congregational Church and Ecclesiastical Society Records, 1729–1882

Scotland [orig. Windham Third Church], Congregational Church Records, 1732–1915

Sherman [orig. New Fairfield North Church], North Congregational Church Records, 1744–1921

South Windsor [orig. Windsor Second Church], First Congregational Church Records, 1694–1898

Voluntown and Sterling, Congregational Church Records, 1723–1914

West Hartford [orig. Hartford Fourth Church], Congregational Church Records, 1713–1924

Account Books and Letterbooks

Account Book of James Harris, Saybrook, Day Book 3, 1733–1747

Account Book of George Stillman, Wethersfield, 1725–1784

Account Books of Jacob Witter, Norwich, 1758–1811

Letterbook of John Ellery, Jr.

Town Clerk's Office, Guilford, Connecticut

Proprietors Records

Yale University (Sterling Memorial Library), New Haven

Chauncey Family Papers
William Griswold Lane Memorial Collection
Talman Family Papers
"The Record of the Votes and Doings of the Proprietors of the Common field in Guilford called the Great Oxpasture [1729–1811]," Connecticut Miscellaneous Mss., Ser. III: Towns (Guilford)

PRINTED SOURCES, TREATISES, AND PAMPHLETS

Legal Sources

Acts and Laws of His Majesties Colony of Connecticut in New-England. New London, Conn., 1715.
Acts and Laws of His Majesty's English Colony of Connecticut in New-England in America. New London, Conn., 1750.
The Book of the General Laws of the People Within the Jurisdiction of Connecticut. Cambridge, Mass., 1673.
Fane, Francis. *Reports on the Laws of Connecticut.* Edited by Charles M. Andrews. New Haven, Conn., 1915.
Johnson, William Samuel. *The Superior Court Diary of William Samuel Johnson, 1772–1773.* Edited by John T. Farrell. Washington, D.C., 1942.
Lacy, Norbert B., ed. "Records of the Court of Assistants of Connecticut, 1665–1701." M.A. thesis, Yale University, 1937.
Records of the Particular Court of Connecticut, 1639–1663. Connecticut Historical Society, *Collections,* 22. Hartford, Conn., 1928.
Shurtleff, Nathaniel B., ed. *Records of the Governor and Company of the Massachusetts Bay in New England.* 5 vols. Boston, 1853–54.
Trumbull, J. Hammond, and Hoadly, Charles J., eds. *The Public Records of the Colony of Connecticut, 1636–1776.* 15 vols. Hartford, Conn., 1850–90.

Treatises

Beawes, Wyndham. *Lex Mercatoria: Or, a Complete Code of Commercial Law.* 1st ed. London, 1752; 6th ed. London, 1813.
Kyd, Stewart. *A Treatise on the Law of Awards.* 1st ed. Dublin, 1791; 2d ed. London, 1799.
Malynes, Gerard de. *Consuetudo, vel, Lex Mercatoria: Or, The Ancient Law-Merchant.* London, 1622.
March, John. *Actions for Slaunder . . . To which is added, Awards or Arbitrements.* 1st ed. London, 1647; 2d ed. London, 1648.
Swift, Zephaniah. *A System of the Laws of the State of Connecticut.* 2 vols. Windham, Conn., 1795–96.

Pamphlets, Tracts, and Other Sources

Alexander, James. *A Brief Narrative of the Case and Trial of John Peter Zenger.* 2d ed. Edited by Stanley N. Katz. Cambridge, Mass., 1972.

Eliot, Jared. *Give Cesar his Due. Or, The Obligation That Subjects are under to their Civil Rulers.* New London, 1738.

[Hawles, Sir John.] *The English-mans Right, a Dialogue Between a Barrister at Law and a Jury-Man.* London, 1680.

Hooker, Thomas. *A Survey of the Summe of Church-Discipline.* London, 1649.

Hutchinson, Thomas. *The History of the Colony and Province of Massachusetts Bay.* 3 vols. Edited by Lawrence S. Mayo. Cambridge, Mass., 1936.

A Just and Impartial Narrative of the Controversy Between The Rev. Mr. Samuel Fisk the Pastor, and A Number of the Brethren of the First Church of Christ in Salem. Boston, 1735.

Letter Relating to the Divisions in the First Church. Boston, 1734.

Mather, Cotton. *Ratio Disciplinae Fratrum Nov-Anglorum: A Faithful Account of the Discipline Professed and Practised; in the Churches of New-England.* Boston, 1726.

A Platform of Church Discipline. Cambridge, Mass., 1649.

Remarks on some Contents of a Letter relating to the Divisions of the first Church in Salem. Boston, 1735.

Stiles, Ezra. *The Literary Diary of Ezra Stiles.* 3 vols. Edited by Franklin B. Dexter. New York, 1901.

Stoddard, Solomon. *An Answer to Some Cases of Conscience Respecting the Country.* Boston, 1722.

[Wise, John.] *The Churches Quarrel Espoused.* New York, 1713.

SECONDARY WORKS

Abel, Richard L. "A Comparative Theory of Dispute Institutions in Society." *Law & Society Review* 8 (1973): 217–347.

Allen, David Grayson. *In English Ways: The Movement of Societies and the Transferal of English Local Law and Custom to Massachusetts Bay in the Seventeenth Century.* Chapel Hill, N.C., 1981.

Appleby, Joyce Oldham. *Economic Thought and Ideology in Seventeenth-Century England.* Princeton, N.J., 1978.

Atiyah, P. S. *The Rise and Fall of Freedom of Contract.* Oxford, 1979.

Bailyn, Bernard. *The New England Merchants in the Seventeenth Century.* Cambridge, Mass., 1955.

———. *The Peopling of British North America: An Introduction.* New York, 1986.

———. *Voyagers to the West: A Passage in the Peopling of America on the Eve of the Revolution.* New York, 1986.

Barnes, Thomas. "Thomas Lechford and the Earliest Lawyering in Massachusetts, 1638–1641." In *Law in Colonial Massachusetts, 1630–1800*, edited by Daniel R. Coquillette, 3–38. Colonial Society of Massachusetts, *Publications*, 62. Boston, 1984.

Baxter, William T. *The House of Hancock: Business in Boston, 1724–1775*. Cambridge, Mass., 1945.

Bender, Thomas. *Community and Social Change in America*. New Brunswick, N.J., 1978.

Beutel, Frederick K. "Colonial Sources of the Negotiable Instruments Law of the United States." *Illinois Law Review* 34 (1939): 137–50.

Bidwell, Percy Wells, and Falconer, John I. *History of Agriculture in the Northern United States*. Washington, D.C., 1925.

Black, Barbara A. "The Judicial Power and the General Court in Early Massachusetts, 1634–1686." Ph.D. diss., Yale University, 1975.

Black, Robert C., III. *The Younger John Winthrop*. New York, 1966.

Boyer, Paul, and Nissenbaum, Stephen. *Salem Possessed: The Social Origins of Witchcraft*. Cambridge, Mass., 1974.

Bronson, Henry. *A Historical Account of Connecticut Currency, Continental Money, and the Finances of the Revolution*. New Haven Colony Historical Society, *Papers*, 1. New Haven, Conn., 1865.

Bushman, Richard L. "Family Security in the Transition from Farm to City, 1750–1850." *Journal of Family History* 6 (1981): 238–56.

_____. *From Puritan to Yankee: Character and the Social Order in Connecticut, 1690–1765*. Cambridge, Mass., 1967.

Caulkins, Frances Manwaring. *History of Norwich, Connecticut: From Its Possession by the Indians, to the Year 1866*. Hartford, Conn., 1866.

Clark, Christopher. "Household Economy, Market Exchange and the Rise of Capitalism in the Connecticut Valley, 1800–1860." *Journal of Social History* 13 (1979): 169–89.

Cockburn, J. S. *A History of English Assizes, 1558–1714*. Cambridge, 1972.

Cohn, E. J. "Commercial Arbitration and the Rules of Law: A Comparative Study." *University of Toronto Law Journal* 4 (1941): 1–32.

Cook, Edward M., Jr. *The Fathers of the Towns: Leadership and Community Structure in Eighteenth-Century New England*. Baltimore, 1976.

Cranch, William. "Promissory Notes Before and After Lord Holt." In *Select Essays in Anglo-American Legal History*, 3:72–97. 3 vols. Boston, 1907–9.

Crowley, J. E. *This Sheba, Self: The Conceptualization of Economic Life in Eighteenth-Century America*. Baltimore, 1980.

Daniels, Bruce C. *The Connecticut Town: Growth and Development, 1635–1790*. Middletown, Conn., 1979.

_____. "Economic Development in Colonial and Revolutionary Connecticut: An Overview." *WMQ*, 3d ser. 37 (1980): 429–50.

_____. "Long Range Trends of Wealth Distribution in Eighteenth-Century

New England." *Explorations in Economic History* 11 (1972–73): 123–35.

Davis, Andrew McFarland. "A Connecticut Land Bank." Colonial Society of Massachusetts, *Publications*, 5:96–111, 6:6–11. Boston, 1898–1900.

Dawson, John P. *A History of Lay Judges.* Cambridge, Mass., 1960.

———. "The Privy Council and Private Law in the Tudor and Stuart Periods." *Michigan Law Review* 44 (1950): 393–428.

Demos, John. *Entertaining Satan: Witchcraft and the Culture of Early New England.* New York, 1982.

———. *A Little Commonwealth: Family Life in Plymouth Colony.* New York, 1970.

Dunn, Richard S. *Puritans and Yankees: The Winthrop Dynasty of New England, 1630–1717.* Princeton, N.J., 1962.

Everitt, Alan. "The Marketing of Agricultural Produce." In *The Agrarian History of England and Wales, 1500–1640*, edited by Joan Thirsk, pp. 466–592. Cambridge, 1967.

Felstiner, William L. F. "Influences of Social Organization on Dispute Processing." *Law & Society Review* 9 (1974): 63–94.

"Fight in a Hartford Suburb: Residents v. Rattlesnakes." *New York Times*, 17 July 1985, B1.

Flaherty, David H. "Criminal Practice in Provincial Massachusetts." In *Law in Colonial Massachusetts, 1630–1800*, edited by Daniel R. Coquillette, pp. 191–242. Colonial Society of Massachusetts, *Publications*, 62. Boston, 1984.

———, ed. *Essays in the Early History of American Law.* Chapel Hill, N.C., 1969.

Foster, Stephen. *Their Solitary Way: The Puritan Social Ethic in the First Century of Settlement in New England.* New Haven, Conn., 1971.

Geertz, Clifford. "Local Knowledge: Fact and Law in Historical Perspective." In Geertz, *Local Knowledge: Further Essays in Interpretive Anthropology*, 167–234. New York, 1983.

Gildrie, Richard P. *Salem, Massachusetts, 1626–1683: A Covenant Community.* Charlottesville, Va., 1975.

Gilmore, Grant. *The Ages of American Law.* New Haven, Conn., 1977.

Gluckman, Max. *The Judicial Process Among the Barotse of Northern Rhodesia.* 2d ed. Manchester, England, 1967.

Golding, Martin P. "The Nature of Compromise: A Preliminary Inquiry." In *Compromise in Ethics, Law, and Politics: Nomos XXI*, edited by J. Roland Pennock and John W. Chapman, pp. 3–25. New York, 1979.

Grant, Charles S. *Democracy in the Connecticut Frontier Town of Kent.* New York, 1961.

Green, Thomas Andrew. *Verdict According to Conscience: Perspectives on the English Criminal Trial Jury, 1200–1800.* Chicago, 1985.

Greenberg, Douglas. *Crime and Law Enforcement in the Colony of New York, 1691–1776*. Ithaca, N.Y., 1976.

Greven, Philip J., Jr. *Four Generations: Population, Land, and Family in Colonial Andover, Massachusetts*. Ithaca, N.Y., 1970.

Gross, Robert A. "Culture and Cultivation: Agriculture and Society in Thoreau's Concord." *Journal of American History* 69 (1982): 42–61.

_____. *The Minutemen and Their World*. New York, 1976.

Hall, David D. *The Faithful Shepherd: A History of the New England Ministry in the Seventeenth Century*. Chapel Hill, N.C., 1972.

Hartog, Hendrik. *Public Property and Private Power: The Corporation of the City of New York in American Law, 1730–1870*. Chapel Hill, N.C., 1983.

Haskins, George L. *Law and Authority in Early Massachusetts: A Study in Tradition and Design*. New York, 1960.

_____, and Ewing, Samuel E., III. "The Spread of Massachusetts Law in the Seventeenth Century." *University of Pennsylvania Law Review* 106 (1958): 413–18.

Henretta, James A. *The Evolution of American Society, 1700–1815: An Interdisciplinary Analysis*. Lexington, Mass., 1973.

_____. "Families and Farms: *Mentalité* in Pre-Industrial America." *WMQ*, 3d ser. 35 (1978): 3–32.

_____. "The Morphology of New England Society in the Colonial Period." *Journal of Interdisciplinary History* 2 (1971): 379–98.

Heyrman, Christine Leigh. *Commerce and Culture: The Maritime Communities of Colonial Massachusetts, 1690–1750*. New York, 1984.

Holden, J. Milnes. *The History of Negotiable Instruments in English Law*. London, 1955.

Holdsworth, William S. *A History of English Law*. 16 vols. 7th ed. London, 1966.

Horwitz, Morton J. *The Transformation of American Law, 1780–1860*. Cambridge, Mass., 1977.

Innes, Stephen. *Labor in a New Land: Economy and Society in Seventeenth-Century Springfield*. Princeton, N.J., 1983.

Isaac, Rhys. *The Transformation of Virginia, 1740–1790*. Chapel Hill, N.C., 1981.

Jedrey, Christopher M. *The World of John Cleaveland: Family and Community in Eighteenth-Century New England*. New York, 1979.

Johnson, Herbert A. *The Law Merchant and Negotiable Instruments in Colonial New York, 1664–1730*. Chicago, 1963.

Jones, William C. "An Inquiry into the History of the Adjudication of Mercantile Disputes in Great Britain and the United States." *University of Chicago Law Review* 25 (1958): 445–64.

Katz, Stanley N. "The Politics of Law in Colonial America: Controversies over Chancery Courts and Equity Law in the Eighteenth Century." In *Perspectives in American History*, 5 (1971), edited by Donald Fleming and Bernard Bailyn, pp. 257–84.

———. "The Problem of Colonial Legal History." In *Colonial British America: Essays in the New History of the Early Modern Era*, edited by Jack P. Greene and J. R. Pole, pp. 457–89. Baltimore, 1984.

Konig, David Thomas. *Law and Society in Puritan Massachusetts: Essex County, Massachusetts, 1629–1692*. Chapel Hill, N.C., 1979.

Kuflik, Arthur. "Morality and Compromise." In *Compromise in Ethics, Law, and Politics: Nomos XXI*, edited by J. Roland Pennock and John W. Chapman, pp. 38–65. New York, 1979.

Langbein, John H. Review of J. S. Cockburn, *A History of English Assizes, 1558–1714. American Journal of Legal History* 18 (1974): 88–94.

Larned, Ellen D. *History of Windham County, Connecticut*. 2 vols. Worcester, Mass., 1874–80.

Lemon, James T. *The Best Poor Man's Country: A Geographical Study of Early Southeastern Pennsylvania*. Baltimore, 1972.

———. "Spatial Order: Households in Local Communities and Regions." In *Colonial British America: Essays in the New History of the Early Modern Era*, edited by Jack P. Greene and J. R. Pole, pp. 86–122. Baltimore, 1984.

Lockridge, Kenneth A. *A New England Town, The First Hundred Years: Dedham, Massachusetts, 1636–1736*. New York, 1970 [expanded ed. New York, 1985].

———. "Social Change and the Meaning of the American Revolution." *Journal of Social History* 7 (1973): 403–39.

Lucas, Paul R. *Valley of Discord: Church and Society along the Connecticut River, 1636–1725*. Hanover, N.H., 1976.

Macaulay, Stewart. "Non-Contractual Relations in Business: A Preliminary Study." *American Sociological Review* 28 (1963): 55–67.

McGiffert, Michael. "American Puritan Studies in the 1960's." *WMQ*, 3d ser. 27 (1970): 36–67.

Main, Gloria L. *Tobacco Colony: Life in Early Maryland, 1650–1720*. Princeton, N.J., 1982.

Main, Jackson Turner. "The Distribution of Property in Colonial Connecticut." In *The Human Dimensions of Nation-Making: Essays on Colonial and Revolutionary America*, edited by James Kirby Martin, pp. 54–104. Madison, Wis., 1976.

———. *Society and Economy in Colonial Connecticut*. Princeton, N.J., 1985.

Mann, Bruce H. "Parishes, Law, and Community in Connecticut, 1700–1760." Ph.D. diss., Yale University, 1977.

Marcus, Gail Sussman. " 'Due Execution of the Generall Rules of Righteousnesse': Criminal Procedure in New Haven Town and Colony, 1638–1658." In *Saints and Revolutionaries: Essays on Early American History,* edited by David Hall, John M. Murrin, and Thad W. Tate, pp. 99–137. New York, 1984.

Martin, Margaret E. *Merchants and Trade of the Connecticut River Valley, 1750–1820*. Smith College Studies in History, 24. Northampton, Mass., 1939.

Merrill, Michael. "Cash Is Good to Eat: Self-Sufficency in the Rural Economy of the United States." *Radical History Review* 4 (1977): 42–71.

Miller, Perry. "The Marrow of Puritan Divinity." Colonial Society of Massachusetts, *Publications*, 32:247–300. Boston, 1937.

_____. *The New England Mind: From Colony to Province*. Cambridge, Mass., 1953.

Milsom, S. F. C. "Law and Fact in Legal Development." *University of Toronto Law Journal* 17 (1967): 1–19.

Mitchell, Isabel. *Roads and Road-Making in Colonial Connecticut*. Connecticut Tercentenary Commission Pamphlets, no. 14. New Haven, Conn., 1933.

Morgan, Edmund S. "The American Revolution Considered as an Intellectual Movement." In *Paths of American Thought*, edited by Arthur M. Schlesinger, Jr., and Morton White, pp. 11–33. Boston, 1963.

Morris, Richard B. *Studies in the History of American Law, with Special Reference to the Seventeenth and Eighteenth Centuries*. New York, 1930.

Murrin, John M. "Magistrates, Sinners, and a Precarious Liberty: Trial by Jury in Seventeenth-Century New England." In *Saints and Revolutionaries: Essays on Early American History*, edited by David Hall, John M. Murrin, and Thad W. Tate, pp. 142–206. New York, 1984.

_____. "Review Essay." *History and Theory* 2 (1972): 226–75.

Mutch, Robert E. "Yeomen and Merchants in Pre-Industrial America: Eighteenth-Century Massachusetts as a Case Study." *Societas* 7 (1977): 279–302.

Nader, Laura. "Choices in Legal Procedure: Shia Moslem and Mexican Zapotec." *American Anthropologist* 67 (1965): 394–99.

Nash, Gary B. "Social Development." In *Colonial British America: Essays in the New History of the Early Modern Era*, edited by Jack P. Greene and J. R. Pole, pp. 233–61. Baltimore, 1984.

Nelson, William E. *Americanization of the Common Law: The Impact of Legal Change on Massachusetts Society, 1760–1830*. Cambridge, Mass., 1975.

_____. *Dispute and Conflict Resolution in Plymouth County, Massachusetts, 1725–1825*. Chapel Hill, N.C., 1981.

Nettels, Curtis P. *The Money Supply of the American Colonies before 1720*. Madison, Wis., 1934.

Nobles, Gregory H. *Divisions throughout the Whole: Politics and Society in Hampshire County, Massachusetts, 1740–1775*. New York, 1983.

Oberholzer, Emil, Jr. *Delinquent Saints: Disciplinary Action in the Early Congregational Churches of Massachusetts*. New York, 1956.

Olson, Albert Laverne. *Agricultural Economy and the Population in Eighteenth-Century Connecticut.* Connecticut Tercentenary Commission Pamphlets, no. 40. New Haven, Conn., 1935.

Parker, Wyman W. *Connecticut's Colonial and Continental Money.* Hartford, Conn., 1976.

Pettit, Norman. *The Heart Prepared: Grace and Conversion in Puritan Spiritual Life.* New Haven, Conn., 1966.

Phillips, Philip G. "Synthetic Courts—A General Introduction." *University of Pennsylvania Law Review* 83 (1934): 119–31.

Plucknett, T. F. T. *A Concise History of the Common Law.* 5th ed. Boston, 1956.

Pope, Robert G. *The Half-Way Covenant: Church Membership in Puritan New England.* Princeton, N.J., 1969.

Pound, Roscoe. *The Formative Era of American Law.* Boston, 1938.

Powell, Sumner C. *Puritan Village: The Formation of a New England Town.* Middletown, Conn., 1963.

Price, Jacob M. *Capital and Credit in British Overseas Trade: The View from the Chesapeake, 1700–1776.* Cambridge, Mass., 1980.

Pruitt, Bettye Hobbs. "Self-Sufficiency and the Agricultural Economy of Eighteenth-Century Massachusetts." *WMQ*, 3d ser. 41 (1984): 333–64.

Roeber, A. G. *Faithful Magistrates and Republican Lawyers: Creators of Virginia Legal Culture, 1680–1810.* Chapel Hill, N.C., 1981.

Rothenberg, Winifred B. "The Market and Massachusetts Farmers, 1750–1855." *Journal of Economic History* 41 (1981): 283–314.

———. "A Price Index for Rural Massachusetts, 1750–1855." *Journal of Economic History* 39 (1979): 975–1000.

Ruffino, Julio. "Disputing Over Livestock in Sardinia." In *The Disputing Process: Law in Ten Societies*, edited by Laura Nader and Harry F. Todd, Jr., pp. 209–46. New York, 1978.

Rutman, Darrett B. "Assessing the Little Communities of Early America." *WMQ*, 3d ser. 43 (1986): 163–78.

———. *The Husbandmen of Plymouth: Farms and Villages in the Old Colony, 1620–1692.* Boston, 1967.

———. *Winthrop's Boston: Portrait of a Puritan Town, 1630–1649.* Chapel Hill, N.C., 1965.

Saladino, Gaspare J. "The Economic Revolution in Late Eighteenth-Century Connecticut." Ph.D. diss., University of Wisconsin, 1964.

Salmon, Marylynn. *Women and the Law of Property in Early America.* Chapel Hill, N.C., 1986.

Sayre, Paul L. "Development of Commercial Arbitration Law." *Yale Law Journal* 37 (1928): 595–617.

Shammas, Carole. "How Self-Sufficient Was Early America?" *Journal of Interdisciplinary History* 13 (1982): 247–72.

Shipton, Clifford K. *Sibley's Harvard Graduates.* 17 vols. Cambridge, Mass., 1873–1975.

Simpson, A. W. B. *A History of the Common Law of Contract: The Rise of the Action of Assumpsit.* Oxford, 1975.

———. *An Introduction to the History of the Land Law.* 2d ed. Oxford, 1985.

Smith, Joseph H. *Appeals to the Privy Council from the American Plantations.* New York, 1950.

Stark, Bruce P. "The New London Society and Connecticut Politics, 1732–1740." *Connecticut History* 25 (1984): 1–21.

Starr, June, and Yngvesson, Barbara. "Scarcity and Disputing: Zeroing-In on Compromise Decisions." *American Ethnologist* 2 (1975): 553–66.

Steiner, Bernard C. *A History of the Plantation of Menunkatuck and of the Original Town of Guilford, Connecticut.* Baltimore, 1897.

Tracy, Patricia J. *Jonathan Edwards, Pastor: Religion and Society in Eighteenth-Century Northampton.* New York, 1982.

Trakman, Leon E. "The Evolution of the Law Merchant: Our Commercial Heritage." *Journal of Maritime Law & Commerce* 12 (1980): 1–24.

Trubek, David M. "Toward a Social Theory of Law: An Essay on the Study of Law and Development." *Yale Law Journal* 82 (1972): 1–50.

Trumbull, Benjamin. *A Complete History of Connecticut, Civil and Ecclesiastical.* 2 vols. 1818. New London, Conn., 1898.

Underdown, David. *Revel, Riot, and Rebellion: Popular Politics and Culture in England, 1603–1660.* Oxford, 1985.

University of Pennsylvania Law Review Symposium on The Public/Private Distinction, 23 Jan. 1982. *University of Pennsylvania Law Review* 130 (1982): 1289–1609.

Walker, Williston. *The Creeds and Platforms of Congregationalism.* New York, 1893.

Walton, Gary M., and Shepherd, James F. *The Economic Rise of Early America.* New York, 1979.

Warren, Charles. *A History of the American Bar.* Boston, 1913.

Watson, Alan. *The Evolution of Law.* Baltimore, 1985.

Weaver, Glenn. *Jonathan Trumbull: Connecticut's Merchant Magistrate (1710–1785).* Hartford, Conn., 1956.

Weber, Max. *Economy and Society: An Outline of Interpretive Sociology.* Edited by Guenther Roth and Claus Wittich. 2 vols. Berkeley, Calif., 1978.

Wroth, L. Kinvin. "Possible Kingdoms: The New England Town from the Perspective of Legal History." *American Journal of Legal History* 15 (1971): 318–30.

———, and Zobel, Hiller B., eds. *Legal Papers of John Adams.* 3 vols. Cambridge, Mass., 1965.

Yngvesson, Barbara. "The Atlantic Fishermen." In *The Disputing Process: Law in Ten Societies*, edited by Laura Nader and Harry F. Todd, Jr., pp. 59–85. New York, 1978.

_____. "Responses to Grievance Behavior: Extended Cases in a Fishing Community." *American Ethnologist* 3 (1976): 353–73.

Zuckerman, Michael. *Peaceable Kingdoms: New England Towns in the Eighteenth Century*. New York, 1970.

INDEX